SUBJECT LIBRARIANS

This book is dedicated to our partners – Roger Dale, Nick Matthews and Jane Robinson – with thanks for their support and encouragement. We would also like to record our thanks to colleagues at Bournemouth University for their help and ideas, especially Su Kensley for help in preparing the manuscript.

Subject Librarians
Engaging with the Learning and Teaching Environment

Edited by
PENNY DALE, MATT HOLLAND AND MARIAN MATTHEWS
Bournemouth University, UK

ASHGATE

© Penny Dale, Matt Holland and Marian Matthews 2006

Penny Dale, Matt Holland and Marian Matthews have asserted their right under the Copyright, Designs and Patents Act, 1988, to be identified as the editors of this work.

Published by
Ashgate Publishing Limited
Gower House
Croft Road
Aldershot
Hampshire GU11 3HR
England

Ashgate Publishing Company
Suite 420
101 Cherry Street
Burlington, VT 05401-4405
USA

Ashgate website: http://www.ashgate.com

British Library Cataloguing in Publication Data
Subject librarians : engaging with the learning and
    teaching environment
    1. Area specialist librarians 2. Academic libraries
    I. Dale, Penny II. Holland, Matt III. Matthews, Marian
    027.7

Library of Congress Control Number: 2006925025

ISBN 0 7546 4095 7

Printed and bound in Great Britain by MPG Books Ltd, Bodmin, Cornwall.

Contents

PART I THE SUBJECT SPECIALIST IN HIGHER EDUCATION

PART II SERVING DIFFERENT CONSTITUENCIES

List of Figures

Notes on Contributors

The Editors

Penny Dale is Subject Librarian for the School of Conservation Sciences at Bournemouth University, where she has worked in different capacities since 1990. Her particular interest is staff development, she organises the staff development and training programme for the library service and contributes to the Bournemouth University staff development programme. The highlight of her career to date was being awarded the Alison Northover Bursary for staff development in 2003; this enabled her to present a paper on engaging widening participation students in information literacy at the Libraries Without Walls 5 Conference.

Matt Holland is an expert in the field of subject support within academic libraries. He has postgraduate qualifications in librarianship from the University of Northumbria and the University of Central England, and in Management Studies at Bournemouth University. He has worked at the University of the West of England and is currently the Subject Librarian for the Media School at Bournemouth University. His other areas of interest are in Media Archives and he has participated in a number of Arts and Humanities Research Board projects in this area.

Marian Matthews is Academic Programmes Co-ordinator for Bournemouth University Graduate School. She is Programme Leader for the new Postgraduate Certificate in Research Degree Supervision and also designs and contributes to Research Methodology and Skills for research students. Marian is involved in the strategic development of the Graduate School including review panels, quality assessment and the implementation of the e-learning environment for doctoral students. She is Bournemouth University Link Tutor for one of the partner colleges. For several years Marian was subject specialist for Finance and Law, fostering and supporting independent learning skills through the delivery of curriculum-linked information and research skills as well as engaging in virtual learning environment development projects. Her research interests and publications extend to information literacy, internet accountability, the application of the web in the learning process and supervision issues. She holds an MSc in Education and is a member of The Higher Education Academy.

The Contributors

Sally Brown is Professor of Higher Education Diversity in Learning and Teaching at Leeds Metropolitan University. She was formerly Director of Membership Services at the Institute of Learning and Teaching in Higher Education.

Jill Beard is Deputy University Librarian at Bournemouth University, where her responsibilities include the development of support for the academic community and the evaluation and enhancement of service quality. She is a member of the University's Quality Assurance and Enhancement Group, chairing validation events and representing Academic Services on Quality Assurance Agency preparation steering groups. Her research interests focus mainly on health information; she was a co-author of the first Library and Information Co-operation Council health panel accreditation scheme for libraries and recently led a research project called Healthinfo4u to enable access to the full text of health journals by the general public.

Jenny Campbell Faculty Liaison Librarian for the following Schools: Chemical Engineering and Advanced Materials; Civil Engineering and Geosciences; Electrical, Electronic and Computer Engineering; Mathematics and Statistics; Mechanical Systems and Engineering.

Margaret Feetham is the Information Librarian for Law at Southampton Solent University, a university college recently granted university status, and combines subject responsibilities with responsibility for the design and maintenance of the library website. Interests include the delivery of electronic resources for which she received HEFCE funding to research the off-campus experience of students accessing library resources. Recognising the increasing importance of teaching information literacy skills, she has added membership of the Higher Education Academy and a MA in Education to her Librarianship qualifications and CILIP membership.

Trudi Knight is a member of the Library Systems Team at the University of Greenwich, where her responsibilities include the maintenance and design of the library website. Her particular areas of interest are website accessibility and usability. She has previously held support roles in libraries and in university administration. She recently gained her Master's in Computing and Information Systems from the University of Greenwich and is currently seeking accreditation as a WebCT trainer.

Maggie Leharne is a Senior Academic Services Librarian at the University of Greenwich. Since qualifying as a librarian she has worked in a number of educational institutions in the further and higher education sectors, both as a subject librarian and in serials management. She is currently involved in developing services and support for off-campus library users. Particular areas of interest include information literacy and e-learning, for which she is studying for a Certificate in e-Learning, e-Teaching and e-Training.

Pete Maggs is currently Faculty Liaison Librarian, Humanities and Social Sciences, at the University of Newcastle. Previously he has worked at both the Universities of Southampton and Exeter. He holds postgraduate qualifications in Librarianship from the University of Wales, Aberystwyth and in Management Studies from the Open University. He is section editor of the Social Science Information Gateway (SOSIG) and author of the 'Internet Geographer' tutorial on the Resource Discovery Network's Virtual Training Suite. He administers and teaches Information Literacy at a wide range of levels at Newcastle – including the role of Module Leader on the University's Humanities and Social Sciences Faculty Postgraduate Research Training Programme.

Kate Marshall is Academic Services Librarian for the Humanities at the University of Greenwich, where she is involved with supporting teaching and learning through academic liaison and information skills development. Her particular areas of interest include e-learning and information literacy and she is currently working towards accreditation by the Higher Education Academy. She is committed to continuing professional development and has recently submitted an application for Chartered Membership of the Chartered Institute of Library and Information Professionals (CILIP). Having gained experience in support roles at Manchester Metropolitan University and the University of Sheffield, she gained her Master's in Information Management from the University of Sheffield in 2000. She gained experience in research, training and serials management within the business information sector before returning to the academic sector in 2004.

Buhle Mbambo is University Librarian of the University of Zimbabwe. She joined the University of Zimbabwe from the University of Botswana where she served as subject librarian for 12 years. She is well experienced in library support to faculty. Furthermore, she is well versed in issues of international librarianship. She is a standing committee member of the International Federation of Library Associations and Institutions (IFLA) Africa section. She serves on the Advisory Board of Electronic Information for Libraries (eIFL). She is Country Co-ordinator of the Programme for Enhancement of Research Information. She is passionate about consortium development in higher education as a strategy for enhancing library operations in higher education, and is current chairperson of the Zimbabwe University Libraries Consortium. Her research interest is in women and information technology application in developing countries.

Janet Peters began her career at the University of the West of England, in audiovisual and systems librarianship. She then moved to the University of Glamorgan as the Head of Bibliographic Services. On moving to the University of Wales, Newport, she established Subject Librarian posts to create closer links between the Library and the academic departments. Since 2002 the Library has converged with the IT and Media Services Department and the Centre for Learning Development to provide a single support structure for student learning. Janet is currently University Librarian and Senior Assistant Director of Information Services at Cardiff University. Professionally active throughout her career, she is currently a member of the Society of College, National and University Libraries (SCONUL) Working Group on Information Literacy and Learning and various regional collaborative schemes.

Jane Ryland has worked as a professional librarian in the UK, US and Australia in a variety of contexts, including public, health and academic libraries. Her interest in partnership started when she was working as a Subject Librarian at Bournemouth University and she has been the University Library's partnerships specialist since July 2003.

Kerry Shephard is an educational developer and, since 2000, Learning Technologies Co-ordinator at the University of Southampton's Centre for Learning and Teaching. He has a research and teaching background in higher education in the biological sciences and broad interests in developing and evaluating innovative approaches to support learning. He leaves the UK in 2006 to become Director of the Higher Education Development Centre, University of Otago, Dunedin, New Zealand.

Frank Trew is University Librarian at the American International University in Richmond, London. He is a graduate of both Oxford and London Universities with a postgraduate qualification in librarianship from Thames Valley University. He is also Subject Librarian for the arts and social sciences, and has been instrumental in developing

Foreword

Sally Brown

Higher Education is currently experiencing a period of unprecedented change. The ways in which students go about the learning business differ greatly now from approaches in the twentieth century. We see a much more diverse student population in terms of age profile, social background, ability and expectations. Nowadays students are likely to have more varied modes of study and numerous external responsibilities making calls upon their time. The very nature of learning facilitation has changed, with a stronger emphasis on the uses of information technologies and the rapid growth in electronic information resources and networked information, requiring specialist support in the development not only of students' information retrieval skills, but, more importantly, the ability to judge, evaluate and use information from a wide variety of sources.

The roles of subject specialists working in libraries in Higher Education have undergone commensurate change. They have become much more involved in the total student learning experience, with fostering and supporting independent learning skills becoming an ever-more central part of the subject specialist librarian's working life. Role boundaries are blurring, as information specialists start working ever more closely with academic staff, both in the classroom and on funded projects, involving mutual up-skilling and support. They are now increasingly seen in higher education institutions as powerful change agents, advocates for good practice, sources of wisdom and brokers of productive partnerships.

At a time when higher education practitioners generally have been reviewing the whole nature of professionalism, library subject specialists have recognised the need for ever greater flexibility, for stronger specialisation (at the same time as more effective multi-tasking) and for valuing their own ongoing training and lifelong learning. In the UK, the Institute for Learning and Teaching in Higher education (now part of the Higher Education Academy) has championed professional accreditation for teaching and learning support staff, and the library subject specialist group have been in the vanguard of this national movement. Internationally similar moves are being explored in New Zealand, Australia, Canada, South Africa and elsewhere.

Library subject specialists are today contributing significantly to the enhancement of the Higher Education learning environment, as this valuable and timely book demonstrates. It provides invaluable information for new and experienced library professionals and engages productively with current debates on what really matters in universities and colleges. I wholeheartedly welcome its publication.

Editors' Introduction

Penny Dale, Matt Holland and Marian Matthews

Subject librarians are in our view key players in academic libraries in the UK and around the world. They are the link between the academic community and the library, between students and the library and between the library and the wider world of information. However, the significance of this role, the everyday experience of subject librarians at work and their contributions to the profession are not fully reflected in the literature. The idea for this volume came from a desire to fill the gap and provide, in effect, snapshots of the work and responsibilities of subject librarians and to encourage discussion and reflection on the way that the role is developing. The themes of this book; lifelong learning, widening participation, information literacy and collaborative working, have an impact across the profession. We hope it will also appeal to staff in other student support services and give insights into the work of subject librarians which will inform the partnerships to support student learning that we see as an important development in the future. Finally, and perhaps most importantly, we believe that the themes, concerns and suggestions for moving forward that underpin the book will be of interest to students of librarianship and information science.

The first part of the book explores the drivers in higher education that impact on the role of subject librarian and shape the changing environment in which they work. This is followed by a closer look at our user communities, including a chapter describing the international context with an emphasis on Southern Africa. The themes of the book are brought together in the conclusion.

We felt it was important to hear the voice of the practitioners, so almost all of the contributors work in academic libraries and address their topics from a wide knowledge drawing on a wealth of personal experiences. Contributors who are not subject librarians bring wider perspectives to the book. Kerry Shephard, from the Centre for Learning and Teaching at the University of Southampton brings the viewpoint of an academic to the debate on the contributions that librarians have to make to the learning and teaching agenda. Jill Beard was a subject librarian at Bournemouth University; now as part of her role of Deputy University Librarian she manages the subject librarians and oversees the quality processes in the library. Janet Peters is Director of Library and Information Services at University of Wales, Newport, and takes a strategic view of how subject librarians can respond to the needs of asynchronous learners. Buhle Mbambo, Librarian of the University of Zimbabwe, was formerly a subject librarian in both Zimbabwe and Botswana, and her perspective on the role of subject librarianship in Southern Africa adds to the literature of an area where the contributions of librarians to the information literacy agenda are developing. Finally Marian Matthews, one of the editorial team, was a Subject Librarian and is now Academic Programmes Co-ordinator in the Graduate School at Bournemouth University. The chapter Marian has written with Kerry in many ways synthesises the possibilities of the relationship between librarians and academics.

From the beginning, we wanted to involve practitioners from across the higher education sector in the UK. To this end we approached librarians from old as well as new Universities, large and small institutions, and perhaps most significantly people without a record of publishing as well as some more established contributors. We hope that we have succeeded in these aims, with contributions from some long established universities such as those of Wales and Newcastle; as well as one of the very newest institutions to gain university status, Southampton Solent. Some of our authors have extensive writing and publishing experience, whilst for other contributors the book has offered a vehicle for first time publication.

At this point we would like to add a few words about style. We wanted the voices of all our contributors to stand out, to speak for themselves, so our editorial input into language used has been as minimal as possible. In some cases this has led to duplication or repetition of terms. For example we have referred to 'subject librarians', but in some chapters the terms 'subject specialist' or 'information advisor' have been used. Similarly we have made no attempt to differentiate between 'information literacy' and 'information skills', 'user education' and 'library orientation' but have let each author describe, and where necessary, defend why they have chosen a particular term.

The Subject Specialist in Higher Education

The first half of the book defines the scope of subject librarianship, and begins with a review of the literature. **Margaret Feetham's** literature review looks at the history of subject librarianship in the context of organisational change, growing use of the Web and the changing role of the subject librarian. She identifies a number of conflicts in the subject specialist role; the tension between functional and subject specialist roles, the dilemma of academic status, the financial cost of the subject specialist and the threat of disintermediation in the context of increasing end user access to resources. Margaret refers to the flexibility of the subject specialist role and the ability of subject specialists to cope with change. She also describes the increasingly important part that they play in delivering the learning and teaching agenda, alongside their perhaps more traditional skills of disseminating subject information and facilitating access to institutional and nationally created educational resources.

This chapter bridges past and present thinking, and leads into a series of chapters describing the environments in which subject librarians are working at the beginning of the twenty-first century. The chapter by **Penny Dale** with **Maggie Leharne, Trudi Knight and Kate Marshall** considers professional engagement in the contexts of working with library and information professionals and other support staff, as well as with academic staff and students. The challenges of enabling effective learning in academic libraries, of establishing and maintaining professional relationships with academic staff and other colleagues, and the vital need for continuing professional development are described in the context of the post-modern learning environment of higher education. The need for collaboration and partnerships is highlighted, and the potential for extending the uses of communities of practice are touched on.

The Quality Assurance Agency Subject Review pre-2002 was a unique exercise, examining in detail subject provision across the whole of UK higher education. **Jill Beard** takes the lessons learned from this experience as benchmarks for the future of engagement with the quality process. She sees the processes of quality review as offering subject librarians catalysts for change as learning resources are ranked high on the quality assurance agenda. This chapter taps into the evidence of Subject Review from published Quality Assurance Agency reports, draws on the experiences of subject librarians and looks forward to the future shape of the Quality Assurance Agency process and its likely impact on libraries and subject support.

Kerry Shephard takes an academic's view of the contributions that subject librarians make to learning and teaching. He observes that far-reaching though the impact of the Dearing Report has been, it is only one in a series of watersheds and the changes that higher education has experienced since 1997 will have an equivalent, if not greater, impact on higher education and subject librarians. Kerry asks us to reconsider how librarians and other learning support professionals engage with the practicalities of learning and teaching, particularly in the contexts of e-learning, quality assurance and widening participation.

The delivery of higher education in further education institutions is an area in which Bournemouth University has acquired considerable expertise, and we are pleased to include a chapter by our colleague **Jane Ryland** on the challenges and opportunities presented by the growth of Foundation degrees in partner colleges. Following the success of the Dorset South Somerset and South Wiltshire (DSW) project funded by the Higher Education Funding Council for England, and the subsequent establishment of a specialist librarian's post with a partnership focus, Jane now has a wider role, liaising with partner colleges to promote communication and best practice across a range of library and academic support services. Jane's chapter explores some of the issues faced by libraries delivering support to higher education students in further education colleges, and offers some solutions and opportunities for change.

The contribution of subject librarians to learning and teaching is linked, possibly inextricably, with the development of the virtual learning environment. **Marian Matthews** draws on her experience of developing a virtual learning environment for business and law and her more recent work to develop flexible learning to support doctoral students. Marian considers the contribution of e-resources to the virtual learning environment, and wonders how evaluation and feedback of web-based learning can be used to enhance students' learning experience.

This section concludes with a joint chapter from **Kerry Shephard and Marian Matthews** that considers the process of liaison and negotiation that takes place between subject librarians and academic staff. There is some evidence that these relationships are changing. Communication technologies such as the World Wide Web enable frequent interaction, and desk top access raises the profile of the Library as a provider of access and support. Technology based projects aimed at creating digital content require input from the subject librarians who are drawn into closer collaborations with academics and researchers. The digital and resource-based learning strategies in higher education place an ever-greater premium on a user focused library service. Subject librarians are also engaging in a whole new set of relationships with colleagues in support services who in turn are competing or co-operating with them for the attention of academics. This chapter examines the relationships between subject librarians and academics, drawing out the key points but also looking to future trends.

Serving Different Constituencies

We are very aware that for many subject librarians, undergraduates are still the largest constituent group who regularly provide new challenges in terms of acquiring information literacy. **Pete Maggs and Jenny Campbell** have written a case study of the University of Newcastle. The experiences at Newcastle have implications for the whole of the higher education sector, especially when we consider how good information-handling skills impact on student satisfaction, lifelong learning and employability. The Society of College, National and University Libraries' 'Seven Headline Skills Model' (the Seven Pillars) is used to map how information skills are delivered at Newcastle from induction to Master's level, with particular reference to benchmarking and quality assurance.

Asynchronous learners are those whose learning is not dependent on traditional on-campus. **Janet Peters** considers what has been done to promote learning opportunities for the increasing number of students who do not have the luxury of full-time, focused study on a university campus. She looks at the role of subject librarians, working with academic course teams to ensure that learning resources are available in a flexible way to ensure equitable provision of information. Using two case studies, Janet explores topics as diverse as access to physical resources, e-access, information literacy and learners with special needs.

Matt Holland considers the support and contributions subject librarians provide for research degree programmes. He reflects on the journey from Follett to the Research Libraries Network, and considers initiatives covering activities as diverse as access, guidelines and codes and the delivery of research training that are now in place. Matt includes some examples of good practice in research support. He surveys how researchers use libraries and information services, and considers ways in which they can be supported, even those reluctant to engage in the process.

The final chapter of this section covers international students in the UK. This fast growing group constitutes over 11 per cent of the total student body. **Frank Trew** uses his considerable experience of serving international students to look at academic library experiences from the perspective of a student new to higher education in the UK. Frank's description of the 'librarian as communicator' echoes other contributors' descriptions of librarians as knowledge brokers, but with the added edge of responding to and overcoming language and cultural issues. Communication, whether at the enquiry desk, in a one-to-one advice situation or as part of the information skills programme is discussed as well as the merits and de-merits of multi-lingual provision.

The last chapter describing our constituents is slightly different in that it is devoted to the international scene, with a focus on provision in Southern Africa. The first part of **Buhle Mbambo's** chapter is a review of the literature of the forms and types of academic library support in Africa, Asia and Australia. The transition from predominately functional roles to subject specialisation is discussed, looking at how the pace of change has varied in different countries. The second part of the chapter is a case study of library faculty support in Southern Africa. Buhle notes that within the region the subject based model operates in the majority of universities, but this does not preclude different practices and structures that appear to have little correlation to the size of the University. This reflects the situation in the UK, and some of the comments from her respondents on the relationships between libraries and faculties will also strike a chord with colleagues in the UK.

The final chapter is the editors' conclusion, which we will leave to speak for itself. However at this point we would like to mention **Professor Sally Brown** and thank her for encouraging us to undertake this project in the first place. We hope that the result justifies her enthusiasm for the book and her faith in us as editors. Finally we would like to thank our contributors for the additional work that writing imposed on their already busy lives. We thank them for their patience whilst we slowly progressed the project and most of all for the skill and professionalism that each displays in the very different chapters. At Library School (too many years ago to count!) we discussed S.R. Ranganathan's five laws of library science. Reading the contributions to this book there is no doubt that Ranganathan's words of 1931, 'the library is a growing organism', are still valid more than 70 years later.

References

Ranganathan, S.R., 1931. *The five laws of library science*. The Madras Library Association. London.
Society of College, National and University Libraries (SCONUL), 2000. *The seven pillars of information literacy* [online] http://www.sconul.ac.uk/activities/inf_lit/seven_pillars.html [accessed 13 June 2005].

PART I
The Subject Specialist in Higher Education

Chapter 1

The Subject Specialist in Higher Education – A Review of the Literature

Margaret Feetham

Introduction

The concept of the subject librarian has been defined as a 'librarian with special knowledge of, and responsibility for, a particular subject or subjects …' (Feather and Sturges, 1997). The subject-based model was first introduced into the UK as an alternative to the functional model at University College London by R.W. Chambers (University College Librarian 1901–22), adopted at the University of Leeds in the 1930s under Richard Offor and then spread to other universities. The appointment of subject specialists to improve reader services was recommended in the Parry Report (University Grants Committee, 1967) and remained popular throughout the 1960s and 1970s. This concept was epitomised at the University of East Anglia by Thompson (1975), who, as the English literature specialist, claimed to have built up 'one of the best and least accidental collections in the field'. At the beginning of the 21st century, subject librarians are rising to many challenges including electronic resource provision, liaison with academic departments and information skills training. Consequently, some writers such as Heseltine (1995) and Gaston (2001) argue that the original role of subject librarian has disappeared while others such as Pinfield (2001a) argue that the subject librarian has become more flexible and has adapted to changing circumstances. Parallel concepts have evolved alongside the subject librarian such as the tutor librarian, a term first applied at Hatfield Polytechnic in the 1960s (Harrison, 1990, p. 43) and encompassing the recognition that the role of the academic librarian extended beyond selection and management of materials to embrace user education, and the academic liaison librarian, where emphasis is placed on the working relationship with the faculties.

Even when subject expertise was the dominant criterion, research shows that there were wider requirements, for example, technical and language skills. The role has also generally included a combination of liaison with academic departments; stock selection and maintenance; enquiry work and user education; cataloguing and classification (where not done centrally) and wider functional and managerial responsibilities (Pinfield 2001a, p. 33). Latterly, organisational change and the demands of new technology mean that there has been more emphasis placed on liaison with users; adoption of new enquiry techniques and selection and provision of electronic resources. Information skills training and involvement in learning environments have become more important as have team working skills and project management skills (Biddiscombe, 2002 p. 232).

The changing role of the subject librarian in academic libraries has been discussed in the literature (Fleming 1986; Akeroyd, 2001; Pinfield 2001a, 2001b; Gaston 2001 and Biddiscombe 2002). This chapter looks at the influences, challenges and opportunities facing the subject librarian and how these factors have redefined the role.

External influences

This section will show that changes in the role of the subject librarian over the last few decades reflect changing attitudes to both the organisation and strategy of the academic library. A shift in the concept of what the library means, as Wolff (1995) argued that convergence of services, the technological revolution and knowledge explosion have all resulted in libraries adopting a fundamentally different role over recent decades. Wolff suggested that prior to the 1980s; the focus of libraries was on *holdings*. With the explosion in knowledge aided by technology it is impossible for collections to contain everything and the emphasis changed in the 1980s to ensuring *access* to material, both via electronic resources held remotely and via co-operative access arrangements with other organisations. From 1995, libraries have concentrated on the *use* of the resources and placed greater emphasis on the acquiring of information skills Wolff predicts that by 2010, libraries will be concentrating on learning transformation, playing a leading role in the provision of resources in a format suitable for the new pedagogical approach adopted by the Virtual Learning Environment (VLE).

The organisational model

Major surveys of subject specialisation in university libraries were carried out in 1982 (Woodhead and Martin, 1982) and 1996 (Martin, 1996) and a third survey extended to include the former polytechnic (new university) libraries in 2000 (Reid, 2000). Woodhead and Martin argued that in all libraries, a certain range of work has to be done including stock selection, liaison with academic departments, acquisitions, cataloguing, classification, shelf-arranging, borrowing services, document delivery, enquiry and advisory work, literature searching, current awareness and user education. They suggested that there was a range of organisation models that had been adopted based on a proposal by Scrivener (1974) (Woodhead and Martin, 1982 p. 98; Martin, 1996 pp. 160–161) and that the various models adopted by the libraries at different times have impacted on the role of the subject librarian. Martin's research indicated that by 1996, there had been movement away from the hybrid model (staff with both responsibility for their own subject area and other centralised functions) and three-tier organisational structures (senior staff have subject responsibility, with remaining functions being the responsibility of middle grade staff supported by library assistants) with movement towards a dual model (some senior staff have subject responsibility while others are responsible for the remaining centralised functions) which accommodated 63 per cent of respondents from higher education libraries. One also saw the emergence in the 1996 survey of the subject divisional model (teams of both senior and supporting staff with each team located in and responsible for physically separate parts of the collection and underpinned by centralised functions). Martin (1996) sites several factors for a move from the three-tier model: increased size of operations, increasing professionalism, decreasing importance of book selection and the impact of information technology.

Research by Martin (1996) and Reid (2000) revealed a move towards less hierarchical structures and team working, in which front-line staff are in more direct communication with the decision making process. This often means school/faculty teams with a range of staff levels and – in a converged organisation – different professional backgrounds. This convergence results in librarians embracing new tasks such as mediation of electronic resources, identification of choice of delivery, licensing, interface selection or creation, platform advice, promotion and training.

Centralisation of functions and the rise of the paraprofessional

A number of writers such as Woodhead and Martin (1992), Brophy (1998) and Biddiscome (2002, p. 228), argue that there are several key processes in all academic libraries that do not require a qualified librarian and that while information access and information enquiry service have generally remained the provenance of the subject librarian, other areas of responsibility such as acquisition, cataloguing and classification and document supply services have been increasingly devolved to central functional and paraprofessional staff (Pinfield, 2001a, p. 34; Biddiscombe, 2002, p. 228). Sandler (1996) quoted in Corrall (2004, p.26) also points to an 'ascendant class of IT savvy librarians and paraprofessionals' and a decline in the numbers of professionally qualified staff employed, a position predicted in the Fielden Report on Human Resource Management in Academic Libraries (John Fielden Consultancy, 1993 paras. 3. 24– 3.30).

Convergence of services

Martin quotes Richard Heseltine (Martin, 1996, p. 147) as predicting the end of the subject librarian because Heseltine argued that the delivery of end-user services will become more systemised and result in the convergence of learning support services. For users, the distinctions between library, computer centre and media resources centres will fade as students start to use and access learning resources from a variety of locations. Ultimately Heseltine predicts 'service convergence round broad functional responsibilities' will overtake the generic model of subject librarianship.

The Fielden Report commissioned by the Higher Education Funding Council (John Fielden Consultancy, 1993) as a result of the Follett Report (Joint Funding

Council, 1993) reported that convergence had been the main driver of change in the organisation of library services in the US and UK over the previous eight years. The study identified two different types of convergence – 'organisational or formal convergence' in which two or more services are brought together for managerial purposes (paras. 2.25–2.27) and 'operational or informal convergence' (paras. 2.28–2.30) in which the detailed functions and operations of the services are changed or are brought together. The report suggested that it was not necessary to have organisational convergence to have operational convergence – it could be sufficient for the heads of the two services to undertake joint strategic planning.

Although the concept of convergence first originated in the US in the 1980s, it was not until the late 1980s and early 1990s that changes relating to operational convergence really became visible in the UK, mainly resulting from the opportunities arising as a result of the retirement of the librarian or head of computing services. The 1988 issue of the *British Journal of Academic Librarianship* is devoted entirely to the topic. The first UK university to 'merge the major academic services at an operational level' (Harris, 1988) and have a merged service with a single executive head (Lovecy, 1994. p1) was the University of Salford which merged its computing services with the library to form an academic information service. Other early adopters included Roehampton Institute and Liverpool John Moores University (Sykes and Gerrard, 1998).

Further research by Lovecy in 1994 indicated that different models of convergence had been adopted by different universities ranging from the 'meeting between the heads of the services' at one end of the spectrum to 'the single service administered by one officer in which many staff cannot claim to be either Library or Computing staff'. The Fielden Report (John Fielden Consultancy, 1993) predicted that operational convergence would be the norm with integrated library and information service strategic plans and joint network management. Fielden also prophesised the start of 'academic convergence through learner support' (para. 3.17), defined as 'activities within library and information services that exist to support individual learners', with the professional staff expected to play a greater role in learner support and liaison with academic staff. Typically this included user education, mediated access to databases and tailored navigational support (help given by information librarians with subject-specific knowledge to staff or students wanting to use the most appropriate resources for their subject).

Morgan and Atkinson (2000) estimate that as many as 60 institutions have converged in the UK. In 1995 the University of Birmingham amalgamated four separate units: library, academic computing service, television service and computer-based learning, which, with the additional of language laboratories and lecture theatres in 1998 became the largest converged service in an academic institution in the UK (Shoebridge, 1998). The University combined staff from all the different parts into multifunctional academic discipline-based teams, making it a real example of operational convergence. Most convergences in the late 1980s onwards were with computing services although, since 1995, a different configuration has appeared with libraries choosing to align themselves with learning support departments, thereby placing the focus on the learner rather than seeking operational efficiency. Some library departments have merged, demerged and subsequently aligned themselves with different services, for example the Universities of Luton, De Montfort and Northumbria. In such cases, the library services have moved away from close partnerships with computing services, often based on the fact that historically libraries were heavy users of IT services, to more closely align themselves with learning support departments, better recognising the role that libraries play in the learning process.

The challenge of disintermediation

According to Biddiscombe (2002, p. 228), we are seeing a two-fold change in libraries as paraprofessional staff take over the tasks of professional librarians and end-user empowerment, mostly as a result of the World Wide Web, means that end users can increasingly satisfy most of their information needs and demand access to academic services away from a fixed location .

The ability of students to directly access materials results in disintermediation. Sturges (2001, p. 63) argues that the introduction of the online database and later the CD-Rom originally enhanced rather than decreased the librarian's role as most early databases were only bibliographic and the assistance of the librarian was still required to interpret the information in the database and locate the original article. The emergence of full text databases and greater familiarity with Internet technology, however, offers the user more independence and has therefore reduced the demand for a librarian as an intermediary. Furthermore, database suppliers providing in-house training staff or training up students to provide training to other students are all challenges to the role of the librarian. Both Mougayar and Sawhney, however, quoted in Biddiscombe (2002, p.229), see a continued role for the 'informediary', providing the 'mechanism for aggregating customers and suppliers, thereby facilitating exchanges, creating and capturing value in the process'.

The 'Google factor' (the preference for students to resort first to the Internet) presents a challenge to the subject librarian. Armstrong (2001) and colleagues working on the Justeis project – 'Monitoring and evaluating user behaviour in information seeking and use of information technology and information services in UK Higher Education' found that students initially went to websites first and made low use of library sources such as bibliographic databases, electronic journals and web databases. A survey of electronic information resources used by undergraduate and postgraduate students (Lonsdale and Urquhart, 2001, p.36) revealed that search engine use was identified as the first choice and cited by 75 per cent of users compared with e-mail (27 per cent), OPAC (23 per cent) and web based databases (10 per cent). Similar results were derived from the 'Formative Evaluation of the Distributed National Electronic Resource' (EDNER) project (Griffiths and Brophy, 2001) where 45 per cent of students used the Google search engine to locate material on set tasks, compared with 10 per cent for the Online Public Access Catalogue (OPAC) and 9 per cent for Yahoo. Nevertheless Sturges still argues that there will be a continuing role for the librarian (Sturges, 2001, p. 63), for while skilful independent researchers will largely continue to ignore the function of the librarian, the vast majority of people will continue to prefer to receive the most important parts of the information they need through an intermediary.

As long ago as the mid-1980s, Fleming (1986) discussed the potential of developments in information handling skills courses and uses of information technology allied to the need for greater integration of user education into the curriculum.

The challenge for the librarian is to prove the role that they can play, what Sturges (2001, p.65) calls reintermediation. Marfleet and Kelly (1999) describe this as the demystification of information retrieval in which the librarian must recognise the greater independence of the end user and, rather than fight it, use their energies instead to enhance services. The librarian is still required to be the intermediary between the vendor and the supplier, make decisions on how the resource should be accessed and provide training to the end user. Finally search engines still work on the principle of keyword searching, a concept generally unfamiliar to many information users which emphasises the need for skilled searches, normally with the assistance of the librarian.

Both Akeroyd (2001, p. 93) and Corrall (2004) point out that the increased use of the Virtual Learning Environment (VLE), seen by so many as an opportunity for libraries, could also lead to disintermediation. Libraries have traditionally provided access to electronic resources via the library homepage, information skills training materials and subject gateways. The ease with which academics can now link to electronic resources, often provided by the library, but without communicating or consulting with the library staff over resource descriptions, threatens the library's role. VLEs also tend to offer course restricted access and this may be at odds with the institute-wide provision adopted traditionally by libraries. McLean (2002) quoted in Corrall (2004, p.19) argues, however, that such situations can also offer opportunities to those librarians prepared to collaborate closely with academics and educational technologists and accept a redefinition of boundaries between the library and other domains.

Government policy: widening participation and tuition fees

As part of the widening participation agenda, the Government has set targets of 50 per cent entering higher education within the next 10 years. Amongst this larger population entering higher education have been those who have not been previously exposed to independent learning or environments where information literacy is encouraged. This observation has resource and staffing implications for libraries as they meet the challenge of ensuring that such students are not disadvantaged by their lack of information literacy skills. Students are also becoming increasingly demanding of library resources and services as they seek to get what they regard as 'value for money' in return for their tuition fees. In conclusion, the role of the subject librarian has been affected by organisational change and the trend for convergence of services, and cultural changes within society as the Internet revolutionises the way we access information and more people enter higher education.

Changing emphasis in the role of the subject librarian

Having established the external influences that are reshaping the role of the subject librarian, we will now analyse the effect these influences have had on different aspects of the subject librarian's role.

The subject librarian as subject expert

Over time there has been a change of emphasis relating to the subject knowledge of the subject librarian. Traditionally the subject librarian may have had a first or second degree in the subject area that they support but increasingly librarians have been asked to cover a wider subject remit than the subject in which they have a qualification. Recent surveys indicate that many librarians do not necessarily have a qualification in the subject they support. This change reflects not only the organisational trends within libraries but also a broader shift in traditional disciplines with a wider range of degrees now on offer. The SPTL/Academic Law Library Survey 2000/2001 (Jackson, 2002) revealed that of 62 responding institutions, only 15 respondents had at least one member of staff with an academic or professional qualification in law. A survey of academic law librarians in British and Irish Universities in 2000/1 (Young, 2002) looked at the extent to which law librarians have responsibilities other than law. Out of the 66 respondents, only 21, or 31.8 per cent, had no other responsibilities. A total of 35 additional subject responsibilities were noted ranging from accountancy and business to sociology, government, social work and education. Many of the law librarians also had responsibility for European Documentation Centres, official publications and special collections. Taking into consideration operational responsibilities such as desk duties; acquisitions; cataloguing; management of staff and information systems, nearly two-thirds or 60.8 per cent of respondents had responsibilities other than law although the degree of time taken with those roles varied.

Pinfield (2001a, p. 38) argues that while advantageous to have a first degree in a related discipline, what is crucial is that the subject librarian has an appreciation of teaching and research techniques in their subjects, and in the structure of the literature and in key terminology and concepts. This opinion is reinforced by Battin, whom Corrall quotes (2004, p.33) in support of her belief that the new electronic environment will place a greater need for the subject librarian to have a deep knowledge of a discipline's primary questions. Writing from an academic's viewpoint, Toft (2004, p.43) places emphasis on the subject knowledge, commenting that academics primarily want librarians with specialist knowledge with whom they can communicate at the same level as with colleagues. Simester (2000) suggested that the conceptual separation of academic departments from the library needs to be reviewed: he argued that for universities to produce high quality research and teaching, there needs to be good co-operation between academic departments and library and that the current division between academic and support departments may be both artificial and counter productive.

The subject librarian as liaison librarian

The increasing emphasis on liaison with both academic departments and student users is reflected in the recent use of new titles for subject librarians – Faculty Liaison Librarian, Academic Liaison Librarian etc. Woodhead and Martin's surveys in 1982 (Woodhead and Martin, 1982) and 1996 (Martin, 1996) have shown a shift away from a term denoting a subject specialist. Terms in use in 1982 included: subject librarian; subject consultant, reference librarian, tutor librarian and liaison librarian. Although the second survey in 1996 indicated that half the respondents were still using the term subject librarian, a wider range of alternative terms were coming into use including: faculty librarians; subject support officers, academic librarians, link librarians, information librarians and information specialists. Reid (2000) suggests that the newer terms both indicate a 'proper caution about pretending to specialist knowledge that the bearer may not have' and an emphasis on 'information' and 'support'.

The subject librarian as information expert

Lester, quoted in Woodhead and Martin (Woodhead and Martin, 1982, p. 102), speaking at a SCONUL Information Services Group Conference on Subject Specialisation in 1982, argued that ' ... our libraries increasingly need 'information specialists' and not 'subject specialists' ... an academic must find in his or her subject specialist librarian, first and foremost someone with a wide and competent knowledge of librarianship; who knows, or at least knows where to find out, about those specialised areas of librarianship that the academic is ignorant of.

The librarian's familiarity with Internet searching and metadata offers opportunities for skilled practitioners to apply accurate and helpful descriptions to resources. Rikowksi quoted in Sturges (Sturges, 2001 p. 66) sees a new role for the subject librarian as providing a 'bridge' between the subject matter and the emerging technologies. He believes that library staff can, in co-ordination with others, play a leading role in helping faculty understand both how to access information and integrate technology and new information resources into the curriculum. Wolff (1995, p. 85) also believes that as most librarians adapt to new technology, usually in advance of academics, they may become an important source of student learning about technology, its limits, uses and integration into all elements of life. Such developments also allow librarians to position themselves as specialists who complement academics. Court and Rayner (2001, p. 234) quote a librarian who believes that with the growth of information sources available, subject librarians are becoming 'specialists within their fields and increasingly complementary to academic staff whose subject specialties are becoming narrower'.

The subject librarian as hybrid librarian

Developments in technology have acted as an agent of change over the years. Libraries were early adopters of technology with the library management system and have continued to take advantage of developments to use it as a means of providing bibliographic information and latterly full text online content. We now have the hybrid library, defined by Rusbridge (1998, p. 18) as integrating 'access to all … kinds of resources … using different technologies from the digital library world, and across different media'. The role of the librarian has consequently changed from custodian of a physical collection to that of supporting the networked information user. With the emergence of the Internet, academic users now expect 24/7 access to resources from anywhere, made all the more possible by disintermediation.

The move from holdings of information in-house to electronic access to remote sources has changed the emphasis of work from physical collection management to facilitating and managing electronic resources. Librarians, who have traditionally had expertise in negotiating one-off access contracts to print materials have had to take on all the complexities of electronic provision including differing formats, variable pricing models, usage restrictions and ownership rights.

The systems librarian has now been joined by the e-journals coordinator, HERON advisor and special project co-ordinators. In some libraries, such responsibilities are being fulfilled as additional functions of substantive posts; elsewhere new posts have been created such as the eServices Collections and User Support Manager as at the University of Sheffield (Tattersall, 2004). In some circumstances such posts are fixed term posts to allow resources to be placed into getting projects started, for example the JISC funded Exchange of Learning (X4L) programmes.

While subject librarians have traditionally found themselves out on their own as early adopters of technology, there are now a range of departments within an institution utilising web resources and educational technologies necessitating co-ordination with other departments such as learning support departments. Many libraries, taking advantage of the skills that their subject librarians have developed in handling electronic resources, have extended their remit to cover the electronic distribution of institutional information such as student handbooks, exam papers and reading lists. According to Corrall (2004) some are even getting involved in digital asset management, scholarly communications and institutional publishing via open access projects.

Against a background of free and easy access to both quality Internet resources such as the Resource Discovery Network (RDN), and sometimes less authoritative documents found using general search engines, the challenge for librarians according to Brophy (1998) will be to ensure that they continue to 'define a role for themselves in relation to electronic information resources that is regarded as legitimate and necessary by academics and which justifies a continuing allocation of the institution's budget'.

The subject librarian as tutor librarian/learning facilitator

Many writers argue the future role for the librarian is that of an educator or learning support professional (Biddiscombe, 2002 p. 230). Librarians are already taking on the role of the initial mediator and facilitator of resource-based open learning, with increasing responsibilities for first line instruction and supervision of students.

Prado (2002, p. 203) argues that until recently, the only barrier to accessing documentary information was alphabetisation but now an equally powerful new barrier has emerged: technological skills. It is no longer sufficient for the librarian to make the information available; the students need to acquire the information handling skills in order to be able to use it effectively. Since the 1990s there has been increasing emphasis on information literacy, defined by the American Library Association Presidential Committee on Information Literacy (American Library Association, 1989) as the ability '... to recognise when information is needed and have the capacity to locate, evaluate and use effectively the needed information'. Encompassing both IT and information skills, according to the SCONUL model (SCONUL,1999) information literacy programmes should provide at the minimum, bibliographic instruction and at best, should be integrated into all curricula as a learning outcome of higher education. Attempts to fully integrate information skills into academic curricula have met with mixed success but the adoption of VLEs amongst higher education institutions currently offers the opportunity for engagement with academic staff in the provision of resources and training.

The Association of University Teachers in its report on building the academic team (Association of University Teachers, 2001) recognised the contribution made to student learning by academic related staff, and especially librarians, calling on employers to view academic related staff as partners with academic staff in providing higher education. Increasingly, it is not sufficient for the librarian to 'train' students in the use of library resources but have a real understanding of the pedagogy of teaching. Many librarians have felt the need to gain formal educational qualifications to become valued by academics – Court and Rayner (2001) cite one librarian as saying 'It is important that we are seen as equal team members – this is why I went for the PGCE a couple of years ago.' Others have become members of the Higher Education Academy. Relevant qualifications are likely to become increasingly important as librarians position themselves as learning support professionals. Biddiscombe (2002, p. 230) sees such staff as becoming less library- based in the future with weakening links to the traditional library structure.

The subject librarian as collaborator

Having recognised that no one library can encompass all knowledge within its collections, the subject librarian has started to work collaboratively (mainly but not exclusively with other academic libraries) to widen access to resources and find common solutions to common problems. The ELIB projects are an example of co-operative working on hybrid library projects which developed out of the Follett Committee recommendations (1993) that funds and effort be devoted to the concept of the hybrid library. Later projects have concentrated on looking at the integration of systems and services in both the electronic and print environment. Simester (2000) argues that subject specialists often have more in common with subject librarians in other universities than with their own colleagues and that librarians should be considering a more collaborative approach to work, as already adopted by academics.

The Future

The digital librarian

As libraries move away from the hybrid – print and electronic access – approach, one may see the emergence of the cyberarian or digital librarian , defined by Sreenivasulu (2000, p.12) as 'a specialist information professional who manages and organises the digital library, combines the functionality for information, elicitation, planning, data mining, knowledge mining, digital reference services, electronic information services, representation of information, extraction and distribution of information, co-ordination, searching … and retrieval'. Sreenivasulu goes on to say that the ultimate goal of a digital librarian is to 'facilitate access to information just-in-time to the critical wants of end users and additionally to facilitate electronic publishing'. Digital librarians will need to have knowledge of 'searching, web authoring, archiving digital documents, meta-indexing, speech recognition, searching of images and digitisation amongst many other skills'.

Future challenges

New models of library provision mean that it will no longer be possible to predict information requirements in advance – the current 'just in case approach' will be replaced by 'just in time' (Fourie, 2004 p. 67). Courses' use of information will be more dynamic, with teachers changing the emphasis rapidly in response to changing developments. The best library services will succeed where they become an integral part of the learning process and the subject librarian is more involved with course planning.

Wolff (1995, p. 88) argues that the next stage of development for the library is to serve as a full partner in transforming the act of learning.

> The main point is the library needs to be taken out of its confining role as support service and seen as a central element in any institution's response to the learner of the future' and the next challenge is that 'Technology and the information explosion will affect not only the quantity of information available and our access to it but the very

definitions of knowledge and learning ... learning will change as will process – what does it mean to prepare students for a future where there will always be more readily accessible information on any topic than can be mastered? ...where the content as well as the underlying foundational principles of the disciplines ... may change at least once (if not more often) during the individual lifetime?' (Wolff, 1995, p.88).

As has been demonstrated, the academic librarian is expected to embrace new technologies and working practices as well as maintaining a working knowledge of the subjects they support.

Conclusion

Librarians have sought to acquire the skills that Pinfield (2001b, p. 11) identifies as necessary for the modern subject librarian. They have become comfortable with a wide range of formats; adopted an intermediary role using both their good knowledge of sources and user requirements and ability to negotiate with suppliers, and become enablers – proactively connecting users with the information they require. In addition, they have become educators – teaching information skills and information literacy and a publisher of training materials (Fourie, 2004 p. 67)

Many are already working with teams outside the library, building the new partnerships with pedagogic experts, document managers, publishers and other information businesses, both internal and external to the organisation within which they work, that Akeroyd (2001) and Biddiscombe (2002) see as essential for future development of the role. They have become team players, project managers and innovators, working with colleagues in library and IT services and with academics.

The subject scholar is no longer the most appropriate model for many organisations. Indeed Reid (2000) argues that the transition has already been made, with subject knowledge having become a secondary concern and subject responsibility, in reality, being no more than a convenient means of assigning limited areas within which knowledge of resource need and availability can be developed to a 'high degree of compass and depth'.

Finally Gaston (2001, p. 33) argues that, rather than disappear, subject librarians have continuously adapted their roles around a liaison function, which has always differentiated them from other members of the library. If one views academic liaison as the key role of a subject librarian, then a coherent thread of continuity between the past, present and future is clearly identifiable.

References

American Library Association, 1989. *Presidential Committee on Information Literacy: Final Report.* [www] Available from http://www.ala.org/Content/ NavigationMenu/ACRL/Publications/White_Papers_and_Reports/Presidential_

Committee_on_Information_Literacy.htm [Accessed 10 December 2003].

Akeroyd, J., 2001. The future of academic libraries. *Aslib Proceedings,* 53(3), 73–84.

Armstrong, C., 2001. Low ICT Use by Students. *Library Association Record,* 103(6), 358–9.

Association of University Teachers, 2001. *Building the academic team. A report on the contribution of academic-related staff to the delivery of higher education.* London: Association of University Teachers.

Battin, P., 1998–2001, Librarianship in the Twenty-First Century. *Syracuse University Library Associates Courier,* XXXIII, 43–61.

Biddiscombe, R., 2002. Learning Support Professionals: The Changing Role of Subject Specialists in UK Academic Libraries. *Program: Electronic Library and Information Systems,* 6(4), 228–35.

Brophy, P., 2000. Towards a generic model of information and library services in the information age. *Journal of Documentation,* 56(2), 161–84.

Corrall, S., 2004. Rethinking professional competence for the networked environment. *In* M. Oldroyd (ed.), *Developing academic library staff for future success,* London: Facet Publishing, pp. 15–39.

Court, S. and Rayner, A., 2001. When is a librarian a teacher? *Library Association Record,* 103(4), 234–5.

Feather, J., and Sturges, P., 1997. *International encyclopedia of information and library science.* London: Routledge.

Fisher, B., 2004. Converging on staff development. *In* M. Oldroyd (ed.), *Developing academic library staff for future success,* London: Facet Publishing, pp. 61–81.

Fourie, I., 2004. Librarians and the claiming of new roles: how can we try to make a difference? *Aslib Proceedings,* 56(1) 62–74.

Fleming, H.,1986. User education in academic libraries in the UK. *British Journal of Academic Librarianship,* 1 (1), 18–40.

Fleming, H., 1990. Educating the future end-user of online information services. *In* H. Fleming (ed.)*: User education in academic libraries.* London: Library Association, pp. 139–64.

Gaston, R., 2001. The changing role of the Subject Librarian with a particular focus on UK developments, examined through a review of the literature. *The New Review of Academic Librarianship,* 7, 19–36.

Griffiths, J. and Brophy, P., 2001. Student searching behaviour in the JISC information environment. *Adriane* [online] 33. Available from: http://www.ariadne.ac.uk/issue33/edner/ [Accessed 9 August 2004].

Harris, C., 1988. Academic information services at the University of Salford. *British Journal of Academic Librarianship,* 8(3) 147–52.

Harrison, C., 1990. User education in further and higher education compared and contrasted. *In* H. Fleming (ed.) *User education in academic libraries.* London: Library Association, pp. 43–54.

Heseltine, R., 1995. The challenge of learning in cyberspace. *Library Association Record.* 97(8), 432–3.

Jackson, C., 2002. SPTL/BIALL Academic Law Library Survey 2000/2001. *Legal*

Information Management, 2(2), 38–49.

John Fielden Consultancy, 1993. *Supporting expansion: a report on human resource management in academic libraries for the Joint Funding Councils' Libraries Review Group.* Bristol: HEFCE.

Joint Funding Councils' Libraries Review Group, 1993. *Report* (Follett Report). London and Bristol: HEFCE.

Lonsdale, R., and Urquhart, C., 2001. Electronic information resources for higher education: something amassed or amiss? *UKOLUG Newsletter* 12(3), 35–7.

Lovecy, I., 1994. Convergence of libraries and computing services. *Library and Information Briefings*, 54, 1–11.

Marfleet, J., and Kelly, C., 1999. Leading the field; the role of the information professional in the next century. *Electronic Library*, 17(6), 359–64.

Martin, J., 1996. Subject specialization in British university libraries: a second survey. *Journal of Librarianship and Information Science*, 28(3), 159–69.

McLean, N., 2002. *Libraries and e-learning: organisational and technical operability* [online] Available from: www.oclc.org/research/publications/archive/mclean_neil_20020308_rev.doc. [Accessed 21 August 2004].

Pinfield, S., 2001a. The changing role of subject librarians in academic libraries. *Journal of Librarianship and Information Science* 33(1), 32–8.

Pinfield, S., 2001b. Managing electronic library services: current issues in UK higher education institutions [online]. *Ariadne*, 29. Available from http://www.ariadne. ac.uk/issue29/pinfield/intro.html. [Accessed 21 August 2004].

Prado, R. De, 2000. Do users dream of electronic libraries? *Electronic Library*, 18(3), 202–9.

Reid, B., 2000. Organizational models for managing academic information. *In* B. Reid and Foster, W. (eds), *Achieving cultural change in networked libraries*, Aldershot: Gower, 15–26.

Rikowski, R., 2000. The essential bridge: a new breed of professional? *Managing Information,* 7(3), 40–5.

Robertson, D., 1998. *The new renaissance: computers and the next level of civilization.* Oxford University Press: New York.

Rusbridge, C., 1998. Towards the hybrid library, *D-Lib. Magazine*, July-August 1996 [online]. Available from http://www.dlib.org/dlib/july98/rusbridge/07rusbridge. html [Accessed 05 August 2004].

Scrivener, J., 1974. Subject specialization in academic libraries: some British practices. *Australian Academic and Research Libraries,* 5(3), 113–22.

Shoebridge, M., 1998. Case study: managing converged reference services at the University of Birmingham. *In* T. Hanson and J. Day, *Managing the electronic library. A practical guide for information professions.* London: Bowker Saur.

Simester, A., 2000. Collection development and exploitation in the Hybrid Library: an academic perspective [online]. *In 3rd CURL Conference, University of Newcastle-Upon-Tyne, 3–4 April 2000.* Available at http://www.curl.ac.uk/ Presentations/2000%20conference/simester%203rd.html. [Accessed 15 August

2004]

Society of College, National and University Libraries, 1999. *Information skills in Higher Education: a SCONUL position paper* [online]. Available from http://www.sconul.ac.uk/activities/inf_lit/papers.html [Accessed 05 January 2004].

Sreenivasulu, V., 2000. The role of a digital librarian in the management of digital information systems (DIS). *The Electronic Library*, 18(1), 12–20.

Sturges, P., 2001. Gatekeepers and the other intermediaries. *Aslib Proceedings*, 53(2), 62–7.

Sutton, A., 2000. Convergence: a review of the literature. *In* B. Reid. and W. Foster, (eds), *Achieving cultural change in networked libraries*, Aldershot: Gower, 63–75.

Sykes, P., and Gerrard, S., 1998. Operational convergence at Roehampton Institute London and Liverpool John Moores University. *The New Review of Academic Librarianship* 3, 67–89.

Tattersall, M., 2004. A day in the life of an e-resources librarian. *Serials* 17, 3, 210–211.

Thompson, J., 1975, The argument against subject specialisation, or Even a good idea can fail. *ARLIS Newsletter* 22, 3–6.

Toft, Z., 2004. What can librarians for us? An academic's perspective. *Update,* 3(1), 42–43.

University Grants Committee, 1967. *Report of the committee on libraries*. London: HMSO.

Wilson, T., 1998. Redesigning the university library in the digital age. *Journal of Documentation,* 54(1), 15–27.

Woodhead, P., and J. Martin, 1982. 'Subject specialization in British university libraries: a survey. *Journal of Librarianship*, 14(2), 93–108.

Wolff, R., 1995. Using the accreditation process to transform the mission of the library. *New Directions for Higher Education,* 90, 77–91.

Young, H., 2002. Law Librarians' survey: are academic law librarians in decline? *Legal Information Management*, 2(2), 50–55.

Chapter 2

Professional Engagement – The Subject Specialist in Higher Education

Penny Dale with contributions from Maggie Leharne,
Trudi Knight and Kate Marshall

Introduction

Professional engagement works on a number of levels in higher education institutions (HEIs) contributing to personal development, individual and institutional recognition, wider professional engagement and informing communities of practice. All HEIs are unique to some extent, although there are points of commonality amongst parts of the sector; for example new as opposed to old universities or single campus compared to multi-campus institutions. Because of this variation and differences in job descriptions and responsibilities, the parameters of professional engagement vary both for individuals and for institutions. This chapter will attempt to indicate the areas where professional engagement occurs, identify some of the challenges and offer some indicators of possible developments and opportunities. Libraries according to Radford (1998) are 'the ultimate realization of a place where each item within it has a fixed place and stands in an a priori relationship with every other item'. This rigidity is in stark contrast to the students who are using academic libraries, as Prensky (2001) observes 'today's students are no longer the people our educational system was designed to teach'. The chapter will also consider the role of the librarian as knowledge broker, working collaboratively with academics to support students, (Thomas et al. 2004, p. 25). The importance of Continuing Professional Development (CPD) and the contributions of communities of practice to individuals and to the information profession (Wenger 1998, p. 73) will provide the underlying theme to the chapter.

Institution-based engagement

Formal and informal interaction with colleagues in the information and other professions provides subject librarians with opportunities for personal and professional development. Whilst some of this engagement is structured and very public, other contacts are not only unstructured but happen almost accidentally and without the participants sometimes being fully aware of their importance. Unless these engagements are properly identified and recorded, there is a danger that the contribution of individuals' CPD, to their institution, to the information profession and to other professions is lost. In the increasingly competitive environment of higher education (Hughes, 2000) any omission can constitute a wasted opportunity to raise the profile of an individual or their service; the experience at the University of Wales described later in this chapter has been a salutary one. Training diaries, logs, and learning journals (Moon 1999, p. 39) are all mechanisms that subject librarians can use to maintain motivation, inform their appraisals, develop their CV, and where appropriate contribute to research and publication. The Chartered Institute of Library and Information Professionals (CILIP) launched a framework in 2005 to encourage CPD and better reflect the breadth and depth of professional engagement that is undertaken by information professionals. At this very early stage the success of this development remains to be seen.

The many and increasing forms of electronic communication have facilitated the development of professional contacts. Librarians and other information professionals have for some years used JISCmail and its predecessor Mailbase as a forum for debate as well as for information sharing and dissemination. More recently weblogs have provided additional and sometimes alternative means of communicating and sharing project news. These can be on an intranet, as at the University of Greenwich, where a weblog was used on an e-learning project as well as on the World Wide Web (WWW) as a means of disseminating information across the profession, of which Sheila Webber's Information Literacy Weblog (Webber 2005) is an example. There are other tools, for example podcasting which is a way of publishing sound files to the internet, allowing users to subscribe to a feed and receive new audio files automatically (Wikipedia, 2005). The use and development of such tools will change to a greater or lesser degree not only how we engage with our users, but also how we engage with our own and other professions. Virtual communities of practice within the information professions continue to flourish on JISCmail while online communities such as Informationcity provide a range of online services including networking, training and (perhaps a worrying development) retail opportunities. The Higher Education Academy (HEA) and the regional development agencies provide interdisciplinary and regional examples of how information professionals can work with other colleagues in virtual communities of practice, but the full potential of cross-sectoral communication is probably still to be fully exploited.

Development is a two-way process; as well as being receivers of developmental opportunities professional staff also have a duty to provide learning and developmental opportunities to colleagues. Personal professional development and the responsibility to 'encourage colleagues…, to maintain and enhance their professional knowledge and competence' is embodied in CILIP's Ethical Principles and Code of Professional Practice (2003).

Staff Development programmes within an institution provide opportunities for CPD as well as opportunities for contribution to training sessions, research seminars and conferences. In-house training sessions are relatively safe environments in which newly qualified professionals can develop their presentation skills and allow themselves to get used to the culture of their organisation (Hyde, 2000), whilst more experienced staff can use colleagues as internal peer reviewers for work destined for wider promulgation. The contribution of subject librarians to the learning and teaching agenda encompasses working with academic colleagues on curriculum development, embedding information literacy into teaching programmes, and involvement with the HEA. Successful competition for national awards such as the National Teaching Fellowships indicates the level of engagement with other disciplines and brings added richness to subject librarianship. This is wider than the all-important relationships with academic disciplines which will be dealt with elsewhere in this chapter, as it includes other support staff. This synergy is growing in importance as support staff no longer provide relatively isolated islands of service but work together to provide a seamless service to enhance the learning environment (Hart, 2004). Examples include support for additional learning needs, IT support and staff development. Experienced information staff who contribute to the wider student support arena can benefit from re-invigorating ideas and new contacts as a result of these interactions.

Regional, national and international engagement

Beyond the home institution there are a number of regional and sub-regional groups; the M25 Group, North West Academic Libraries (NoWAL), and the Scottish Academic Libraries Cooperative Training Group (SALcTG) are examples but there are many groups, effectively communities of practice, offering opportunities for librarians to further their own development and contribute to wider issues that concern them and the profession. CILIP has regional and special interest groups that respond to professional issues be they subject, functional or regional. The Framework of Qualifications (2004) laid down some important directions for the profession; encompassing support and mentoring, chartering, and continuing professional development with the intention of '... raising the status of the professional body to one that views its validation as a current dynamic activity, not one rooted in history'.

The role of CILIP and the debate concerning its value to the information profession has been described by, amongst others, Corrall (2002) and Owen (2003), as well as extensively (and frequently less positively) in online discussion lists during 2004/5. On an international level, the International Federation of Library Associations and Institutions (IFLA) provide diverse opportunities for professional engagement with information professionals from around the world. The value of conferences organised by these, and other, professional bodies is considerable, both in terms of professional development and networking. However the cost of sending staff to these events means that institutions are increasingly selective, and attendance even to present a paper cannot be assured. The information community has responded to this in part by the creation of awards and bursaries to encourage wider participation.

This practice extends to some institutions and subject librarians need to be proactive, and apply as appropriate to ensure that external opportunities are available to them.

Many subject librarians in the UK are also members of the HEA, established in 2003 by the merger of the Institute for Learning and Teaching in Higher Education, the Learning and Teaching Support Networks and the National Coordination Team for the Teaching Quality Enhancement Fund. This forum enables subject librarians to engage not only with other information professionals involved with learning and teaching but also the wider academic community. Powis (2004) noted that 'involvement in teaching bodies enhanced our credibility within our organisations and gave us a shared language to speak with academics...'

CILIP, SCONUL, IFLA, HEA and other professional organisations give subject librarians opportunities to work in communities of practice as defined by Lave and Wenger (1991, p. 98) as '...an activity system about which participants share understandings concerning what they are doing and what that means in their lives and for their community. Thus, they are united in both action and in the meaning that the action has, both for themselves, and for the larger collective'. Subject librarians have responded to the academic community, the 'larger collective', through involvement with both centrally funded projects such as those run by the Joint Information Systems Committee (JISC) and the Resource Discovery Network (RDN), and institutionally funded projects such as the KnowledgeShare project (Dale et al., 2005) to develop group bibliographic software at Bournemouth University. Mentoring schemes, CILIP special interest groups, and regional groupings provide further opportunities for participation based on confidence, understanding and co-operation, shared language and mutual support (Price 2005).

The literature describing different aspects of professional engagement amongst subject librarians is extensive, but what seems to be lacking is wide and sustained debate and reflection upon the value of these activities. Other professions within the social sciences appear to engage more freely in this type of analysis. This may be because of the nature of the literature (or even the nature of subject librarians!), it might also be an indicator of the post-modern environment in HEIs that drives a continual reinvention of the role, leaving little space or purpose for this level of analysis. Harley et al. (2001) identify student attitudes, the WWW and consumerism as indicators of post-modernism in academic libraries. The information literacy debate, the introduction of a realistic CPD framework and the possibilities presented by electronic communication might signal an opportunity for subject librarians to review the purpose and value of professional engagement.

Engagement with academic staff

Whilst engagement has connotations of participation, sharing or collaboration, it also has an alternative definition as a meeting of opposing forces. The literature suggests that the reality lies somewhere between these two definitions with the extent and quality of engagement dependent upon factors such as the skills and personal attributes of the subject specialist, institutional structures, and the attitude of academic staff.

Recruitment and development of subject librarians should focus on reinforcing interpersonal skills and innovation together with a commitment to continuing professional development and current awareness. In this way subject specialists will be encouraged to create and embrace opportunities for engagement with academics, proactively selling the library, its services and the contribution that they can make to the learning and teaching activities of the institution. Hughes (2000) discusses the notion of the 'competitive space' as academic librarians now find themselves working in competition as providers of information services and support, and need to be outgoing and creative in order to successfully meet this challenge.

As noted earlier in this chapter, institutional structure in HEIs also necessarily influences the level of engagement between subject specialists and academic staff. Since the publication of the findings of The National Committee of Inquiry into Higher Education (1997) (hereafter the 'Dearing Report'), higher education has increasingly focused on supporting independent learning. This change in the academic climate, as well as funding issues, rising student numbers and government policy initiatives such as widening participation, has stimulated many university libraries to respond by restructuring in recent years, developing proactive, user-focused services.

For example, Wilson (2003) suggests that since the Dearing Report 'information services within higher education have undergone enormous change' and found that 48 per cent of surveyed respondents' job titles had indeed changed. Pinfield (2001) also highlights this change suggesting that 'in recent years, the roles of subject librarians have been reprioritised in many libraries', with an increasing emphasis on faculty liaison 'which has often been reflected in the new titles for subject librarians: "Faculty Team Librarian", "Liaison Librarian", even "Learning Advisor".'

Restructuring does not, however, always have a positive impact on subject specialists' engagement with academic staff. The University of Wales, Bangor, Executive (2005) has proposed a radical restructuring of library provision arguing that 'support to the academic and student communities from the qualified subject librarians, whatever its contribution to the teaching and research roles of the institution, is hard to justify in value-for-money terms at a time when the process of literature searches is substantially deskilled by online bibliographical resources'. Under the proposed structure a single 'User Support Officer' will replace the majority of subject specialist positions. If adopted, this structure is likely to significantly impact on the engagement of the library with academic staff, as a single user-support officer is unlikely to be able to engage to any significant extent with academics.

A useful analysis of institutional structure is provided by the Deliberations project (London Metropolitan University, 2005) which identified three primary models of liaison between academic staff and librarians. In the 'Running Behind' model, liaison is characterised by unco-ordinated communication and a reactive response to teaching and learning requirements. In the 'Partnerships' model, liaison is more formalised with the librarian proactively engaged with the academic departments, whilst in the 'Sharing Assessment' model, the librarian is sufficiently involved in the academic structure to contribute to the assessment process. In reality the engagement experience of any individual subject specialist is likely to be a mixture of these three models, with the level of collaboration with academic staff varying according to academic level, discipline and the attitude of individual academics.

How academic staff perceive the library is crucial to the quality of professional engagement. Whyley and Callender (1997) reported that many support staff 'felt that the academics they worked with did not recognise the importance of the service they provided'. While academics may understand the value of traditional library activities such as collection development and promotion of services, evidence suggests that information literacy skills training is undervalued. In a US survey of academics Yang (2000) found that while significant numbers of academics ranked activities such as 'updating faculty of the services available in the library' and 'ordering books or serials for faculty' as 'very important' only 17.5 per cent of respondents considered 'conducting bibliographic instruction to the students' to be an important aspect of the librarian's role. Similarly, Gonzales (2001) found that 'the fact that faculty members received library research instruction from a librarian did not relate positively to the faculty members' decision to ask a librarian to give instruction to their students'.

Nimon (2002) supports the view that to succeed in having the learning support role – information literacy – taken seriously, librarians must 'be equipped with refined skills and the conceptual knowledge which enables them to perform with an educational competence, and professional confidence, equal to that of their academic peers'. It is a view echoed by Bell and Shank (2004) who highlighted the fact that academic librarians lag in 'understanding of pedagogy and adoption of instructional design theory and practice'. Training and development in this area will enable the subject specialist to develop knowledge and understanding of teaching and learning to facilitate engagement with academic staff.

The subject specialist should also investigate institutional sources of funding for initiatives, such as e-learning, which could be used to consolidate their professional skills and engagement with academic staff, especially if these are sources of funding for which non- academic staff have not been traditionally considered. Publishing, especially in non-library journals, will also raise the professional profile of the subject specialist. One way to gain recognition for the teaching role of the subject specialist is to seek accreditation by the HEA, 'means by which existing professionalism in diverse institutional contexts to support continuous professional development and evaluation of practice can be recognised and rewarded'.

Maintaining current awareness of issues relating to teaching and learning and building a strong professional relationship with institutional directors of research, learning and quality will enable the subject specialist to effectively market their skills and knowledge to academic staff. The Quality Assurance Agency in Higher Education (QAA) (2001) places emphasis on encouraging 'students to reflect upon and evaluate their own learning experiences and plan for their own development' through 'Personal Development Planning'. Kempcke (2002, p. 538) points out that information literacy 'serves both vocational and more traditional academic purposes'. The QAA goal to encourage students to 'become more effective, independent and confident self-directed learners' is at the heart of information literacy programmes and thus there is scope for subject specialists to engage with academic staff and work as knowledge brokers towards a shared agenda.

The subject specialist also has a knowledge brokerage role in supporting the research and teaching information needs and interests of academics. The librarian must establish what these needs are so as to determine what information is appropriate, and then develop the skills to effectively disseminate this information. This may be either formal – (for example, participation at programme committee meetings, staff notice boards within a School, creation of webpages and blogs) or informal through socialisation.

Projects funded by the JISC (Joint Information Systems Committee), such as Big Blue Connect (2003) and *JISC Usage Surveys: Trends in Electronic Information Services* (or JUSTEIS) (JISC 2004) have identified a skills gap with regard to academics' information handling competences. Yang (2000) noted, in a study of academic staff perceptions of library-faculty liaison, that when encountering problems in conducting their own research only 12.5 per cent of respondents would consult their subject specialist in the first instance, and that the majority preferred to use either the library or the Internet to locate information themselves. Price (1999) describes the 'Invisible College' where 'conferences, discussions over coffee and phone calls to colleagues have been joined by e-mail as the most effective ways of keeping up with the field.' In the same paper Price quotes research by Barry and Squires (1995) which suggests that 'academics only learn and use the IT-assisted information systems where they perceive themselves as having a need that can be met by that system'. This highlights the important role subject specialists can have in developing the information literacy skills of academic staff. This support could be through formal development opportunities such as leading or participating in staff training events, to more informal methods such as personal communication, newsletters, and e-mail.

The subject specialist also has a key role in providing academic staff with current awareness of the resources and services offered by the library. Anecdotal evidence suggests that student misconceptions about library services can in part be attributed to out-of-date information provided by academic staff. In keeping academic staff aware of service developments and effectively marketing new services, misconceptions amongst staff and students can be challenged and corrected.

To be successful, engagement between subject specialist and academics has to be a continuing and collaborative process. As Nimon (2002) has said 'cooperation between academics and librarians to promote mutual goals commonly occurs, but there is evidence that more can be done not only to improve general understanding of the potential contribution of librarians but simultaneously to enhance it'. Successful engagement with academics can only promote the role subject specialists have to play in developing Webber and Johnston's (2004) concept of the Information Literate University.

Engagement with students

Information skills programmes provide perhaps the most formal contacts that subject librarians have with students and these contacts and the issues of information literacy that go with them are covered substantially elsewhere in this book, notably Chapter 3. Information literacy is about more than information skills (Price 2005). On one level it is about being able to find information in a timely and efficient manner, but it is also about knowing what to do with the information once it is found. Bundy (2005) points out that Information literacy is not the same as information skills or user education. Harley et al. (2001) suggest that librarians are operating in a post-modern condition characterized by consumerism, superficiality and knowledge fragmentation and that 'bibliographic instruction' must recognize this. The challenge is therefore to equate Harley's assertion that 'most students are not interested in knowing how a library is organized, or which reference sources to use. They simply want the information required for their course assignments' with the need to encourage deep thinking and reflection (Biggs 2003, p. 16). The framework that Harley et al. (2001) suggest to resolve this apparent conflict concentrates on facilitating critical thinking and spending less time on explaining resources, organisations and structures. Oberman (1991) observes that context promotes critical thinking, and that student learning needs to be a progression towards self-reliance. At Bournemouth University the library induction programme has evolved into an academic services wide induction, with an emphasis on the context; who to ask, where to look and how to find out, rather than the specifics of using any of the services. Post-induction information skills programmes are embedded closely into teaching programmes and subject librarians have undertaken a benchmarking exercise to map onto the QAA framework. In a model from the US, the University of Maryland (UM) has all information literacy sessions based on marked assignments, and library induction programmes are no longer delivered. Information skills programmes at UM are delivered by a range of staff including paraprofessional and technical staff, freeing professional staff time for the preparation of learning materials and getting students involved in the research process.

It is probably unrealistic to expect students to learn all they need to know from formal situations, whether 'real' in the sense of real time information skills sessions or 'virtual' via a virtual learning environment (VLE). Informal opportunities can present themselves at the enquiry desk or from a chance meeting in the corridor or coffee shop. Some institutions have adopted 'rovering'(Gill and Newton 2002) as a means of reaching enquirers who do not approach the enquiry desk, whilst attendance at course committees is another way of making informal, as well as formal, contact.

Engagement with students: widening participation

Widening participation, lifelong learning, legislative changes and financial imperatives are contributing factors to the diversity of students with whom subject librarians are engaging. From 2006 top-up fees will add to the increasingly consumerist culture of HEIs although fee-paying students have played an increasing part in the UK university system for some time, not only at postgraduate levels but at undergraduate levels as institutions compete for the revenue generated by international students. Overseas students, mature students, distance learners, students with additional learning needs and the many others who come into the wide and imprecise category of widening participation may have particular, yet very different, problems engaging with the concept of information literacy. There is also the possibility that *all* students are part of the widening participation agenda; a delegate at one of the Libraries Without Walls conferences observed that we are all distance learners now. What is certain is that most students today think and process information differently from their predecessors: Prensky (2001) refers to 'digital natives' or students who have grown up surrounded by the toys and tools of the digital age. Unless subject librarians can understand their different and diverse needs, many students will not engage with information literacy, perceiving it as unconnected with their study, work or professional practice (Rutter and Dale 2004, p. 87). If students see information skills simply as a means to an end, they are taking the surface learning approach as described by Marton and Saljo (1984) and they will have missed an opportunity to acquire good information handling skills that are transferable to both the workplace or study at Master's level and beyond.

Harley et al. (2001) identify two 'paths' that librarians could create to bridge the gap between 'those most in need of research assistance and guidance and those most able to provide it'. Their first path is to attract more students and find ways of engaging them once they are inside academic libraries, whilst the second path is to explore ways of delivering resources and services outside libraries. Martell (2000, p. 104) predicts that librarians will deal with users almost exclusively in a virtual environment; this assertion is supported by the growth of means of electronic communication; VLEs, blogs, podcasts and so on. Engagement with students is fast becoming one of human and computer interaction. The design and accessibility of websites, the management of electronic books, journals, issues surrounding authentication and interoperability are all as important to the process as a knowledge of approaches to learning and different styles of learning (Biggs, 2003, p. 17). However, there are still students whom Prensky (2001) describes as 'digital immigrants' who have not grown up with a high level of exposure to technology, who are wary of it or who simply cannot afford it, so engagement with students continues on a real as well as virtual level.

Conclusion

In conclusion there are some themes that indicate possible opportunities for subject librarians and the ways in which they engage not only with academic and other professional colleagues but also with students and the development of information literacy. One theme is postmodernism, as by examining the contexts in which students learn, subject librarians can 'enable the reader ... to frame knowledge without constraints rather than on understanding an imposed, external organization of that knowledge' (Anderson, 1992, p. 114). Developments in electronic communications will facilitate this process, but subject librarians must be prepared to fully engage as knowledge brokers with information literacy at the core of learning and teaching, and to do this, opportunities for training and CPD need to be available. Currently, there are no CILIP-accredited courses at either undergraduate or postgraduate level that cover learning and teaching, therefore to gain these skills librarians have to either commit to a PG Cert or PG Dip in Learning and Teaching or find their way through distance learning, short courses offered by professional organisations or, in some institutions, in-house training. Once the skills are in place, HEA accreditation is a way of giving them validity and recognition. However there is a arguably a need for further provision, perhaps using short courses and distance learning, to enable subject librarians to acquire the learning and teaching skills and pedagogy. Information literacy in the learning and teaching agenda is seen as a political development by Owusu-Ansah (2004) and Bundy (2005) who have called for librarians to challenge the educational system and drive change, whilst Webb and Zhang (1997) urged librarians to make a 'revolutionary response' and move from organisation to the production of knowledge in order to counter the new technologies that threaten the existence of libraries. The role of communities of practice is established in the library profession; however in the climate of change and challenge that subject librarians are working in there might be scope for some re-evaluation and perhaps consolidation. The communities of practice of which subject librarians are part need to reflect the role of knowledge brokers, and support not only subject librarians but also students, academics and other support staff.

References

Anderson, G., 1992. Dimensions, context and freedom. The library in the social creation of knowledge. In Barrett, E. (ed.), *Sociomedia: multimedia, hypermedia, and the social construction of knowledge*, Cambridge, MA.: MIT, pp. 107–124.

Barry, C. and Squires, D., 1995. Why the move from traditional information-seeking to the electronic library is not straightforward for academic users: some surprising findings. *Online Information Proceedings*, December, 177–187.

Bell, S. and Shank, J., 2004. The blended librarian: a blueprint for defining the teaching and learning role of academic librarians. *College and Research Libraries News*, 65 (7), 372–375.

Biggs, J., 2003. *Teaching for quality learning at university*. 2nd ed. Buckingham: SHRE.

Bruce, C., 1997. *The seven faces of information literacy*. Adelaide: Auslib Press.

Bundy, A., 2005. Changing and connecting the educational silos: the potential of the information literacy framework. *LILAC 2005*. 5 April 2005 *Imperial College*. London: LILAC.

Chartered Institute of Library and Information Professionals, (CILIP) 2003. *Professional Ethics* [online]. Available from: http://www.cilip.org.uk/

professionalguidance/ethics [Accessed 18 April 2005].

Chartered Institute of Library and Information Professionals, (CILIP) 2004. *Framework for Professional Qualifications* [online]. Available from: http://www. cilip.org.uk/qualificationschartership/FrameworkofQualifications/ [Accessed 15 July 2005].

Corrall, S., 2002. The inclusive library: rethinking information services for the network society. *Library and Information Update*, 1 (9), 24–5.

Dale, P. et al., 2005. KnowledgeShare: bibliographic software to support collaborative work. In B. Newland, et al. (eds.), *Flexible Learning: How far have we come?* 5–6 July 2004, Bournemouth University. Poole: Learning Design Studio, *Bournemouth University*, 24–31.

Gill, M., and Newton, A., 2002. Longing to be free of the enquiry desk? *SCONUL Newsletter*, 25 43–45.

Gonzales, R., 2001. Opinions and experiences of university faculty regarding library research instruction. Results of a web-based survey at the University of Southern Colorado. *Research Strategies*, 18 191–201.

Harley, B. et al., 2001. The postmodern condition: students, the web and academic library services. *Reference Services Review*, 29 (1), 23–32.

Hart, L., 2004. Managing merged services. *Multimedia Information and Technology*, 30, (1), 154–155.

Higher Education Academy, 2004. *Proposals for national professional standards for supporting learning in higher education.* [online]. Available from: http://www. heacademy.ac.uk/regand accr/StandardsModelsFinalPaper.pdf [Accessed 21 April 2005].

Hughes, C., 2000. Information services for higher education. A new competitive space. *D-Lib Magazine* [online], 6 (12). Available from: http://www.dlib.org/dlib/ december00/hughes/12hughes.html [Accessed 20 April 2005].

Hyde, M., 2000. Developing your career inhouse. *Records Management Bulletin*, 99, 15, 17–18.

Informationcity. 2005. The online community for library and information professionals. Available from: http://informationcity.com. [Accessed 11 May 2005]

Joint Information Systems Committee (JISC) 2004. JISC Usage Surveys: Trends in *Electronic Information Services* [online]. Available from: http://dil.aber.ac.uk/ dils/research/justeis/cyc2rep.pdf [Accessed 19 April 2005].

Kempcke, K., 2002. The Art of War for Librarians. *Portal*, 2 (4), 529–551.

Lave, J. and Wenger, E., 1991. *Situated learning: Legitimate peripheral participation.* Cambridge: Cambridge University Press.

London Metropolitan University, 2005. *Deliberations Project: Linking course provision to resources* [online]. Available from: http://londonmet.ac.uk/ deliberations/courses-and-resources/course-provision.cfm [Accessed 17 April 2005].

Manchester Metropolitan University, 2003. *Big Blue Connect, final report* [online]. Available from: http://www.library.mmu.ac.uk/bbconnect/finalreport.pdf

[Accessed 19 April 2005].

Martell, C., 2000. The disembodied librarian in the digital age, part ii. *College and Research Libraries*, 61 (2), 99 –113.

Marton, F., and Saljo, R., 1984. Approaches to learning. In F. Marton, D.J. Hounsell, and N.J. Entwistle, (eds) *The experience of learning*, Edinburgh: Scottish Academic Press.

Moon, J., 1999. *Learning journals: a handbook for academics, students and professional development*. London: Kogan Page.

National Committee of Inquiry into Higher Education (NCIHE), 1997. *Higher Education in the Learning Society: Report of the National Committee (Dearing Report)* [online]. Available from: http://www.leeds.ac.uk/educol/ncihe/ [Accessed 17 April 2005].

Nimon, M., 2002. Developing lifelong learners: controversy and the educative. *Australian Academic & Research Libraries* [online], 33 (1). Available from: http://www.alia.org.au/publishing/aarl/33.1/full.text/nimon.html [Accessed 17 April 2005].

Oberman, C., 1991. Avoiding the cereal syndrome, or critical thinking in the electronic environment. *Library Trends*, 39 (3), 199–202.

Owen, T.B., 2003. Lessons in information literacy. *Information World Review*, 191 24.

Owusu-Ansah, E., 2004. Information literacy and higher education: placing the academic library in the centre of a comprehensive solution. *Journal of Academic Librarianship*, 30 (1), 3–16.

Pinfield, S., 2001. The changing role of subject librarians in academic libraries. *Journal of Librarianship and Information Science*, 33 (1), 32–38.

Prensky, M., 2001. Digital natives, digital immigrants. *On the horizon* [online], 9 (5). Available from: http://www.twitchspeed.com/site/Prensky%20-%20Digital%20 Natives,%20Digital%20Immigrants%20-%20Part1.htm [Accessed 1 December 2004].

Price, G. 1999. User education in higher education: helping academics join the learning environment. *In* IATUL, *The future of libraries in human communication*. 17 –21 May 1999. Technical University of Crete, Chania, Crete. Available from: http://www.iatul.org/conference/proceedings/vol09/papers/price.html [Accessed 17 April 2005]

Price, G., 2005. Keynote address. *LILAC 2005*. 4–6 April 2005 *Imperial College* London.

Quality Assurance Agency in Higher Education (QAA), 2001. *Guidelines for HE progress files* [online]. Available from: http://www.qaa.ac.uk/ academicinfrastructure/progressFiles/guidelines/progfile2001.asp [Accessed 21 April 2005].

Radford, G., 1998. The bibliotheque fantastique. *Library Trends*, 46 (4), 616–634.

Rutter, L. and Dale, P., 2004. Ways to engage widening participation students. *In* P. Brophy, et al. (eds.) *Libraries without walls 5: the distributed delivery of library and information services*, London: Facet.

Thomas, L., et al., 2004. *Learning brokerage: building bridges between learners and providers*. London: Learning and Skills Development Agency.

University of Wales, Bangor 2005. *Proposed restructuring of the library provision at UWB: a consultation paper* [online]. Available from: http://www.bangor.ac.uk/is/iss069/website/strategyfinal.pdf

Webb, J., and Powis, C., 2004. *Teaching Information Skills: Theory and Practice*. London: Facet.

Webb, T., and Zhang, B., 1997. Information dropshipping. *Library Hi-Tech*, 57–58, 145–149.

Webber, S., 2005. *Sheila Webber's Information Literacy Weblog* [online]. Available from: http://ciquest.shef.ac.uk/infolit/ [Accessed 18 April 2005].

Webber, S. and Johnson, B., 2004. Perspectives on the information literate university. *SCONUL Focus* [online], 33 (Winter), 33–35. Available from: http://www.sconul.ac.uk/pubs_stats/newsletter/33/12.pdf

Wenger, E., 1998. *Communities of practice*. Cambridge: Cambridge University Press.

Whyley, C., and Callender, C., 1997. *Report 4, Administrative and support staff in higher education: their experiences and expectations*. National Committee of Inquiry into Higher Education. Available from: http://www.leeds.ac.uk/educol/niche/ [Accessed 18 April 2005].

Wikipedia. 2005. The free encyclopedia. Available from: http://en..org/wiki/ [Accessed 11 May 2005].

Wilson, R., 2003. Learner support staff in higher education: victims of change? *Journal of Librarianship and Information Science*, 35 (2), 79–86.

Yang, Z., 2000. University Faculty's Perception of a Library Liaison Program: A Case Study. *Journal of Academic Librarianship*, 26 (2), 124–128.

Chapter 3

Quality Assurance, Quality Enhancement

Jill Beard

Introduction

The process of audit and review can be a catalyst for librarians to create some of the most productive partnerships with academics and others who provide services to students. However it is often seen as a source of anxiety, but if viewed as an opportunity not a threat, the experience can be turned to advantage by subject librarians and library quality managers and so facilitate continual service enhancement for students and faculty.

Interacting with the process of audit and review is challenging with so many variations on a theme. This chapter reflects on the processes used during the past ten years and the reader will need to apply lessons learnt to the current system. The lessons are positive ones; proactive involvement in the process of review delivers benefits to the library and improved services to students. Underpinning the quality review process, however, has to be a robust mechanism to gather feedback from users and the commitment to respond to challenging feedback at all levels of the library service.

Quality assurance and learning resources

In 1995 Jean Sykes, when Chair of the Society of College, National and University Libraries (SCONUL) Working Group on Quality Assurance, described in a conference paper delivered at Bournemouth University the two types of quality assessment then being undertaken in the UK (Sykes,1996). Audit led by the Higher Education Quality Council (HEQC) was UK-wide and looked at a university's procedures. In contrast, assessment was managed differently by the four national funding councils and looked at the teaching quality of academic departments. The process known as Teaching Quality Assessment (TQA) was set up in 1993 to complement the Research Assessment Exercise (RAE). The process has evolved, with each revision claimed by those who manage quality assurance to be an improvement or simplification of the system. The rigour and burden of the early quality assurance processes was criticised by academics who were sceptical about its credibility whilst looking for simple and transparent processes (Laughton, 2003). The inclusion of a focus on learning resources has raised the profile of library services and their relationship with users. Each variation in the process has presented a challenge to those working in libraries to maintain the emphasis. Nevertheless senior librarians lobbied hard to ensure learning resources remained in the audit process, thus demonstrating to reviewers the significance of an effective relationship between teaching staff and their libraries, a relationship which is central to quality enhancement of the services we deliver.

In 1995 the SCONUL Working Group on Quality Assurance and Libraries provided its first guidance note for teaching quality assessors. It should be noted that from the first edition it included libraries and IT and was endorsed by the Universities and Colleges Information Systems Association (UCISA). The document proved invaluable as a checklist to form an agenda for discussion with the TQA subject teams and enhanced the dialogue between faculty and library services. In 1996 Jean Sykes, on behalf of SCONUL, compiled the first guidance note for assessors to be used in their training and to inform their questioning when on review visits (SCONUL 1996). Having learning resources highlighted in assessor training also enhanced the discourse about learning resources that took place within institutions during visit preparations.

A major rationalisation of the quality infrastructure took place in 1997 with the formation of the Quality Assurance Agency for Higher Education (QAA). The agency took on responsibility for both audit and review. Universities were engaged in both audit of the institution and the extensive review of subjects. SCONUL lobbied and achieved continued use of the *Aide-mémoire for reviewers evaluating learning resources*. A note of caution raised by Sykes in 1996 remains worthy of serious consideration not only at the institutional level but also in the subject context throughout any engagements scheduled until 2005/6:

> ...it has become clear that the degree of prominence which will be given to the library service during audit will depend almost entirely on the written documentation submitted by the University itself. (Sykes 1996).

Quality assurance in England and Northern Ireland since 1993

Before moving on to discuss current practice, it is helpful to document the major phases and developments in the audit of institutions and the assessment of the quality of academic delivery. The ways in which academic quality has been judged and reported on has varied between the different parts of the UK, and the focus here is on the experience in England and Northern Ireland,

Teaching Quality Assessment and Subject Review 1993–2001

1993–1995 Teaching Quality Assessment This was led by the Higher Education Funding Councils (HEFC) and looked at the student learning experience and student achievement in each subject area awarding the grade of excellent, satisfactory or unsatisfactory. There was no SCONUL guidance for the review of learning resources.

1995–2001 Universal Subject Review This was QAA-led from 1997 and covered six aspects of provision, each graded 1–4 with the higher the number the better the grade. Learning Resources was one of the strands and reviewers received the SCONUL aide-mémoire. (SCONUL 1996) Institutions had to provide extensive 'base room' documentation for the review teams on all aspects of the review.

Academic Quality Audit from 1991

1991–1997 First round of audits of institutions led by HEQC and its predecessor the *Academic Audit Unit*.

1997–2002 Second round of audits known as Continuation Audits undertaken by the QAA with an institution-wide focus on the learning infrastructure, communication and quality.

2003–2005 Since being announced in 2001 *Institutional Audit* was developed into the prime approach with the focus on quality assurance processes. A Self Evaluation Document (SED) was prepared before audit and student views documented in a Student Written Submission (SWS), complemented by selected Discipline Audit Trails (DAT) to test those processes. This process is supported by Academic Review of subjects as part of a transitional period, mostly for directly funded HE in FE programmes, but with some residual subject coverage in HEIs. This is described as a 'lighter touch' due for completion in 2006. From 2006 audits will be on a six-year cycle. Supporting Institutional Audit is the Collaborative Provision Audit (CPA) scheduled for 2006 for those institutions with significant collaborative provision. The focus is on the effectiveness of the awarding institutions' quality assurance structures and mechanisms for collaborative programmes.

QAA as agent for other organisations

2003–2006 Major review of healthcare The QAA is carrying out a major review of National Health Services (NHS) funded programmes.

How library services contribute to quality audit

The QAA, in their publication *A brief guide to quality assurance in UK higher education*, described the context for institutional audits to be undertaken in all HEIs between 2003 and 2005 to ensure institutions are:

> providing higher education awards and qualifications of acceptable quality and appropriate and academic standard; and (where relevant) exercising their legal powers to award degrees in a proper manner' (QAA, 2003a)

The QAA also articulated two definitions for 'standards' and 'quality' in higher education. Both are important to understanding the evolution of audit and review and the role that libraries can contribute to the enhancement of quality. In Scotland the word enhancement already features in their title for review process *Enhancement led institutional review*:

> Academic standards are a way of describing the level of achievement that a student has to reach to gain an academic award … It should be at a similar level across the UK …Academic quality is a way of describing how well the learning opportunities available to students help them achieve their award. It is about making sure that appropriate and effective, support assessment and learning opportunities are provided for them. (QAA, 2003a).

Institutions are expected to have internal quality assurance processes for attaining standards and assuring and enhancing the quality of their provision. The development of the *Code of practice for the assurance of academic quality and standards in higher education* (QAA 2004a) has ten sections each with precepts or principles that should be able to be demonstrated in audit. Many of these ten points lend themselves to being supported by subject librarians. Point 6 in the code is programme approval, monitoring and review. Subject librarians should be reassured that any involvement in course planning is contributing to a key element of institutional quality. Institutional Audit makes this involvement an absolute necessity. Point 4 in the code of practice sets out the context for external examining (QAA 2004b). Whatever the form of engagement with the QAA, therefore, subject librarians must ensure they see the reports regularly and respond to any action planning, monitoring and feedback for any issues relating to learning resources.

The other eight sections also give pointers where subject librarians can make a contribution, especially if they can provide best practice examples in assuring the quality and standards in HE. They are: postgraduate research programmes; collaborative provision; students with disabilities; academic appeals and student complaints on academic matters; assessment of students; career education, information and guidance, placement learning, recruitment and admissions.

Current practice

Bournemouth University case study 1: evidencing good practice

An example of best practice from Bournemouth University, which has been used with success in Intuitional Audit, the review of Foundation Degrees and Academic Review of a subject (Equine Studies 2005) being taught in FE, is the appointment of a Peripatetic Support Librarian. The postholder works to support information skills training, staff development and support in partner colleges working with librarians and academic staff teaching to HE awards. The remit has recently been expanded to co-ordinate support for other services under the broad remit of Academic Services,

ICT, Learning Support, and Staff Development. This is described in greater depth in Chapter 5.

Case study 1 illustrates how many of the quality assurance processes librarians engage with will directly or indirectly enable an institution to demonstrate innovation and best practice when it comes to the writing of the SED. It may require persistence to ensure these examples are included. This challenge will be revisited when discussing the importance of what may be said in the SED.

The Mission of the QAA may have been described in many different ways since 1997, but the current version is simple and concise and must underpin why subject librarians and library quality managers should continue to work with those in their institutions who have been and will continue to be working in partnership with the QAA to continuously improve higher education:

> Our mission is to safeguard the public interest in sound standards of higher education qualifications and to encourage continuous improvement in the management of the quality of higher education. We do this by working with higher education institutions to define academic standards and quality, and we carry out and publish reviews against these standards. (QAA 2005a).

Guidelines for Progress

This chapter can only be a snapshot in time and the reader must refer to the latest guidance given by the QAA and as the transitional phase 2002–2005 draws to a close we can expect to see new guidance emerging. The reader should take reassurance that if the following advice is acted upon, libraries will continue to contribute to quality enhancement and the profile and value of their work should be seen as being central to the learning experience of the student. Libraries should ensure that their service is:

- involved in strategic planning groups that may be formed when any engagement is announced;
- included in the range of learning resource activity, giving examples of innovation and best practice in the SED and addressing issues before the auditors ask about them;
- equipped with quality assurance processes that are transparent and fit with institutional processes;
- involved with student feedback and the resulting action plans are documented and shared.

Keeping track of the quality assurance agenda at this time of change is challenging but there is some help to digest this information. The QAA for example publish a regular bulletin, *Higher Quality* available on the QAA website and sent in hard copy to all institutions. There is no prescribed way to acquire knowledge of your institution's current approach to QAA activity. However, to ensure the nuances of current practices are understood it is beneficial for least one member of the library or its parent division to be involved in the institutional quality assurance processes, for example attending briefings and serving on steering groups established for any audit or review events. As an example from Bournemouth University, Academic Services held membership on the following:

- the Institutional Audit Steering Group, including being part of the Institutional Audit SED drafting team and DAT planning groups;
- the Major Review in Healthcare Steering Group;
- the Institutional Collaborative Audit Steering Group;
- the Institution's ongoing Quality Assurance and Enhancement Group, which includes responsibility for chairing or acting as internal independent member at validation events and examination boards.

SCONUL continues to lobby and provide advice to members on how best to engage with audit and academic review. The section on their website devoted to quality assurance has guidance notes for both institutional audit and academic review.

Institutional Audit

As mentioned, Institutional Audit is the review currently prevailing in England and Northern Ireland. Between 2003 and 2005, all HEIs will have taken part in an audit. It is expected that after this the audits will be repeated in a six year cycle. The judgments from Institutional Audit are expressed as 'broad confidence', 'limited confidence' or 'no confidence'. The greater the confidence that derives from the audit, the lighter the touch of any subsequent Academic Review of subjects is supposed to be. The interim arrangements for the Academic Review of subjects will focus on those delivered in further education institutions (FEIs) and the remaining subjects from the original cycle of subject review. Some of the methodology for the institutional audit and academic review models came from a limited series of developmental engagements 2002–2005. These were based on an SED and SWS. The developmental nature perhaps led to the lowest engagement with library services and a fear that all the good work and opportunity gained from the rigours of Subject Review might be lost. However, lobbying from SCONUL, and the timely publication of the findings of the first rounds of Institutional Review (QAA, 2005b) ensured learning resources provision was still acknowledged as a key component to be considered. The contribution is not only to the process-driven agenda of Institutional Audit, but also to the three chosen Discipline Audit Trails (DATs) that examine the institution's internal quality assurance processes at the subject level. Learning resources are also included in the agenda for the supposedly lighter touch Academic Review for subjects. SCONUL's advice note, *Guidelines for QAA Institutional Audit in England* not only outlines the timetable for Institutional Audit, which helped many libraries engage in the process within their institution, but also provides extensive advice on making a contribution to the SED.

Institutional Self Evaluation Document

The SED is the benchmark document submitted by the institution at the start of the review process, against which the institution will be judged. Institutions follow guidelines and advice from the QAA on the key issues to be addressed and SCONUL has provided the following advice about what to include in a library submission to the institutional SED:

- your service's contribution to the institution's quality assurance and your own department's own quality processes;
- evaluation of your service and actions resulting;
- liaison with academic departments, teaching programmes and academic staff, including contributions to academic staff development;
- awareness of programme needs;
- your service's contribution to teaching programmes and student learning;
- how your service helps shape the student learning environment;
- how you consult student and staff views of your service including any links with the students union. (SCONUL, 2004)

In another example from Bournemouth University, the SED contained references to library and ICT activities in 12 paragraphs which were positioned in the following different sections of the SED: learning and teaching; assurance of quality; learning support; some challenges relating to learning resources; student guidance support and supervision; collaborative provision.

Student Written Submission

SCONUL advice that library services ask to see the SWS is confirmed by the experience at Bournemouth University. When the SWS is seen before audit a reasoned response can be prepared and shared with the Students' Union, who will have prepared the report, and those who may be asked questions about its findings in meetings during the visit. The preparation of a timely response also illustrates a commitment to responding to feedback and enhancing service quality.

Discipline Self Evaluation Document for Discipline Audit Trails (DATs)

The QAA select three discipline areas shortly before the scheduled institutional audit visit and each DAT requires a brief SED. Librarians are strongly advised, despite the tight time scales and restrictions on word counts, to work in partnership with the drafting teams to ensure brief information is included on the strategy for building up appropriate collections, facilities, support etc., as well as the nature and quality of liaison, how services are integrated into the delivery of teaching and learning and how student feedback is obtained. If there is an example of how feedback has been used to direct quality enhancement then it is important to include this.

Bournemouth University case study 2: Preparing for and handling the visit

Intranet access was provided to the learning resources strategy and other strategic documents for the groups who would be meeting the auditors. The subject librarians attended the rehearsals for the DAT meetings to brief those who would be able attending on any possible learning resources questions from the SEDs and SWS, including the reply we had already prepared for the Students Union. Three of the university-wide meetings had a representative from Academic Services attending, all of whom answered questions on any aspect of service. The meetings were the overall Quality Assurance meeting, the Staff Development meeting and the Quality Assurance and Enhancement group meeting, the latter illustrating how well integrated the library was into the quality monitoring processes of the university. The assessors' judgments were based on the written submissions and any questions and answers in the institution-wide meetings.

During the actual visit it is unlikely that there will be a tour of facilities. As the SCONUL note concludes:

> Do not expect a visit to the resources areas. The audit team will be static and they will expect evidence to be brought to them. They may not even ask you to respond to student or staff comments on your services (SCONUL 2004).

Academic Review of Subjects

Academic Review of subjects is part of the transitional arrangements to accompany Institutional Review in some HEIs during the period from 2002. It is also being used for directly funded higher education provision in further education colleges in England. The broad timetable for the subjects to be reviewed is provided on the QAA website, individual institutions will negotiate the precise timing and it is important that decisions on what is being reviewed and when are communicated to the interested parties.

SCONUL, through Jeremy Atkinson, the current chair of the SCONUL/UCISA Working Group on Quality Assurance, have negotiated an updated *Aide-mémoire for reviewers evaluating learning resources*, (SCONUL/UCISA, 2003).

The objective of the SCONUL aide-mémoire is to give a better understanding of the brief points highlighted in the QAA reviewer's aide-mémoire (Appendix B of the *Handbook for Academic Review: England 2004*) (QAA, 2004c). The handbook makes it clear that the review is based on the institutions self evaluation which should demonstrate in the context of learning resources review:

the adequacy of human and physical learning resources and the effectiveness of their utilization. In particular, the evaluation should demonstrate a strategic approach to linking resources to intended learning outcomes at programme level.

The reviewers are asked to consider:

- staffing levels and the suitability of staff qualifications and experience, including teaching and non-teaching staff;
- professional updating to keep abreast of emerging, relevant subject knowledge and technologies;
- staff development opportunities, including induction and mentoring, and whether opportunities are taken;
- journals and electronic media;
- access times and arrangements, and induction and user support provision; computing hardware, and both general and subject-specific software availability, and currency;
- accessibility, including times of opening and opportunities for remote access, and induction and user-support provision;
- specialist accommodation, equipment and consumables;
- adequacy, accessibility, induction, user support and maintenance;
- suitability of staff and teaching accommodation in relation to the teaching and learning strategy and the provision of support for students.

All of the above give scope for showcasing and critically evaluating learning resources in the SED. It is important to be accurate with statements that can be verified including where possible, links to any supporting evidence The SED evidence may also act as a trigger in any staff meetings and/or tours to highlight and discuss service provision. Exaggerated claims cause the review team to doubt the reliability of the institutions view of itself. It is recognised however that where changes are in progress at the time of the review, the evidence may not yet be available to illustrate the effectiveness of any new activities or procedures. The QAA encourages institutions to comment in the SED on how they are managing the process of change. The sections in the SED will follow the advice given in the *Handbook for Academic Review: England 2004* (QAA 2004c) and will cover: the overall aims and outcomes of the subject provision curricula; assessment; achievement; teaching and learning; student progression; learning resources; maintenance and enhancement of standards and quality. Institutions are encouraged to also consider those facets of the code of practice which relate to quality and standards and to consider the questions suggested for reviewers in the aide-mémoire.

The SCONUL/UCISA aide-mémoire provides points of reference for the assessor and hints for the subject librarian who is likely to be identified by the assessors as a key person in the review of learning resources in Academic Review. The sections are on:

- strategy, planning and liaison
- evaluation and feedback

- provision for the courses being evaluated
- relevance of learning materials
- availability and accessibility
- user support.

The contribution to the SED should address these issues. Assessors may also ask questions about them in meetings or on tours of resources. Recent experience suggests that, although Institutional Audit does not include tours because of the focus on process, the 'lighter touch' Academic Reviews will involve tours. Review teams seem to be receptive to the value of seeing the learning resources and this presents a wonderful opportunity to discuss how you ensure the resources are effective and how they are being utilised. It is advisable to communicate with your institutional review facilitator and explain why you believe a tour can help showcase all the learning and teaching innovations, especially those flagged up in the SED. If the lead assessor does not request a tour the institutional facilitator may well then suggest one when they meet the lead assessor at the preliminary meeting.

All reviews follow the same basic approach: presentation of the SED; visit from the lead assessor to discuss the review; dialogue between the institutional facilitator and the review panel chair to arrange the programme for the visit including visits to placement, partnership, or work-based learning as appropriate. Additional documentation required is identified and the detail of who will meet the assessors in which meetings is agreed. As there will just be one meeting covering all aspects of the review it is possible, but not certain, that the meeting with staff will include learning resources staff. There will also be a meeting with students and when appropriate a meeting with employers. The student meeting will include learning resources and their deployment. The reviewers will be looking to triangulate any comments made when they meet staff or go on tours.

The advice given to reviewers is that everything that is said during the visit is on the record and there should always be two of them present on any tour, it is therefore sensible to adopt the same approach and have a small group leading any tour that can represent all the constituencies of learning resources. The lead person would normally be the head of learning or teaching or an equivalent postholder in the discipline area under review. It would be expected that the subject librarian would also be involved. If you rehearse it is possible to ensure all your key enhancement activities will be highlighted even if direct questions are not forthcoming.

Major review of healthcare programmes

The major review of healthcare programmes has its own newsletter *News for healthcare education*, which gives hints, tips and feedback on how the reviews have been progressing and the lessons learnt. There is a separate handbook for the major review (QAA, 2003c) and a complete section on the QAA website devoted to the

Partnership Quality Assurance Framework for Healthcare Education in England (QAA, 2004d).

The language used makes it clear that the process is very much about continuous quality enhancement and as much about the quality of education in healthcare practice environments as in the HEI. With so many partners in the delivery of healthcare education it becomes more challenging to ensure the contribution of learning resources is recognised in the SED and the review programme. All the ideas given about involvement in Academic Review are still relevant but the emphasis on education for clinical practice may appear to lessen the perceived importance of the HEI central provision. Subject librarians should demonstrate in their SED contribution how their information literacy and collection development activities are related to intended learning outcomes, subject benchmarks and are making a difference to accessing learning resources both in practice and the HEI.

The schedules for the review visits are congested, with two of the four days spent visiting practice and partnership locations with each team covering four locations on each day. It was understandable therefore that the QAA and NHS agreed that if the NHS libraries were accredited using the Health Libraries and Information Confederation (HeLicon) scheme they would require no further visit (Health Libraries and Information Confederation, 2002).

The Scheme was originally designed by the Library and Information Co-operation Council (LINC) Health panel and the author of this chapter was one of the authors of that original scheme. (Beard, 1996). The current version is the second to be produced under the auspices of HeLicon and provides a useful benchmark on the all-round performance of a library service. Although it can be used in HE it is most effective in an exclusiviely NHS setting. Accreditation includes the preparation of a portfolio of evidence. The visit includes discussion with library staff and stakeholders such as senior Trust Managers, including the Chief Executive, and users of the service. This accreditation is usually part of a three year cycle. One of the precepts of major review, which is explicitly a part of the Partnership Quality Assurance Framework, is for HEIs to ensure the ongoing quality monitoring and enahncement and it may be desirable to consider how to take HeLicon accreditation as a benchmark and build an annual enhancement review into HEI institutional/library quality assurance processes.

Bournemouth University case study 3: A major healthcare review

A senior library staff member was invited to be on the steering group and to contribute to the writing of the SED. Contributions featured in 16 of the paragraphs appearing under the headings of achieving learning outcomes by students; curricula; learning and teaching; learning resources and their effective utilization; maintenance and enhancement of standards and quality. A theme chosen for particular focus was e-learning and so the examples of innovation were drawn from this area including the diverse range of e-resources and e-support. Mention was made of an ongoing impact study and the interim results were available and displayed on the student portal, which the assessors could access and on posters around the faculty and library. The positives, high usage and enthusiasm for more e-learning, as well as an ongoing need for training, were highlighted. A tour of learning resources was requested by the lead assessor and a period of two and a half hours was made available to showcase the wide range of e-learning and clinical skills support. The tour was an opportunity to mention new or forthcoming additional enhancements to e availability for the healthcare students. It also gave the assessors the chance to explore how student feedback was working and how the services in the NHS hospitals linked with the services from the University. The tour was carefully rehearsed to ensure the route gave opportunities to focus on all the aspects of learning resources from the student office and lecture theatres to the PC labs, the library and clinical skills facilities. Where visits were to be made to a sub-campus and the University Centre managed by a partner college, there were additional briefings arranged which included feedback about the University resource visit.

Collaborative Audit

Where HEIs have significant partnership activity the Institutional Audit will not be sufficient to assure the quality of provision. A collaborative audit will take place after Institutional Audit and will look at the effectiveness of the awarding institution's quality assurance structures and mechanisms for collaborative programmes. The guidance is given on the QAA website (QAA, 2004e).

One area specifically mentioned for consideration is the experience of students as learners in collaborative provision. Subject librarians will have a significant role in explaining how students of their institution studying in a collaborative provision access learning resources, how they are supported in acquiring the skills of information literacy, how the quality of the experience is monitored and how the student feedback is obtained and acted upon.

The Code of Practice for the assurance of academic quality and standards in higher education, section 2: Collaborative provision and flexible and distributed learning (including e-learning) issued in September 2004 is also being used as one of the tools adding guidance to this type of review. At the time of writing no case evidence exists to give advice on how best to interact with this phase of review. All the best practice from all the other methods will contribute to best practice in this area. What is clear is the obligation of the HEI to be responsible for the academic standards of all awards granted in its name. An HEI must know about all collaborative partnerships and they should be managed in accordance with formally stated policies and the awarding institution is ultimately responsible for ensuring the quality of learning opportunities offered through a collaborative arrangement is adequate to enable a student to achieve the academic standard required for its award (QAA 2004f).

Quality enhancement and institutional procedures

What is clear from the discussions about all the different methods of audit and review is that the library must have sound processes for assuring the quality and enhancement of the services it provides. Whatever methods exist must also be part of the institution's processes. Reference has already been made to involvement in programme planning and review. If the subject librarian has significant experience of involvement in supporting programme development perhaps there may be opportunities to contribute as an independent member of any institutional quality assurance groups. The experience gained could enhance subsequent involvement in external audit and review.

Evaluation of services

The subject librarian can work with other colleagues to ensure there is adequate student feedback, that it is documented and suitable action plans are developed and delivered. There is not space in this chapter to discuss all the possible methods for obtaining evaluation and if possible some measures on the impact of the activities undertaken. What is important to stress is that the feedback must be sought on a regular basis and in a variety of ways from taught sessions, to suggestion schemes, focus groups, surveys and of course the student written submission.

Conclusion

Jean Sykes' concluding remarks at the *Routes to Quality* conference held at Bournemouth University in 1995 have stood the test of time:

> Clearly quality assurance will continue to take a prominent place in the HE agenda in the coming years. Equally clearly HE Librarians and computing directors will need to ensure a continued involvement for learning resource services in the quality processes and procedures. They can work on this from two directions: on the one hand by pressing internally for an appropriate role for the library and computing services in the institution's quality procedures, and on the other hand by ongoing discussion with any HE quality agencies which might emerge in the future. (Sykes 1996)

It is clear that the QAA will engage more and more with the HEIs as they work to develop quality assurance measures that encourage enhancement of the student experience. The protocols and methods outlined in this chapter may change but the principles of engagement and the need for regular and robust local procedures to illustrate how the standards and quality are being upheld will remain. Indeed it can be argued that if there is effective external quality audit it can be a powerful lever for institutional change and improvement to institutional quality management (Scott and Hawke 2003). If the subject librarian looks back over the last ten years and reflects upon when audit has taken place, then it is clear that the engagement with faculty has led to an opportunity to improve services to the student. Audit and review are two of the best catalysts for change the subject librarian can engage with.

References

Beard, J., 1996. The Bournemouth Experience: Health care libraries and accreditation. *In* B. Knowles (ed.), *Routes to quality*, BUOPOLIS 1. Proceedings of the conference held at Bournemouth University 29–31 August 1995.

Health Libraries and Information Confederation (HeLicon), 2002. Accreditation of libraries in the healthcare sector: A checklist to support assessment, 2nd ed. [online]. Available from: http://www.nelh.nhs.uk/librarian/Accreditation_ Checklist_2nd_Edition_2002.pdf [Accessed 15 April 2005].

Laughton, D., 2003. Why was the QAA approach to teaching quality assessment rejected by academics in UK HE?' *Assessment & Evaluation in Higher Education*, 28 (3), 309–21.

Quality Assurance Agency (QAA), 2003a. A brief guide to quality assurance in UK higher education QAA 032 06/03. [online]. Available from: http://www.qaa. ac.uk/aboutus/heGuide/guide.asp. [Accessed 08 August 2004].

Quality Assurance Agency (QAA), 2003b. Handbook for enhancement-led institutional review: Scotland [online]. Available from: http://www.qaa.ac.uk/ reviews/ELIR/default.asp. [Accessed 08 August 2004].

Quality Assurance Agency (QAA), 2003c. Handbook for major review of healthcare programmes. QAA 034 05/2003 [online]. Available from: http://www.qaa. ac.uk/reviews/institutionalAudit/collaborative/supplement/CPASupplement.pdf [Accessed 04 March 2005]

Quality Assurance Agency (QAA), 2004a, Code of practice for the assurance of academic quality and standards in higher education [online]. Available from: http:// www.qaa.ac.uk/academicinfrastructure/codeofpractice/default.asp [Accessed 04 May 2004]

Quality Assurance Agency (QAA), 2004b. Code of practice for the assurance of academic quality and standards in higher education. Section 4: External examining – August 2004 [online]. Available from: http://www.qaa.ac.uk/ academicinfrastructure/codeOfPractice/default.asp [Accessed 04 August 2004]

Quality Assurance Agency (QAA), 2004c. 'Handbook for academic review: England 2004' [online] Available from: http://www.qaa.ac.uk/reviews/academicReview/ acrevhbook2004/HandbookAcademicReview.pdf [Accessed 25 April 2005].

Quality Assurance Agency (QAA), 2004d. The Partnership Quality Assurance Framework for Healthcare Education in England [online]. Available from: http:// www.qaa.ac.uk/health/framework/default.asp [Accessed 25 March 2005].

Quality Assurance Agency (QAA), 2004e. Supplement to the Handbook for institutional audit: England: collaborative provision audit [online]. Available from: http://www.qaa.ac.uk/reviews/institutionalAudit/collaborative/supplement/

CPASupplement.pdf [Accessed 02 February 2005].

Quality Assurance Agency (QAA), 2004f. Code of practice for the assurance of academic quality and standards in higher education. Section 2: Collaborative provision and flexible and distributed learning (including e-learning) – September 2004 [online]. Available from: http://www.qaa.ac.uk/academicinfrastructure/ codeofpractice/default.asp [Accessed 04 March 2005].

Quality Assurance Agency (QAA), 2005a. QAA Home page [online]. Available from: http://www.qaa.ac.uk/aboutus/ [Accessed 21 March 2005].

Quality Assurance Agency (QAA), 2005b. Institutional audit: England – key features and findings of the first audits QAA 07604/05 [online]. Available from: http://www.qaa.ac.uk/reviews/institutionalAudit/outcomes/Outcomes_initial.pdf [Accessed 06 March 2006].

Scott, G. and Hawke, I., 2003. Using an external quality audit as a lever for institutional change *Assessment & Evaluation in Higher Education*, 28, (3), 323–31.

Society of College, National & University Libraries (SCONUL), 1996. The Quality Assurance Agency for Higher Education – Aide-mémoire for reviewers evaluating learning resources. London [now withdrawn]. Endorsed by the Universities & Colleges Information Systems Association.

Society of College, National & University Libraries and the Universities and Colleges Information Systems Association (SCONUL/UCISA). 2003. 'The Quality Assurance Agency for Higher Education – Aide-mémoire for reviewers evaluating learning resources [online]. Available from: http://www.sconul.ac.uk/ activities/quality_ass/papers/ [Accessed 09 June 2005].

Society of College, National & University Libraries (SCONUL) 2004. SCONUL guidelines for QAA institutional audit in England [online]. Available from: http:// www.sconul.ac.uk/activities/quality_ass/papers/ [Accessed 09 January 2005].

Sykes, J., 1996. Quality issues in higher education: the library perspective. *In* B. Knowles (ed.), *Routes to quality*, BUOPOLIS 1. Proceedings of the conference held at Bournemouth University 29–31 August.

Chapter 4

Learning and Teaching

Kerry Shephard

Introduction

I have been asked to write about learning and teaching in UK higher education, post-Dearing, with a focus, of course, on how it might influence, and be influenced by, the broader roles of subject librarians, the implication being that the Dearing Report (NCIHE, 1997) was a significant milestone in higher education. There is no doubt that the Dearing Report was a significant, broad and far-reaching review of higher education. It would be difficult to find an aspect of higher education that has not been influenced by this review. But I am not personally convinced of the particular significance of the changes occurring in higher education since its publication in 1997. Particular, that is, in relation to other changes that have occurred in recent history, and in relation to likely changes in the future. I am reminded of a publication with the title *Higher education at the crossroads* published in 1980. Its editor commented on recent rapid growth in higher education up to 1980 and went on to say 'More recently however this period of rapid growth, both in the scale of higher education generally and, to some extent in research also, has come to a halt. We are entering a period of restraint, re-evaluation and possibly revitalisation' (Oxtoby, 1980). How difficult it must have been to stand at that junction and guess what lay ahead. I suspect that higher education has always changed and it is always tempting to think that the path ahead is different from the path behind. But did staff working in higher education, or students passing through, notice the crossroads at the time? Or were the lights green allowing a speedy continuation on a long journey? In my experience the lights have been green for many years. Not that the road has been straight, mind you, and Thatcher, Dearing and Blair can be held responsible for some recent scary bends... but the analogy of the road falls down here. Roads generally are too regular. I want to introduce the notion of cataracts, waterfalls, bottlenecks and weirs more familiar to users of waterways (and make only a passing mention here of plugholes). So rather than focus on changes since a particular event, I think it worthwhile to review the fluid nature of learning and teaching in higher education in recent years and in this way introduce some of the key changes that have occurred and generally continued to occur. As I write we can look forward to teaching-only universities, escalating tuition fees and ever-increasing involvement of computers in all aspects of higher education. Clearly, we stand at yet another waterfall.

The major areas that I shall look at are aspects of quality assurance and enhancement, e-learning and, more briefly, the broad overlapping areas of accessibility, widening participation and lifelong learning. Wherever possible I shall avoid describing a simple chronology and base my chapter on my interpretation of the broader provenance of each topic. The chapter is designed to provoke information professionals, and others traditionally (but arguably) on the periphery of learner support in higher education, to reconsider the extent and manner in which they engage with the practicalities of learning and teaching in and around universities.

Quality assurance and enhancement

In this section it would be impractical to describe the full range of developments and impositions allegedly designed to lead to improvements in learner support in higher education. I am sure that some elements of both quality assurance (QA) and quality enhancement (QE) have been effective. We should be aware of Academic Quality Audit (1991–1997), Teaching Quality Assessment (1992-1997), the QAA (Quality Assurance Agency) Quality Audit and Assessment (1997–2000, established on the recommendation of the Dearing Report; NCIHE, 1997) and the QAA Subject Review and Institutional Review (from 2000) and the current 'lighter touch'. (An excellent summary of this complex history is provided online in the University of Aberdeen's Academic Quality Guide; University of Aberdeen, 2004). A description of what is in place now is available on the QAA's own website (QAA, 2004). We should also reflect on the impact and successes of programme specifications and of the QAA's benchmark statements. We should know about institutional learning and teaching strategies and related human resources strategies. Many of these developments link closely to the TQEF (Teaching Quality Enhancement Fund), the central part of HEFCE's (Higher Education Funding Council for England) learning and teaching strategy established in 1998. TQEF supports the LTSN (Learning and Teaching Support Network) and its various subject centres, the FDTL" (Fund for the Development of Teaching and Learning and the National Teaching Fellowship Scheme, designed to develop and disseminate good teaching practice in higher education.

It might not be at the top of everyone's list of QA and QE activities but I put staff teaching skills and related learner-support skills, and mechanisms devised to promote and to quality assure them, at a pole position. It is on this theme that I want to focus here. That is not to say that all good learning depends on good teaching (indeed on any teaching) or that higher learning only takes place as a result of learners being exposed to higher education. But where teachers in higher education do attempt to teach, or to support learning, we would like to think that not only are we good at it, but we are also getting better.

Formal and informal attempts to improve the skills of teachers in higher education have a long history and their origins, of course, predate the Dearing Report In this section I look at the role of the Institute for Learning and Teaching (ILT) in developing programmes of training for new lecturers and more recent plans to work towards a framework of professional teaching standards. It is necessary, however, to put these developments into context by first examining more traditional approaches to develop and improve the teaching skills of academic staff by way of conventional academic staff development.

Traditional staff development

It is perhaps reasonable to state that most teaching staff in most higher education institutions have traditionally benefited from an introductory course on supporting learners, itself supported by an ongoing and often extensive programme of continuing professional development (CPD) opportunities. In many organisations these opportunities are also available to the wider range of professionals who support learners in higher education. Often these formal staff development opportunities support the activities of a mentor or senior colleague as part of a broad induction programme for new staff. Knight and Trowler (1999) studied good and poor aspects of these traditional mentoring and induction routines. These authors noted that these routines are most potent within professional communities that are sites of professional learning, such as departments. They expressed concern that the drive for better mentoring, and for better programmes of preparation for teaching, should not substitute for the promotion of workplace cultures that provide the messages and practices that new academic staff need to experience. Nevertheless, educational or staff developers have traditionally had a major role in developing the teaching skills of new and experienced university teachers.

Educational developers usefully reviewed aspects of traditional professional development in higher education in 1981 (Harding, Kaewsonthi, Roe and Stevens, 1981). This source provides an insight into the (pre-Dearing) values, operation and concerns of educational developers in higher education (Shephard, 2004) It is noteworthy that many issues relevant to that time remain important to staff development today. These include: the role and operation of reward systems for teaching staff engaging in professional development; personal as opposed to institutional goals for changing professional practice; the implications of voluntary as opposed to compulsory professional development; separation of professional development from appraisal and evaluation of staff performance; criteria used for the recognition of professional competence; competing demands on scarce resources; and the organisation and underlying models of staff-development effort. Harding et al. (1981) describe a range of models of continuing professional development, types of continuing professional development activity and approaches to evaluate the effectiveness of continuing professional development that remain valid and important today. Harding et al. (1981) did not obviously anticipate the contribution of educational developers to the current rate of change in higher education. The same authors do develop the theme of institutional change but they fall short of suggesting that its promotion is a central function of educational developers. They suggest, 'The idea that change is necessary and perhaps inevitable may not find general support' (Harding et al., 1981; page 41). By 2001, this reservation was clearly outdated, at least in the UK and among educational developers. Gosline, for example, surveyed members of the Heads of Educational Development Group in the UK and reported, 'all the respondents agreed that it was their role to encourage innovation and change in teaching and learning' (Gosline, 2001). So, not only is change apparently inevitable but it is now the role of educational developers to promote it.

It would be interesting to explore whether or not the motivation to engage in professional development and the extent of such engagement has changed in response to changes in its perceived purpose, but there is little hard data on this. Beetham attempted to assess what motivates academic staff in higher education to undertake professional development activities (Beetham, 2000). Although intrinsic factors such as the quest for personal intellectual stimulation and improved support for students were important factors for some, extrinsic factors (such as career advancement) tended to predominate for many. There are, however, significant differences between institutions in relation to reward and recognition for high standards of teaching. A recent guide to good practice produced by the HEFCE suggests, 'Two-thirds of institutions have built into their strategy mechanisms to recognise and reward excellent teachers. In many cases this is an aspiration rather than a developed plan, and many details of promotion and reward schemes are yet to be worked out'. (HEFCE, 2001; Paragraph 74). It is also difficult to assess how many days each year real teachers commit to continuing professional development. Daniel, drawing on experiences running the Open University in the UK, uses the Investors in People UK standard of ten-days annually as an indication of his expectation of time committed to professional development. In relation to the need to develop new skills to use new learning technologies, he establishes a strategic expectation in stating 'A clear focus on professional development is key to the successful deployment of new technology in teaching' (Daniel, 1996, page 157) and goes on to suggest that half of the time that full-time academic staff are expected to spend on professional development should be spent on aspects of information technology.

There is currently great diversity in institutional provision of professional development in higher education. Educational development centres are based in administrative or support-services settings in some higher education institutions and in academic settings in others (Gosline, 2001). In addition, individual educational developers vary greatly in their approach to professional development. Land (2000) for example, describes twelve orientations to educational development that relate to developers' attitudes, knowledge, aims and tendencies of action.

ILT and programmes of training for higher education teachers

Whatever opportunities existed for continuing professional development for university teachers, prior to 1997, it was clearly considered by many to be inadequate to assure the provision of quality learner support in higher education. Dearing suggested that a major role of his hoped-for Institute for Learning and Teaching (ILT) should be to accredit programmes of training for higher education teachers (NCIHE, 1997, para 34). It is notable that one such accreditation scheme already existed at that time. The Staff and Educational Development Association (SEDA) launched the first teacher accreditation scheme in 1993 and many programmes that were eventually to be accredited by the ILT (later the ILTHE, Institute for Learning and Teaching in Higher Education) started life with SEDA. SEDA recognised institutional programmes that were based on its published framework of objectives and values. This work was subsequently taken forward by ILTHE working collaboratively with SEDA as the ILTHE National Accreditation Framework in 1999. The process has been undoubtedly very successful in accrediting training programmes that now exist in nearly all UK HEIs. There is every indication that completion of an accredited programme will become a requirement for new lecturers in many institutions; perhaps in all. Whether the process has been successful in raising the quality of learner support is less certain although there is some evidence that training programmes for university teachers can improve their teaching skills (Gibbs and Coffey, 2004). Even so, the programmes are not without their own problems. Some programmes are optional for staff but many are compulsory for staff on probationary contacts. Trowler and Cooper present an important analysis of these programmes by developing and assessing the impact of teaching and learning regimes (TLRs) on them (Trowler and Cooper, 2002). TLRs comprise the rules, assumptions, practices and relationships relating to teaching and learning issues in higher education. Trowler and Cooper argue that professional development programmes can fail to account for differences between TLR's of programme tutors and participants and this may lead to resistance to this form of continuing professional development (Trowler and Cooper, 2002). The situation is set to develop further as more institutions establish accredited professional development programmes that specifically address ICT skills to support learning.

Continuing professional development, the HE Academy and a framework of professional teaching standards

Accredited programmes are open to a wide range of professional staff in HE with a learner-support role. There are also mechanisms to support and recognise the professional development of these wider roles within the Professional Development Framework accredited by the Staff and Educational Development Association (SEDA, 2003). Continuing professional development of the broad range of professionals who support learning in HE, and its recognition, will be a core activity for the UK's HE Academy (the ILTHE was incorporated into the HE Academy in May 2004) and it will be interesting to see how the Academy will work with other groups involved in promoting, supporting and recognising CPD in the HE sector. The Chartered Institute of Library and Information Professionals (CILIP), for example, has a new framework of qualifications to be implemented during 2005. Qualifications will be based on continuing professional development with the primary responsibility for assessment for certification and revalidation in the hands of locally based and trained assessment panels (CILIP, 2004). This approach is consistent with that recently piloted by the ILTHE, whose CPD framework asks members to identify their plans for CPD and to record their comments on the value of the professional development activities that they have undertaken (ILTHE, 2004). CPD for teaching staff has a great deal of support from outside of the profession itself. The HEFCE undertook to raise the esteem in which teaching is held within the higher education sector and included the recognition and reward of excellent teaching practice within its recent strategies (HEFCE 2003/35). The Government White Paper, *The Future of Higher Education* (DfES, 2003b) proposed that a set of national professional standards should be agreed by 2004-5 and that all new teaching staff work towards a qualification that meets these standards from 2006. Substantive additional funding has been provided to institutions by HEFCE for this purpose including an extension of the TQEF. As I write this chapter, Universities UK, SCOP (the Standing Conference of Principals) and the HE Funding Councils are proposing that the Higher Education Academy take forward the development of national professional standards in teaching and learning in HE. Current ILTHE accreditation processes and continuing professional development projects will be carried forward into the Higher Education Academy, and it seems likely that the standards framework will eventually supersede these. Current proposals for a framework model include distinct levels through which HE professionals would pass through teaching-related promotion, incremental progression or specific award. The challenge will be to produce a framework of evidence-based standards that is consistent and sector-wide. The underlying rationale for many of these developments can be traced to Dearing's recommendation to establish higher education teaching as a profession in its own right (NCIHE, 1997). At the core of Dearing's recommendation was concern for the student learning experience and the perception that mechanisms should be put in place to reward and recognise teaching, rather than just research, excellence. The actions of the HE Academy seem to be largely consistent with this approach, but some anomalies remain. Professions generally are exclusive bodies, defined at least in part by whom they exclude. But 'The Higher Education Academy is concerned with every aspect of the student experience' (HE Academy, 2004). In attempting to be so inclusive, the HE Academy may find it difficult to meet the aspirations of Dearing to establish higher education teaching as a profession in its own right. This problem may be further complicated by an issue that the ILTHE failed to adequately address; that many HE professionals already belong to other professional bodies such as the Institute of Biology, or CILIP, whose purpose and functions already generally includes education and the promotion of CPD. The introduction to the Institute of Biology's CPD scheme, for example, states, 'Competent professionals routinely maintain and update their expertise in ways appropriate to their role (education, research, management, etc.) and thereby develop the attributes that enable them to act in a professional capacity (Institute of Biology, 2004). Discussions and agreements with these professional bodies would seem to be a priority for the HE Academy.

Electronic learning

It will be very difficult to identify when in recent educational history the concept of electronic learning (e-learning) entered the mainstream of educational thinking. Leaving aside the issue of how we define e-learning, it was not that long ago that many academics, departments and institutions did not allow students to submit assignments that were generated using a word processor. Many issues were at stake including that of equal opportunities and unfair advantages given to those who had access to new technologies and who had developed these new communication skills. How different it is today where many students submit assignments via their computers, and indeed where most use computers and the Internet to help prepare their assignments. In just about all institutions and most subject areas, the use of computers to support learning is normal practice. Going further than that, the skills so shunned by academic staff in the past are now considered to be essential elements of the skills base needed by students to learn and key learning outcomes from the graduate experience itself. e-learning is considered by many to be central to the mission of higher education whether as a contribution to distance learning, to open and flexile learning or indeed to conventional learning in a 'blended' format. It is also an area where a wide range of support staff is commonly involved in learner support, working alongside conventional university academics. Information specialists are, of course, particularly involved. It was perhaps Dearing's review into higher education in 1997 that brought the importance of these IT skills into prominence for the HE sector. IT skills are now considered (along with communication, application of number, working with others, improving own learning and performance and problem solving) as the key skills elements of programmes by the Qualifications and Curriculum Authority.

There has been huge investment into e-learning in UK HE in recent years. Naturally much of this has been to provide the necessary equipment and infrastructure but significant research and development has also occurred to explore how computers can best be used to support learning. Running in parallel for some time with FDTL, the Teaching and Learning Technology Programme (TLTP) has supported a significant range of projects. In many cases the precursors to LTSN subject centres were CTI (Computers in Teaching Initiative) centres. These programmes and centres have had crucial roles in supporting and encouraging use of e-learning as have information specialists working within them.

It is important to note that in many cases it has been necessary for institutions and government to support and encourage the use of computers to support learning. Outside of the relatively small group of 'early adopters', and perhaps the larger group of information specialists, the mainstream of learner supporters in higher education have been relatively reluctant to embrace the use of computers for learner support (Warburton, 2000). Progress has not necessarily been self-propelled by learner-support professionals. Surry and Land (2000) reviewed generic strategies for motivating academic staff to use e-learning, with a particular emphasis on 'reward and recognition' processes. Many initiatives encourage staff to acquire new ICT skills and encourage institutions to ensure that they do. The Higher Education

Funding Council (HEFCE) has attempted to establish good practice in setting human resources strategies. HEFCE recommend that such strategies must 'meet specific professional development and training objectives that not only equip staff to meet their current needs but also prepare them for future changes, such as using new technologies for learning and teaching' (HEFCE, 2002, p. 47, Annex A). Some initiatives apply most directly to particular subject areas. For example, a recent report commissioned by the Joint Information Systems Committee (JISC) on the development and use of virtual learning environments in medical schools makes a wide range of recommendations including the idea that 'support, training and incentives for academics may be necessary to ensure that systems are populated with appropriate content across the curriculum' (Cook, 2001, p. 9). Such encouragement is naturally strategically based. Institutions around the world are embedding ICT within their learning and teaching strategies and linking its use and development with a wide range of other institutional changes, including expansion of student numbers, widening participation, a stress on lifelong learning, and measures for cost efficiency (Conole, 2002; McNaught and Kennedy, 2000). All UK higher education institutions now have learning and teaching strategies and few of these ignore the likely impact of e-learning on learner support in the future.

But, despite the extent of support and encouragement and its undoubted strategic footing, it is often suggested that the use of ICT to support learning in higher education is not progressing as fast as many would wish. Conole (2002, p 14), for example, suggests that in the UK the 'take-up of ICT in teaching is still fairly low' and points to the lack of ICT skills of staff and students, along with resistance to change, as two of several contributory factors. There are parallels abroad. A recent study in the US suggests that faculty (staff) are lagging behind students and institutions in their enthusiasm for online learning (Allen and Seaman, 2003). They also suggest that there are marked differences in approaches to adopt e-learning between private and public institutions. Although there may not be a great deal of evidence to support it, I suspect that few in the UK would ignore a similar difference between our own research-led and teaching-led institutions or indeed between our new universities and older ones.

In addition to the reluctance of staff to adopt online approaches to support learning, the reluctance of the education marketplace to value e-learning products and programmes may yet impose an additional barrier for e-learning to overcome. Early 2004 saw the demise of the UKeU, a collaborative online venture launched not long before with great enthusiasm from some. Although the higher education community waits for the official reasons for its failure it does appear to many that this online institution was trying to market programmes of study that students did not want or certainly were not prepared to pay for.

There are many topics within the sphere of e-learning of general interest but some that particularly involve information specialists and subject librarians. Here is a sequence of events that will be familiar to many.

1. Information specialists are naturally involved in building collections of online

resources

2. Perhaps because of this they often find themselves having to persuade teaching staff that these resources are worth using to support student learning.
3. Having put the effort into understanding the resources (sometimes even building them) the information specialist finds him or herself more able to use them than many of the teaching staff for whom they were designed.

This sequence, combined with the reluctance of teaching staff (for whatever reason) to use online resources, opens the way for the information specialist to adopt at least some of the traditional learner-support roles of the academic. 'I do not have the time', 'I am too busy doing my research', 'You helped to develop it so you are in a better position than me to support student use of that online resource' are phrases more familiar to some than to others but they are highly indicative of new team-based approaches to learner support that are likely to become more prevalent in the future. Naturally, different authors will place a different 'spin' on these phenomena depending on their personal experience and professional allegiance. Pinfield (2001) whilst reviewing the roles of subject librarians, develops the idea that subject librarians have a particular role in the selection of e-resources and identifies 14 criteria used in the selection process (none of which include, by my interpretation, an analysis of need or likely extent of use). Pinfield emphasises the need for advocacy of collections of new library materials by, for example, suggesting ways in which they might be used in learning and teaching. (Note Pinfield's emphasis on 'suggesting', rather than my own 'persuading'.) Pinfield goes on to develop similar notions of teamwork to that above but stops short of formally identifying a teaching role.

All three stages of this slippery slope, or desirable evolutionary trend, depending on your own perspective, provide opportunities for discussion and dissent. On the first I urge constraint. Although some resources are widely used and demonstrably useful, UK higher education is awash with online resources that few want or ever use. Our enthusiasm for building collections or repositories of online resources and learning objects greatly outweighs our enthusiasm for actually using them. A more detailed and scholarly analysis is provided elsewhere (Calverly and Shephard, 2003). On the second I express concern. Teaching staff often ask for evidence that the use of learning technologies and online resources will lead to improvement in the quality of the learning experience enjoyed by students. The dilemma is straightforward. Most academic staff already pride themselves on providing excellent teaching, supported by excellent learning resources. To develop and use extensive web resources, or web conferencing or computer-assisted assessment to support their teaching will require them to invest time into developing and maintaining new skills. This will be time not spent on important research. It seems unlikely that the new learning resources will be less expensive and highly unlikely, in general, that they will save time. Even where information specialists and learning technologists are available to help, these new tools will need considerable time commitment. So unless someone can demonstrate that they will lead to improvements why should academics change? Furthermore many university teachers feel pressurised into changing their practice without a great deal of support or sufficient evidence that this change, alongside so many others, will be worthwhile. The dilemma may be straightforward but the answer is not. Personally I have great enthusiasm for helping to develop and successfully use some online resources, but I have also been involved in developing and using some 'real stinkers'. These are complex issues and I dislike finding myself in a position of 'selling' a technology or resource to a reluctant academic. On the third I direct readers to Chapter 7 (in this book) that considers changing relationships in the university.

Accessibility, widening participation and lifelong learning

It is within these categories that many really innovative developments have occurred in university teaching and learning and, as with e-learning, much of our success has depended on the activities of professionals traditionally on the periphery of learner support. There is a good reason for this. Most learner supporters in our universities have focused, rightly or wrongly, on the mainstream of learners. Clearly some lecturers, some departments and even some institutions have created specific niches for themselves in these non-traditional areas, but traditional activities have dominated the work of most lecturers and continue to do so. Of particular significance is the ongoing imposition of substantial authoritative guidelines and legislation that seek, as examples, quality assured distance learning (QAA 2001) and computer-assisted assessment (BSI, 2002), equitable accessibility (Special Educational Needs and Disability Act, 2001) and the broader application of e-learning (DfES, 2003a) that in turn seek to support widening participation and to enable greater preparation for employment. Universities, particularly research-active universities, seeking to ensure compliance with these instruments increasingly find the additional workload for academic staff to be unsustainable. A team-based approach seems almost inevitable under such circumstances. Attending to the needs of students from disadvantaged backgrounds, of those in the workplace, of disabled- and of adult-learners have therefore become roles primarily for specialists often working within teaching teams. Librarians in particular have not been shy in committing their own considerable skills and experience to these ends.

Nevertheless a significant focus of the White Paper *The future of higher education* (DfES, 2003b) and of HEFCE policy (HEFCE, 2004) is to bring these niche areas far more into the mainstream. 'The social class gap among those entering higher education is unacceptably wide' (DfES, 2003, Para 1.28). 'Participation in higher education will equip people to operate productively within the global knowledge economy. It also offers social benefits, including better health, lower crime and a more tolerant and inclusive society.'(HEFCE, 2004). Other chapters in this volume address aspects of these important developments but here I want to look briefly at a single but important factor; the sustainability of current successes when rolled out into the mainstream. Will our new team-based approaches work when stretched, financially and pedagogically, by this ongoing change? Will we continue to attempt inclusivity or will we be forced to move more towards specialist provision and specialist institutions. Arguably we are already on that route. Teaching-only institutions will, presumably, have more scope to specialise; and let us not forget the particular, and successful, specialisation of the UK's Open University. Government is not oblivious to at least some of the problems involved and promises to 'ask HEFCE to reform the access premium so that universities and colleges will be properly funded for the extra costs of attracting and retaining students from non-traditional backgrounds.'(DfES, 2003, Chapter 6).

And what of the quality of educational provision? Can this be sustained? Thompson (2001) argues strongly that widening participation projects should not be evaluated using the same criteria as conventional learning and teaching developments. Thompson places a premium on innovation, risk taking and experimentation that seems justified for groundbreaking small projects but unreasonable in a broader setting. The issues seem to be particularly stark in the area of assessment, particularly where 'alternative assessments' are involved (Sharp and Earle, 2000; Maclellan, 2004). If higher education is to rise to these formidable challenges then we do need to confront them and not hide from them.

I end on a positive, and fundamentally inclusive, note. Those who work in this area claim that resources that work best for disabled students also work best for more conventional students. Accessible design is good design (see for example, an excellent essay by Veen, 2004). Good teaching is just that, but perhaps you have a different view?

Evaluating change and the impact of change agents

Clearly there has been a great deal of change in UK HE learning and teaching in recent years. Whether there has been more change or less than in previous periods is debatable but perhaps not the most important issue for us here. It is probably much more important to evaluate the success of these changes in improving student learning and to relate these successes to the source of the change and to the activities of the responsible change agents. In particular this approach might enable us to determine how likely future initiatives are to change UK HE for the better.

Of course, the last really big proposal for a higher education shake-up came with the publication of the controversial *The future of higher education* in January 2003 (DfES, 2003). This proposes a wide variety of future changes including the creation of centres of excellence and teaching-only universities. Gale (2004) considered aspects of the proposals in comparison to a broad examination of previous milestone changes in UK HE learning and teaching, with a particular focus on TQEF and TLTP. To this end, Gale cites other analyses of what the TQEF and TLTP achieved. Prior to the TQEF there was no significant national funding for learning and teaching development and no large projects focused on pedagogy. The TQEF promises to have significant positive impact on student learning in the UK and early evaluations of its successes support this. But even large investments in learning do not necessary see increases in a range of measurable performance indicators such as student retention, student achievement, student use of technology and student employability. Annual reports of UK higher education performance indicators are available from the HEFCE website. We must wait to see how effective the extended TQEF will be on these terms. Prior to the TQEF there were many small projects and these were often poorly reported and rarely shared across institutions. The TLTP projects, for example, tended to focus on product rather than implementation and they were difficult to embed into HE. For both programmes of change it is probably fair to say that much of the drive for change arose externally to higher education, but that change agents, including teaching staff, learning technologists, information scientists and many others, operated from within.

Effective educational research and evaluation may help us chose between good and bad in the future but there are different views on the effectiveness of educational research and evaluation and indeed on what needs to be evaluated and on what criteria evaluations are based. Baume (2003) for example, quotes Miller and Partett's assertion in 1974 that ' It is little exaggeration to assert that education research has had a negligible impact on the workings of educational institutions and on the ways in which academic men and women reflect on their professional activities (Miller and Parlett, 1974, preface; 3) and goes on to say 'Almost 30 years later this is still mostly true and probably as true for educational evaluation as for education research.' In part this is a criticism of the way that we conduct educational research and evaluation. In part this may provide an insight into what we do not research or evaluate. But in part it is also a tribute to the robustness of educators and education in higher education. Teaching in higher education has been subject to relentless pressure to adapt, to keep up, to expand, to get better, to do more. Perhaps it has adapted, kept up, got better and does more, but it is relatively and essentially unchanging.

Conclusions

Learning and teaching are important to higher education in the UK and higher education periodically goes through dramatic developmental change to emphasise this. External agents initiate much of this change but many of the change agents reside within higher education itself. Changes are characteristically, and perhaps unavoidably, incompletely evaluated. Current emphasis on the quality of learner support, the adoption of e-learning and widening participation continue themes that trace their origins a long way back.

To continue my analogy of the aqueous; I see higher education as a procession of small green bottles floating down a stream. Inside each bottle is a message that many chose to read or even add to. On their way the bottles encounter waterfalls, meanders and slow glides between yellow patches of water-buttercup. On occasions, groups of bottles accumulate but then break free to continue their journey. Small children poke them with sticks. Every now and again a bigger child throws bricks at them. Well-meaning adults occasionally open the bottles to change the messages but never manage to catch all the bottles at the same time.

References

Allen, I.A., and Seaman, J., 2003. *Sizing the opportunity: the quality and extent of online education in the United States, 2002 and 2003.* Needham, MA: Sloan Corporation.

Baume D., 2003. Monitoring and evaluating staff and educational development. *In* P. Kahn and D. Baume (eds.) *A guide to staff and educational development.* London: SEDA and Kogan, pp.76–95.

Beetham, H., 2000. An Alternative Perspective on CPD. *Educational Developments*, 1(2), 4–6.

BSI (British Standards Institution), 2002. *BS7988:2003. Code of practice for the use of information technology (IT) in the delivery of assessments.* London: BSI.

Calverley, G.J. and Shephard, K.L., 2003. Assisting the uptake of on-line resources: why good learning resources are not enough. *Computers and Education*, 41 (3), 205–224.

Chartered Institute of Library & Information Professionals (CILIP), 2004. *About the new Framework of Qualifications* [online]. Available from: http://www.cilip. org.uk/qualificationschartership/FrameworkofQualifications [Accessed 04 April 2005].

Conole, G., 2002. The evolving landscape of learning technology. *Association for Learning Technology Journal. (ALT-J)* 10 (2), 4–18.

Cook, J., 2001. The role of virtual learning environments in UK medical education. Final Report ILRT JTAP Institute for Learning and Research Technology [online]. Available from: http://www.ltss.bris.ac.uk/jules/jtap-623.pdf [Accessed 04 April 2005].

Daniel, J.S., 1996. *Mega-universities and knowledge media.* London: Kogan Page.

Department for Education and Skills (DfES), 2003a *Towards a Unified e-learning Strategy, Consultation Document [online]. Nottingham, UK* [online]. DfES Publications. Available from: http://publications.teachernet.gov.uk/ eOrderingDownload/DfES-0455-2003.pdf [Accessed 04 April 2005]

Department of Education and Skills (DfES) 2003b. *The future of higher education* [online]. Available from: http://www.dfes.gov.uk/hegateway/strategy/hestrategy/ need.shtml [Accessed 04 April 2005].

Gale, H., 2004. Towards centres of excellence in teaching and learning. *Educational Developments*, 5.(1), 10–12.

Gibbs, G. and Coffey, M., 2004. The impact of training of university teachers on their teaching skills, their approach to teaching and the approach to learning of their students. *Active Learning in Higher Education*, 5 (1), 87–100.

Gosline, D., 2001. Educational Development Units in the UK – what are they doing 5 years on? *International Journal for Academic Development*, 6 (1), 74–90.

Harding, A.G., Kaewsonthi, S., Roe, E., and Stevens, J., 1981. *Professional development in higher education.* Bradford: University of Bradford Educational Development Service.

Higher Education Funding Council for England (HEFCE) 2001. Guide 01/37

Strategies for learning and teaching in higher education, A guide to good practice [online]. . Available from http://www.hefce.ac.uk/pubs/hefce/2001/01_37.htm (Accessed 7/09/04).

Higher Education Funding Council for England (HEFCE), 2002. *Rewarding and developing staff in higher education* [online]. http://www.hefce.ac.uk/pubs/ hefce/2002/02_14/02_14.doc (Accessed 7/09/04).

Higher Education Funding Council for England (HEFCE), 2004. *Widening Participation* [online]. Available from: http://www.hefce.ac.uk/widen/ [Accessed 04 April 2005].

Institute of Biology, 2004. *Continuing professional development* [online]. Available from: http://www.iob.org [Accessed 04 April 2005]

Joint Information Systems Committee (JISC), 2003. *Learning Technology Career Development Scoping Study* [online]. Available from: http://www.jisc.ac.uk/ index.cfm?name=project_career [Accessed 04 April 2005].

Knight, P.T., and Trowler, P.R., 1999. It takes a village to raise a child: mentoring and the socialisation of new entrants to the academic professions. *Mentoring and Tutoring*, 7 (1) 23–34.

Land, R., 2000. Orientations to Educational Development. *Educational Developments*, 1 (2), 19–23.

Maclellan, E., 2004. How convincing is alternative assessment for use in higher education? *Assessment and Evaluation in Higher Education*, 29 (3), 311–321.

McNaught, C., and Kennedy, P., 2000. Staff development at RMIT: bottom-up worked served by top-down investment and policy. *Association for Learning Technology Journal (ALT-J)*, 8 (1), 4–18.

National Committee of Inquiry into Higher Education (NCIHE), 1997. *Higher Education in the Learning Society* (The Dearing Report) Norwich: HMSO.

Oxtoby, R., 1980. *Higher education at the crossroads*. Guildford: SRHE.

Pinfield, S., 2001. The changing role of subject librarians in academic libraries. *Journal of Librarianship and Information Science,* 33 (1) 32–38.

Quality Assurance Agency (QAA), 2001. *Distance Learning Guidelines* [online]. Available from: http://www.qaa.ac.uk/academicinfrastructure/codeofpractice/ distance-learning/default.asp [Accessed 04 April 2005].

Quality Assurance Agency (QAA, 2004). *The Quality Assurance Agency for Higher Education: an introduction* [online]. Available from: http://www.qaa.ac.uk/ aboutus/qaaIntro/intro.asp [Accessed 04 April 2005].

Sharp, K., and Earle, S., 2000. Assessment, disability and the problem of compensation. *Assessment and Evaluation in Higher Education*, 25 (2), 191–199.

Staff & Educational Development Association (SEDA) (2003) *Professional Development Framework (PDF)* [online]. Available from: http://www.seda.ac.uk/ pdf/index.htm [Accessed 04 April 2005].

Shephard, K.L., 2004. The role of educational developers in the expansion of educational technology. *International Journal for Academic Development*, 9 (1), 67–83

Surry, D.W., and Land, S., 2000. Strategies for motivating higher education faculty to use technology. *Innovations in Education and Training International*, 37 (2) 145–153.

Trowler, P., and Cooper, A., 2002. Teaching and Learning Regimes: Implicit theories and recurrent practices in the enhancement of teaching and learning through educational development programmes. *Higher Education Research and Development*, 21 (3), 221–240.

University of Aberdeen, 2004. Academic Quality Handbook [online]. Available from: tp://www.abdn.ac.uk/registry/quality/ [Accessed 04 April 2005].

Veen, G., 2004. I don't care about accessibility [online]. Available from: http://www. veen.com/jeff/archives/000503.html [Accessed 04 April 2005].

Warburton, S.P.M., 2000. Factors affecting changes in educational technology usage within HE establishments; working document [online]. http://www.telri.ac.uk/ Publications/change1.pdf [Accessed 04 April 2005].

Websites

HEA: Higher Education Academy [http://www.heacademy.ac.uk]

HEFCE: Guide to performance indicators in higher education [http://www.hefce. ac.uk/learning/perfind/2003/guide/what.asp]

QCA: Qualifications and Curriculum Authority [http://www.qca.org.uk]

Chapter 5

Relating to Further Education – Partners and Franchises

Jane Ryland

Background

Since the late 1980s, the number of Higher Education (HE) courses being delivered in FE Colleges (FECs) in the UK has grown significantly. Recent government initiatives based on the *Future of Higher Education* White Paper (DfES, 2003a) to extend Higher Education to target 50 per cent of the population (with a focus on skills development, widening participation and accessible learning) have accelerated this growth. These initiatives have been supported in part by the introduction of foundation degrees which are largely delivered in the FECs.

Different types of HE in FEC relationships have developed, including mixed economy, franchise (that is, indirectly funded) and validated courses. For the purposes of this chapter, the focus will be on the franchise relationship as this is arguably the most problematic, but most of the observations are appropriate to any relationship between Higher Education Institutions (HEIs) and FECs. The recommendations in this chapter are based primarily on the experiences of Bournemouth University and its partner colleges.

Like many HE institutions, Bournemouth University has seen a recent growth in the number of students studying in partner institutions, so that they now comprise a significant percentage of the overall student population. Support for these students needs to be consistent and robust in order to ensure parity of experience regardless of geographic location.

Support for HE in FE students at Bournemouth was strengthened by the establishment of the DSW (Dorset, South Somerset, South Wiltshire) Partnership which was substantially funded for a period of three years by HEFCE. One task group was dedicated to library services from which developed a number of initiatives, including enhanced library management systems; the creation of an image database; a passport providing students with information about each partner library and a pilot appointment of an HE in FE library specialist which later became a permanent position. The partnership helped to improve communication across the Partnership, developing a better understanding and providing a forum for sharing good practice.

As a result of this work and other ongoing activity, Bournemouth University Library has become a leading player in the development of a model for effective library support for HE in FE students.

There are many benefits for students studying for an HE award at their local FEC, such as small classes and geographic accessibility. However, there are issues too especially in relation to resources – staffing and resource budgets being the most problematic. Even in HEIs, library budgets can be tight and may be difficult for HEIs to provide adequate support to their students studying in FECs. They therefore need to seek effective and efficient ways of delivering this support.

For the most part, provision of these courses developed in a haphazard way and consequently so did the support. From the perspectives of both HEI and FEC libraries, these partnerships are often seen as problematic for a number of reasons. There are a great many difference between HEIs and FECs and yet an equitable level of delivery is expected. There are differences in learning cultures. For example, HEIs place more emphasis on research and self-directed learning. There are also differences of scale as HEIs are generally better funded and have larger numbers of staff and students which give them additional flexibility. Individual FECs also differ from one another in their practices and methods of delivery so that a single solution may not be appropriate for every library. This chapter seeks to explore some of the issues faced by libraries delivering support to HE in FEC students and offers some solutions and opportunities for change.

Strategic Support

Library services need to be represented at strategic level both at the HEI and the FEC. In the HEIs, a member of library staff should sit on university-wide partnership strategy committees and maintain contact with link tutors and other key staff. In FECs, this involvement can be more difficult to achieve as many staff, apart from the library manager, are seen as administrative staff rather than information specialists (and are often paid as such). HEI librarians can help with this integration process by attending key meetings with their colleagues in FECs, presenting a united library service. They can also persuade the university link tutors to help by inviting college library staff to key meetings and events. In some colleges, only the library manager attends these meetings which can place untenable demands on his or her time. Other staff could be encouraged to attend in their place which would also give them a good opportunity for staff development.

Library staff need to be involved in the validation and planning processes for new courses. Again, the HEI library staff can help by offering advice based on their experiences in planning for HE and by helping to make the contacts with the relevant teaching staff to ensure library involvement from the beginning of the process. The same applies to validation and review events. A checklist can be devised to help academic staff developing new courses to ensure that they have sufficient information about library support.

Both HEIs and FECs need a structured approach to the dissemination of information about proposed new courses, reviews and closures and the library staff need to be part of this. Many HEIs now have an academic department which includes in its remit the delivery of HE in FEC courses. Strong links with this department are useful for obtaining such information.

Since library provision for HE in FEC students has grown up in a rather haphazard way, communication is often similarly haphazard. Usually, communication links exist between the FEC library staff and the HEI subject librarians, but this can be confusing especially where large numbers of subject areas are covered. In order to co- communication, some HEIs, such as De Montfort University (Arnold, 2002, p. 50) and Bournemouth University have appointed an HE in FEC library specialist. This person generally has a co-ordinating role at both strategic and operational levels and ensures that effective two-way communication takes place. They may also have a hands-on role and provide support directly to the FEC library staff. Ideally, the position should be dedicated full-time to the HE in FEC students and should be at a senior level to enable strategic involvement.

The role of the HEI subject librarians is also vital to the success of the partnership. As the experts in their subject area, they can advise FEC librarians on suitable resources, difficult subject enquiries and appropriate training materials. They will also be present at course or school committee meetings at the HEI where partner issues are often addressed.

One of the main advantages for FECs of delivering HE courses is funding. HE students bring in high levels of funding both directly and indirectly in terms of prestige and publicity. Many FEC library managers have been able to improve their facilities and services as a result of the demands of their HE students. For example, increased study space, extended opening hours and improved ICT facilities have been obtained in this way.

However, the process of allocation is not always transparent and many FEC libraries are not allocated a separately identifiable HE budget. HE funds are therefore left unprotected if a college faces financial cutbacks. Some FECs allocate a proportion of HE funds to cover all learning resources, which leaves the library competing with ICT equipment and media equipment, both of which are high profile and expensive.

For many FECs, start-up funds are made available for new courses but ongoing funds are inadequate or non-existent. This is problematic for resources with ongoing subscriptions such as journals and also makes it difficult to keep the stock up-to-date.

This lack of transparency in relation to funding needs to be tackled at management level and funds to provide learning resources for HE students should be protected. Library staff need to work closely with management and academic staff in both the HEIs and the FECs to ensure that that pressure is placed on managers to provide adequate funding.

A critical strategic issue that needs to be addressed is staffing at the FEC libraries. For many FEC library managers it has been difficult to expand their staffing levels to meet the growing demands of HE students. Many still have inadequate staff numbers, an inadequate proportion of qualified staff, too many vacation-only staff and poor salary levels. HEIs and FECs need to work together to address this issue as the FEC library staff are the key to successful collaborative library services.

Addressing student needs

In the mid-1990s, Deborah Goodall (1994; 1996) wrote about library support for franchise students and her work is still highly relevant and essential reading for anyone involved in supporting HE in FEI students. However, the recent introduction of Foundation degrees has added another dimension as the information needs of students studying for these awards have not yet been clearly identified. Their needs are likely to be far more complex than those studying to FE level, but perhaps less complex than students studying towards a Bachelor degree. The vocational and practical nature of the degrees is likely to impact further on the type of information that the students need. More research needs to be done but in the meantime HE institutions need to ensure, if possible, that they have an HE in FEC specialist on their library team.

Not only does the nature of the award have an impact on information needs, but also the nature of the students themselves. Students studying to HE level in an FEC tend to fit a non-traditional student profile, especially in the light of recent government initiatives based on findings of the White Papers *The Future of Higher Education* (DfES, 2003) and *Widening Participation in Higher Education* (DfES, 2003). The term non-traditional is used to describe students who do not match the profile of students who make up the majority of undergraduates in UK universities. Often a single class can include a very wide range of individuals with different life experiences, educational backgrounds and levels of confidence.

The needs of non-traditional students have been well documented (Heery, 1996; Livesey, 2001) and are beyond the scope of this chapter. In the HE in FEC context, the widely differing learning styles and abilities of these students add to the incentive for appointing an HE in FEC specialist and for ensuring a wide range of support mechanisms. Above all, students need a flexible approach and a high level of support. Some students have poor online skills and lack confidence using computers which is an issue of concern in the HE in FEC environment where use of online resources is so critical.

Often these students have less time to develop the skills required to become effective self-directed learners. The duration of many courses is only two years and students often have other commitments that place heavy demands on their time. Their study timetable is often very intense and the traditional FE culture does not help to promote self-directed learning. In fact, some FEC library staff will give the same highly prescriptive support to their HE students as they would to their FE students, which does not help them to become self-directed learners. HEFCE's guidance report, *Supporting higher education in further education colleges: a guide for tutors and lecturers* (HEFCE, 2003), stresses the importance of independent learning at HE level and offers suggestions for good practice. Library staff have to work in close collaboration to ensure that students are receiving an appropriate level of support but are being encouraged to take responsibility for their own information searching.

Many HE in FEC students are making a significant commitment, often making personal sacrifices, when they undertake their course of study. Expectations are therefore high. Library services to these students need to be of a very high standard and should in no way be considered less important than services to other students, even though student numbers may not be high. There are times, however, when expectations go beyond what can be realistically offered. It is therefore essential to manage student expectations from an early stage and to ensure that teaching staff, library staff and other key personnel are giving the same clear message to ensure that students are aware of their entitlement and of the nature of the partnership.

Resourcing HE in an FE environment

Providing sufficient and appropriate learning resources for HE level study can be problematic for many FEC libraries. Funds are often inadequate and the comparatively small HE student numbers mean that the college libraries cannot provide such a wide range of resources as a university library can provide. Unlike HEI libraries, the material that is purchased for other students is often not of an appropriate level for sharing.

In franchise relationships, the percentage of funds distributed to the college in relation to the funds retained by the HEI varies between partnerships. For example, in those partnerships where the HE library receives funds to support students studying in FECs, an intercampus delivery scheme may be possible. The funds can be used not only to operate the scheme but also to prevent unsustainable pressure being placed on the HE library stock. In partnerships where the funds for learning resources are directed predominantly or entirely at the partner college library, HEI and FEC staff can work together to build appropriate collections at the college library and to ensure that an effective interlibrary loan service is available.

Some HE in FEC students have full membership of their university library, which is particularly useful for those studying within a reasonable distance. For others, it can be frustrating especially when lack of parking and public transport can make visiting the HEI difficult. Some FEC libraries offer a postal return service if the students are prepared to visit the university in person. FEC library staff should be given information and guidelines regarding schemes, such as UK Libraries Plus for part-time students. Many FEC libraries have changed their loan periods to make them more appropriate for their HE users while others have a different loan period for these students.

The most significant way that HEI libraries can help to extend the resources of their partner college libraries is by providing access to online resources. The number of databases available off-campus is now extensive so that the majority of resources are readily accessible in the partner colleges and usage can be monitored. There are potential difficulties. For example, technical issues relating to the ICT infrastructure in some colleges can make access difficult. ATHENS administration at a distance can be problematic, especially when some students have both a college and a university ATHENS password. Security can also be an issue where students are studying alongside others who are not entitled to use the resources. Technical solutions are being sought to resolve some of these issues, but good communication between the college staff and the university staff is also essential. Similarly, good communication and effective training are essential in promoting and encouraging use of online resources.

Subject librarians should be encouraged to play their part by advocating the purchase of online books and journals which can be accessed by those students studying elsewhere.

For some types of partnership agreement, such as validated courses, online access to all databases will not be possible. It is, therefore, essential that academic staff talk to library staff at the HEI when developing new courses before they sign any agreements that mention library resources. The HEI library staff will be able to advise whether a particular type of agreement will require them to seek permission for access to online databases.

Other initiatives can be introduced to widen the range of available resources. For example, a group of libraries within a partnership could set up an e-mail discussion group where they can offer to each other materials that may no longer be relevant to their collections. Strong links with other information providers in the area, such as public libraries, museums and archives can further widen the range of information and expertise available to the students.

Since resources are likely to be more limited in the FEC environment, those that are available need to be exploited to their maximum potential. This can be problematic in the FEC environment where students may be less confident about their research or IT skills and where academic staff may have less awareness of the importance of developing these skills, even if time permits. Effective communication and training are essential for overcoming these problems.

Developing library skills

A robust training programme is essential for students to develop their library skills and maximise their use of available learning resources. This can and should be delivered in a variety of ways, such as group sessions, online support, one-to-one sessions and training documentation.

Most students receive at the very least an initial library induction at their FEC. This is a good opportunity for them to see the FEC library, learn about how to use it and meet the library staff. Usually it is a general session that varies little from the induction given to FE students except that they may be given documentation about the university library. It is equally important, however, that students should receive a follow-up session once term is under way to introduce them to the HEI's online resources. Additional sessions may also be run to support a specific project or assignment or as a refresher.

Ideally, training should be delivered by FEC library staff as they will be the first contact for students needing help. It may also be appropriate sometimes for the HE in FEC specialist or university subject librarian to help to deliver a session. For example, they may want to support a new staff member or help with a difficult subject area or just make sure that they are up-to-date with the needs of the students for whom they are ultimately responsible.

Arranging training sessions can be problematic. FEC timetables are often intense and teaching staff do not always want to give up their teaching time for library sessions. Library staff therefore need to work very closely with the teaching staff to raise awareness of the importance of these sessions. Mature student groups may be prepared to liaise with the library staff themselves to arrange a session outside timetabled sessions.

Once sessions have been arranged, the next challenge is to ensure reasonable attendance. The most effective way to ensure attendance is to link the session with an assignment set by the tutor. This not only gives them the incentive of getting a good grade but also places the training in context.

Training should be supported by clear handouts that set out for the students the processes that they need to access the material once they have left the session. Quizzes and examples are useful for practising their skills and as a reminder of what they have learned.

Library skills training is sometimes delivered by the FEC teaching staff. If this is done in close co-operation with the library staff then it is an effective way of ensuring that the students attend and take note. However, if it is done without consultation with library staff, it can do more harm than good. Teaching staff have busy schedules and are often not up-to-date with all the available resources. They may also be unaware of library procedures or unfamiliar with the collection.

Ideally, FEC libraries would have a separate enquiry desk where staff could devote sufficient time to in-depth enquiries and individual support sessions. Similarly, some FECs have created a subject librarian structure to mirror the staffing structure that is common in HE Libraries. In this way, there is always a subject specialist who can advise HE students in more depth than might be appropriate for a generalised FE Library. Unfortunately, most FEC libraries do not have sufficient staff to support such structures which means that individual support is often delivered at busy counters or can only be provided on an appointment basis. Even smaller libraries, however, can allocate certain subject areas to individual members of staff to enable them to build up expertise in a subject. FEC libraries also need to ensure that appropriately qualified staff are available during some evening shifts to support part-time students.

Increasingly, libraries are looking for online solutions to support students, especially those studying at remote locations. While online training packages cannot compensate for the flexibility and responsiveness of a good teacher, they can help to overcome geographic distances. There are also some students who learn better using online materials. Many libraries are therefore becoming involved in their FEC virtual learning environment (VLE) if they exist or with their intranets. VLEs or intranets are ideal places to include links to information resources, such as the library catalogue, databases and websites. They can also be used to host an interactive information skills learning package. If possible, the package should be linked to the mainstream learning environments, but could stand alone as a separate package. HEIs and FECs can share resources and work together to create effective learning packages to suit their student needs.

Study environment

Despite the best efforts of library staff, FEC libraries are often noisy places. They can also be small and over-crowded due to limited budgets and campus space, as highlighted by CILIP's recent *Survey of Library and Learning Resource Provision in Further Education Colleges* (CILIP, 2003). While some HE students find this a stimulating work environment, most do not. It is therefore essential to ensure that a study area, preferably equipped with computers, is available for HE students to work quietly. While some FECs make this area available only for their HE students, others allow any students to use them provided they work quietly.

The spectrum of courses taught in FECs is very wide in terms of level and subject. Library users may include, for example, students as young as 14, students with learning disabilities, workers studying part-time and adult learners. HE students usually make up a fairly small minority of users, but have high demands. This mix of users can create conflict and requires considerable flexibility on the part of the library staff. There is additional concern about young people sharing resources with HE students, such as art and media students, who may be legitimately using materials that are inappropriate for students under 18 years old.

Some FEC libraries have been able to extend their opening hours to support their HE students. Opening hours need to be monitored and reviewed in accordance with changes in the curriculum: it is no good opening the library until 20.00 on a day when evening groups do not have classes.

Training and development for FE library staff

Many staff in FEC libraries find working with HE students rewarding. The students are usually dedicated, enthusiastic and require more intellectually challenging support than FE students. However, library staff are not necessarily equipped with sufficient knowledge of HE resources and demands to deliver effective support. The HE library therefore needs to take responsibility for training FEC staff so that they can deliver training to their students and staff with confidence. Cascading the training in this way is critical. The students are going to see the college library staff when they come to visit the library for their studies, and so they are the key people that they need to get to know through training sessions.

Training of FEC library staff needs to be ongoing to enable them to develop and maintain their skills. As HE students are usually in the minority, the staff do not have the same intense exposure to HE resources as their colleagues at the HEI library and need to update their skills regularly. Staff turnover in FECs tends to be very high and so there is a need for ongoing training to support new staff.

Training also needs to be accessible as FEC library staff are often unable to travel to the university on a regular basis. As FECs have fewer staff overall and fewer professional staff than HEIs, they tend to have more non-professional staff dealing with subject enquiries. Some of these staff have difficulties working with complex online resources and need additional support. As a result, training needs to be tailored to meet individual needs.

The training needs of FE library staff are, therefore, complex. Online solutions can effectively overcome geographic boundaries and provide ongoing support, but are less responsive and less easily tailored to suit individual needs. An alternative solution is for a librarian to be appointed who can travel to the colleges to deliver the training. This highly flexible approach would allow the delivery of training that is tailored to meet the needs of the FEC. This person could also fulfil the role of HE in FEC specialist at the university library.

Core training should be supplemented by additional training activities that can contribute to the overall career development of library staff. Activities can include, for example, mini-conferences, networking days or training events with an outside speaker. Visits to the university library and meetings with appropriate library staff at the university can help to develop a better understanding of the HE environment and provide useful contacts.

However the training is delivered, it is important that the HEI library is sensitive to FE issues. It is all too easy to perceive the relationship as hierarchical with the HEI trying to impose methods of delivery which are not suitable for the FEC environment. Effective communication and a flexible approach can help to overcome this perception. In practice, this can be achieved by developing a strong channel of communication, clarifying the level of support that is required and providing appropriate training.

Working together

The benefits of working in collaboration in the library environment are well documented (Rockman, 2002, p.192). Practical benefits in the HE in FEC context include the opportunity to share resources and expertise and to embark on large-scale projects by spreading the workload. Partnerships tend to enhance efficiency and flexibility and can help libraries to reach a wider audience. Collaboration also helps to develop a mutual understanding. For example, FEC library staff may perceive the HE library as 'having it all' without realising that HE libraries face similar issues if on a different scale. HE library staff may perceive that working in an FEC is similar to working in HE but on a smaller scale, unaware of the fundamental differences, such as the wide range of user needs. Collaboration can help to dispel these misconceptions and provide more effective support for the students.

Many colleges are geographically remote from their partner HEI and so do not benefit from the informal communication channels that often arise naturally in a large organisation. A more structured approach is therefore required, such as developing a peripatetic librarian post, establishing an e-mail list for all staff working within a particular partnership, holding regular meetings and hosting collaborative events.

By working together, library staff can raise the profile of their services within the wider context of the HE and FE institutions. This in turns enables them to work in co-operation with other key personnel, especially teaching staff but also other support staff. As a result, library services become better integrated into the programme as a whole, making them more accessible to the students.

Collaboration needs to go beyond the critical HE/FE partnership. For example, many networks now exist between groups of libraries usually involving one or more HEIs and their partner colleges. Library staff at FECs can feel isolated from other librarians delivering similar services and these networks can help to overcome this. They can also prevent duplication of work as libraries can share ideas and materials. For staff development purposes, the pool of potential mentors for chartership or other activities widens when libraries join forces as a network.

Other collaborative efforts are cross-sectoral and include public libraries and other specialised information providers. For example, a representative from the partnership can visit the public libraries to talk about the needs of the students and deliver basic training in troubleshooting online resources. The public library can be a preferable study environment for some students and can be a source of useful materials in some specialised areas, such as local information.

Formal arrangements can be drawn up. For example, Bournemouth University has an agreement with the Bournemouth Library regarding student use of its outstanding music collection. Similarly, the University of the Highlands and Islands Millennium Institute, which covers a very widespread, rural student population, deposits material in the local public libraries (Mackay, 2001, p.414). The expectations of students need to be well-managed in these circumstances so that the students understand the differences between the role of the public libraries and the role of their FEC library.

There are barriers to collaboration. Significantly, licensing restrictions on online resources are problematic for institutions who wish to work in partnership. It is understandable that publishers would not want to lose potential income but licensing schemes for small consortia such as HE in FEC partnerships would be beneficial to all parties.

Teaching staff

FECs differ from HEIs in that the teaching staff are often less aware of the significance of complex learning resources that are appropriate to HE level studies. Lecturing at FE level is far more textbook-based than at HE level and, until recently, there has been little incentive for FE staff to develop research skills themselves. This is changing as more staff are required to obtain FE teaching awards and partner HEIs are enhancing the support that they give to teaching staff delivering their HE courses. Teaching staff also have very tight teaching schedules in comparison with their colleagues in HEIs, which gives them less time for staff development.

It can be a constant struggle for library staff to persuade teaching staff to learn about library resources beyond the textbook, especially online resources. This leads to the practical difficulty of arranging to 'borrow' their students for a library session and does not help to encourage the students to use the resources. Smaller college libraries generally find it easier to target their teaching staff than larger libraries, because communication flows more readily in a tight-knit community. For the most part, change is happening but it requires patience and tenacity.

The only truly effective solution is for library skills or information literacy to be embedded in the curriculum. That way, the teaching staff are on board by necessity and the students learn the relevant skills with a target-orientated purpose. For most FEC libraries, this is not yet a possibility. In the meantime, other techniques can be employed by library staff, including attending course meetings, targeting champions or key personnel, using staff development sessions, newsletters and offering one-to-one or group support. Many library staff are involved in the development of their college VLE which is an opportunity for them to talk to teaching staff about learning resources and to stress the importance of including learning resources in VLEs.

Quality

While FECs have many features in common with each other, each institution is unique, and there are considerable differences between them. This can cause difficulties for HEIs in relation to setting standards and monitoring quality. The HEI needs to ensure that students are receiving an equitable standard of service while allowing the flexibility of delivery to account for differences between institutions. It also needs to ensure that targets are not set which cannot be achieved by all partners. QAA documentation makes it clear that overall responsibility for quality lies with the awarding institution (QAA, 2004). In 2005/6, the QAA will start carrying out a series of audits dedicated to collaborative provision.

Service level agreements can be an effective way to ensure quality although sometimes it can be difficult to find terms that are sufficiently general to be attainable by all partner libraries yet specific enough to have significance.

Surveys can be a useful tool to obtain feedback, identify issues and monitor progression. Actions need to be agreed across the partnership and each partner should take responsibility for ensuring that actions are completed and the survey results are disseminated appropriately. Despite the best creative efforts of library staff (handing out lollipops as bribes is a popular approach), returns on such a survey can be patchy and the results may not always be a true reflection of the picture across the partnership.

While some qualitative feedback can be obtained from survey forms, it is often brief and difficult to interpret, especially from the HEI being geographically remote from the students and libraries being surveyed. Comments such as 'not enough books' and 'grumpy library staff' are too vague to be useful beyond identifying patterns. Qualitative feedback is more difficult to obtain but can be very useful. One approach is to target a selection of tutorial and for library staff to open up a dialogue with the students for perhaps 15 minutes at the beginning of one of their tutorials.

Regular audits are an effective way of monitoring progress and identifying issues. For example, an audit document could be devised to cover a number of topics, such as strategy, planning, liaison, resources and learning materials. The FEC library managers would complete this and provide evidence to support their statements. This could be followed by a visit from senior library managers from the university. A report and action plan could be drawn up based on the issues agreed by both parties and distributed accordingly. The audit should be a two-way process where the FEC librarians have the opportunity to discuss their concerns. The final document is useful not only for identifying issues for concern but also as a bargaining tool for FEC library managers to use with their resource managers. The audit process is time-consuming and it is probably best carried out once every five years.

Conclusion

The provision of successful library services for HE in FEC students requires an understanding of student needs, appropriate resources and study environment, support from well-trained library staff and co-operation from teaching staff. These elements are, of course, essential in any academic library setting, but are more difficult to achieve in the HE in FEC context because of the complexity of delivery, geographic remoteness, the profile of the courses and the students, different FE/HE cultures and the potentially fragile relationship between the HEI and its partners.

Strong communication links, a mutual understanding and collaboration across the partnership and beyond are all essential to success. Effective support mechanisms are critical, preferably co-ordinated by a librarian dedicated to an institution's HE in FEC students. Robust quality assurance mechanisms are needed to underpin the service and ensure a high quality effective service for HE in FEC students.

References

Arnold, K., 2002. The partnership experience: De Montfort University and its Associate Libraries Network. *SCONUL Newsletter* 27, 49–54.

Chartered Institute of Library and Information Professionals (CILIP), 2003. *UK Survey of Library and Learning Resource Provision in Further Education Colleges*. London: CILIP.

Department for Education and Skills (DfES), 2003a. *The future of Higher Education*.

London: HMSO.

Department for Education and Skills (DfES), 2003b. W*idening participation in Higher Education*. London: HMSO.

Goodall, D., 1996. Academic franchising: some pointers for improving practice. *Library Management* 17, 4–9.

Goodall, D., 1994. Franchised courses in higher education: implications for the library manager. *Library Management* 15, 27–33.

Heery, M., 1996. Academic library services to non-traditional students. *Library Management* 17, 3–13.

Higher Education Funding Council for Great Britain (HEFCE), 2003. *Supporting higher education in further education colleges: a guide for tutors and lecturers* [online]. HEFCE. Available from: http://www.hefce.ac.uk [Accessed 16 December 2004].

Livesey, S., and Wynne, P., 2001. Extending the hybrid library to students on franchised courses: user profile, service implementation issues and management strategies. *Library Management* 22, 21–25.

Mackay, M., 2001. Collaboration and liaison: the importance of developing working partnerships in the provision of networked hybrid services to lifelong learners in rural areas. *Library Management* 22, 411–415.

Quality Assurance Agency (QAA), 2004. Code of practice for the assurance of academic quality and standards. Section 2: Collaborative provision, in higher education and flexible and distributed learning (including e-learning). Available from: www.qaa.ac.uk [Accessed 16 December 2004].

Rockman, I., 2002. Establishing successful partnerships with university support units. *Library Management* 23, 192–198.

Chapter 6

Virtual Learning Environments

Marian Matthews

The change from physical learning environments to virtual learning environments (VLEs) and from print to e-resources is now so rapid that any librarian who has joined the profession in the last ten years will experience more than one transformation of their work practices within a professional lifetime. This chapter draws on the authors'experience of this transformation, specifically contributing to VLEs for business and law and latterly the development of flexible learning to support doctoral students. It describes the evolution of the role of the subject librarian in parallel with the development of e-resources, identifying some of the key milestones. Of necessity the chapter covers a wide range of topics; change management, participating in web-based collaborative projects, database architecture and e-books as well as the move towards embracing the pedagogy of learning as subject librarians become more and more involved in the delivery of e-learning. A recent research study (Rieger et al., 2004), confirmed the strategic importance of a library presence in faculty-created course web sites. Further more this research was instrumental in 'raising academic staff awareness of the issues surrounding usability and functionality of efficient e-learning environments'.

Historical perspective

Dearing, influential in so many recent developments in higher education asks 'are the Universities we need managing the paradigm shift towards the full integration of the learning technologies into the infrastructure of their deliverables?'(NCIHE, 1997). Since Dearing, the pace of technological change has quickened. Universities have had to adapt their goals and mission statements and current students are experiencing changes in their learning environment as they study. Changed also is the view of learning in higher education from a single intense experience to lifelong learning, the continuous acquisition of knowledge and skills. Organisations responsible for the quality assurance of specific subjects and professions were engaging in their own reviews and recommendations of practice and pedagogy. BILETA (British and Irish Legal Education Technology Association) issued reports on information technology for UK law schools in 1991 and 1996. Though mainly concerned with access to CD based packages and dial up access through local area networks to database sources, enlightening comments on pedagogic issues provide a basis for reflection on the developments since then. Currently there are 'fundamental shifts in the meaning of the term university from a centre of learning to a business organisation with measurable productivity'(Doring, 2002). The view that education has intrinsic value, making a contribution to culture and society is being superseded by the view of the university as an organisation delivering graduates with skills that are required to sustain economic growth and development. Key to the latter view is the use of information technology in the efficient delivery of learning. According to Doring '…[in] the race for what is seen as more effective use of funds, the current change to increased flexible delivery has perhaps, in the name of economic expediency, confused information with knowledge'(2002, p4). The interactivity of the Internet (Broad, et al., 2003), the immediacy of access to its contents, the public accessibility to much of its information and the ease of distributing the information via the Internet, however, do provide a different operating environment which demands a succinct paradigm shift and strategies for change.

E-resources

The source material which underpins virtual learning consists of a growing range of dynamic resources which interlink to form a 'web'of learning opportunities. These include graphics, original notes, journal articles, e-books and all manner of data designed to meet the needs of specified users.

Databases

Databases can almost be said to have created the information environment, as we know it today (Neufeld and Cornog 1986). A significant aspect of many of these commercial database services is their huge volume of data; Lexis-Nexis for example holds in excess of 1.4 billion documents, with over 1.3 million subscribers and millions of annual searches. There is a wealth of available technical literature on database theory and design, and some of it helps to understand the current generation of databases which in are in turn embedded into VLEs. From the rigid file systems of the early 1960s the early database systems based on hierarchical and network models were born and provided a logical organisation of data in trees and graphs. Although efficient these types of product used procedural languages, did not have logical independence and were inflexible giving rise to the first large-scale database/ data communication system (Piattini and Diaz, 2000). During the 1970s and 1980s research work and its application focused on query optimisation, high level languages, memory management and indexing techniques. Early versions of databases to the fully automated legal environment (Krause, 1993). As information technology (IT) skills have developed with enhanced access to software and networks, so the traditional modes of access for the huge complex data files have shifted to web access. With this access come other significant considerations such as usage under academic licence for questionable non-academic use or licence implications for profitable companies. Undoubtedly the first benefits of this technology to users were access to, and latterly full text access to, journal articles, conference papers and reports. This process now appears to have achieved a critical mass with the majority of these types of publication routinely delivered in electronic form. The transformation of resources using technology is now making inroads into books and monographs with a significant number of e-book collections commercially available.

Books become e-books

It is probable that traditional skills of the subject librarian, such as the evaluation of the printed book, are being dismantled as techniques such as heuristic evaluation need to be applied to e-books. Key software features now associated with database, e-journals and other information and courseware, need to be evaluated together with an analysis of the various stakeholders involved such as publishers, authors, software and hardware providers. Key elements and characteristics of electronic publishing together with the delineation of the nature of narrative content, subject orientation, quality control and added value (Armstrong and Lonsdale, 2000) have become the benchmark of the robust VLE.

Successful library collection management relies on a wide definition of collaborative activities concerned with conservation and disposal, and access versus holdings. The current growth rate of scholarly publishing (Kennedy,1997) makes it difficult for scholars to sort out the worthwhile from the valueless and Reiger et al. (2004) point out that 'relevancy and sufficiency judgements'should be applied to collection management. When a book, for example, goes into a second edition rather than a reprint, it is usually a sign of significant developments (Naylor, 1999); the only constant now is that things will keep getting different. Publication date and edition statements are crucial in some subject areas, particularly those affected by legal or regulatory changes. Landoni et al. (2000) conducted research into design features and in particular explored the importance of the visual component of the book metaphor for the production of more effective e-books. Much of the early e-book literature focuses on the issues of access, availability, circulation and pricing structures. Ormes'research paper (2001) provides an excellent summary of the hardware options from handheld to desktop readers and a hypothesis on how users will be able to download titles directly from the library catalogue. The paper does not, however, make any in-depth evaluation of the usability of the product, but instead assumes that its ultimate success may depend on careful management and networking. Whilst analysing disadvantages of e-books, the paper tends to focus on integration and rationalisation of the hybrid resource base. It mentions users'resistance to change, but does not examine any of the intrinsic factors which may contribute to that resistance such as convenience and familiarity.

The issues surrounding e-books according to Morgan (2000) are not so much of standards of format but of access and ownership. The economic survival of e-books is unlikely if issues of design flexibility and access are not addressed and there is already a divergence of initiatives responding to anticipated user needs. HERON

(Higher Education Resources On Demand) was a significant initiative under phase 3 of the eLib project, its particular remit being to offer higher education institutions a copyright clearance and digitisation service. This offered a digital resource bank of widely, and by definition frequently used, student texts or selected excerpts which can be integrated into course learning materials. Currently, evaluation and feedback continues to examine usability features such as consistency of approach, navigation, readability and flexibility.

Collaborative projects

This section describes three projects at Bournemouth University that were the result of successful collaborative applications for internal Learning and Teaching Development Initiative funds. The purpose of these initiatives was to provide an adjunct to traditional teaching methods that could be used during facilitated sessions or as self directed learning or revision materials. Criteria common to all of these projects were interactivity to engage the users, careful consideration of learning objectives, outcomes and design features, and consistent look and feel throughout the modules. Each project included a range of learning materials including lecturers notes, discussion forum, excel exercises, an e book and journal literature, and certain materials were only made available at appropriate stages of the course. The use of the VLE to host these three very different resources not only enhanced the quality of the learning experience but also empowered library staff to contribute to the learning and teaching environment.

Project 1: InfoSkills

InfoSkills was designed as a web-based tutorial, to provide a holistic approach to library user education with 24 hour/seven day a week availability and off-campus access. From the first version launched in 2001, it covered core skills such searching the library catalogue as well as introducing wider concepts of information handling, database searching, the use and evaluation of Internet sources and referencing skills. The main objective of the project was to create an interactive, introductory library skills tutorial (Rutter and Matthews, 2002) that would serve as a foundation for subject-focused seminars and workshops. InfoSkills was designed to encourage students to learn to make informed choices about information retrieval and cultivate critical thinking and evaluation skills to underpin the information literacy process. This was felt especially true for the Internet module as the Internet and the library are often viewed as two separate and unrelated entities (D'Esposito and Gardner, 1999). After four years, InfoSkills remains an integral part of the library VLE, developments include the introduction of Master's level modules.

Project 2: Integrated Virtual Learning Environment (IVLE)

The objective of the IVLE and the associated research was to create and evaluate the use of an IVLE for accounting undergraduates. It was envisaged that the unit would provide a flexible interactive learning tool, which would engender a climate of student learning outside of formal contact sessions and facilitate participative discussion and problem solving during seminars. Embracing the new technologies of the Web is currently perceived as one way of maximising the access of appropriate resources within a specific subject environment. This provides flexibility, point-of-use instruction and guides at the time required (Broad and Matthews, 2004): Atton observes (1996) that the momentum of the change by which academic practice is defined and implemented is probably based on the new educational space created by local and global information networks. The research conducted as part of the IVLE development considered the question of how students' preferred learning styles related to their use and perceptions of VLEs. Specifically the research into student learning styles considered whether embracing and adopting the new technologies as an aid to more effective learning and teaching for the student and tutor was pedagogically sound. Research has also considered whether new technologies can create an efficient and robust learning environment which engenders a culture of deeper learning. Studies have shown (Jones and Scully, 1998; Schon, 1983; Tennant, 1997) that students of all ages learn better when they actively engaged in the process, this applies equally to interactivity with a VLE. Student feedback to the IVLE was positive, though many still favoured the traditional textbook. Readers are known to be able to recall the position of text in a paper text (Rothkopf,1971). Landoni et al. (2000) observe 'this fact connects a semantic entity, the information, with a physical one, which has visual and tactile cues. Factors which can influence the sense of text are the page size, legibility, and a low responsiveness while scrolling when looking for more text'. Thus issues of typography and layout remain as crucial in the electronic environment as in the traditional paper book, so the page metaphor should probably remain.

Project 3: Legal Relationships Unit

The Legal Relationships Unit, common to a range of business undergraduate programmes, provided the ideal opportunity to introduce a web-based learning initiative. Materials were rewritten and contextualised from an existing printed workbook which included tutors' notes, problem solving, group and individual work, study skills and the integration of references to primary and secondary legal resources in electronic and traditional format. An increasingly diverse range of learning resources suggests a need to review current practice and incorporate a holistic approach to learning. The learning environment incorporates an additional assessment task designed to demonstrate the student's understanding and application of electronic information sources in accordance with current practice within the unit. An online student discussion facility is used for legal problem solving and enhances the interactive nature of the unit. The unit, together with the learning resources, offered further potential for off-campus delivery. The unit is used to provide an adjunct to traditional delivery patterns and allows time during workshops and seminars to undertake focussed use of resources, exploring search strategies and the appropriate integration and interpretation of traditional sources of law. The relationship of the use made of printed material with the use made of online resources is summarised by Landoni et al. (2000): 'The sense of the text is the feeling users may have of the structural and semantic structure of the text that is being read, i.e. its spatial disposition'.

Security

Whether searching by some of the traditional access routes such as Telnet or latterly via the web, the question of database security remains paramount. The security process began in the 1970s in the business arena, and it was not until the 1980s that issues of commercial security and sensitivity of data became important in government, military and information environments. While some work on mandatory security secure database management systems were initiated in the 1970s (Ferrari and Thuraisingham, 2000), it was a decade later that password systems fully developed. ATHENS, the unique authentication system developed during the mid-1990s, allows an individual user to register for a personal user account ID which then permits access the authorised portfolio of resources via the internet and exclusive for that particular organisation. This represents a huge efficiency saving for the information professionals who manage the complexities of password administration.

> Whilst this is a very efficient mechanism it is, arguably, important that there are adequate controls in place to ensure that the information is not libellous, defamatory, inaccurate, illegal or inappropriate. These issues are not new and most are common to both the Internet and paper based information. The interactivity of the Internet, the immediacy of access to its contents, the public accessibility to much of its information and the ease of distributing the information via the Internet, however, do provide a different operating environment and therefore different audit and control issues arise (Broad et al., 2003).

In its widest context the potential VLE security issues encompass considerations of academic quality and freedom, no different, some might, say from those of the seminar room. Kennedy (1997) attempts to find a balance by comparing academic freedom with its counterpart, academic duty.

> The evidence suggests a kind of dissonance between the purposes our society sees for the university and the way the university sees itself. For although the freedoms necessary for teaching and scholarly work are understood and reasonably well accepted, the counter balancing obligations are vague and even obscure. Duty is to prepare; to teach; to mentor; to serve the University; to discover; to publish; to tell the truth; to reach beyond the walls; to change (Kennedy, 1997)

The WWW has enabled systems characterised by client server architecture in which the clients are potentially the whole population of learners who are distributed, dynamically changing and removed from the immediacy of interaction with the tutor.

Relationships with learners and academics

Despite the complexity of e-learning the main learning outcomes remain clear, these being to encourage the independent learner to achieve a holistic approach to learning through efficient access, location and interpretation of relevant learning resources. In addition, to ensure students have the necessary transferable skills to distinguish and evaluate the most relevant sources to support their tasks. Within higher education as in most other organisations there is use of Held's (1995) frequently quoted phrase 'a chronic intensification of patterns of interconnectedness', mediated by the new information technology (Edwards, 1997). What this means is that technology has become a powerful tool, which can, arguably, also undermine the necessity for a mediator between the learner and what they wish to learn. Usability is central to encouraging users to engage with e-learning materials. Rigorous usability testing that places the user at the centre of the process, for example Nielsen's heuristic evaluation approach (1993), help to ensure systems are modelled on user needs. User support needs to be available but unobtrusive, accurate and robust, consistent and flexible. Most users only touch the manual when things go wrong, by then they are often out of the site or stranded on an inoperable system. Online documentation should be searchable and provide task-orientated step-by-step instructions together with a variety of examples. There are a number of different approaches to user support (Dix, 1998), command assistance, command prompts, context-sensitive help, online tutorials and online documentation. In pedagogic terms however, this support requires more sensitive yet robust management. The autonomous learner first identified by Laurillard (1993) can become the 'isolated or disengaged' learner with educative process displaced and reconstituted.

Increasingly academics would identify a trend in higher education from teacher-centred to student-centred learning with students developing as 'collaborators' in the learning process (Laurillard, 2004). This is indicative of the shifting relationships within academia – and arguably in the notion of superiority identified with the traditional academic status – and is demonstrated by negotiated learning and other innovations. It is critical that we measure and understand the impact of VLEs on the teaching community. Research by Doring (2002) examines the role of academics as change agent and although inconclusive on several aspects, states that in the context of e-learning 'this shift is considered to demonstrate that by lessening the opportunity for authentic dialogue with students, individual academics may actually disengage from the dialogue process and so become a change victim rather than a change agent'.

Also important is to measure and understand the impact of VLEs on the learning community and within that, unpick the elements that closely relate to the subject support function. The Special Educational Needs and Disability Act 2001 affects all education and training but does not specifically mention learning technologies or the Internet. The Act does cover the concept of 'adjustments'for the disabled, 'requiring educators to pre-determine fundamental issues regarding their academic disciplines and the methods used to access and deliver these'(Corlett, 2001).

Landoni et al. (2000) observe that the

> ... sense of engagement is the level of interest the system induces in users. The result of a good level of engagement is a high level of concentration that makes users interested in their task. One source of engagement is the fun of seeing the system react and is related to the novelty of the system; tangibility and responsiveness are also responsible for a good level of engagement. Paper has generally a low level of engagement because it is not interactive and is overly familiar to users.

It follows that conventions of linear arrangement, typography, contents pages, margin notes and indexes are likely to be sought. However, before electronic books are widely accepted (Pack, 2000) they will have to pass the 'Four B'test, which means people will have to be comfortable taking them in the bathroom, on the bus, to the beach and in the bedroom.

Conclusion

The demystification of information retrieval is largely due to the arrival of the Internet (Marfleet and Kelly, 1999) and, as learning shifts towards a seamless integrated environment libraries are migrating their online catalogues, database gateways and associated retrieval tools to the web. Compatibility with any and all potential web-based and traditional environments is a key factor (Beagle, 2000) and databases have become a crucial part of successful data retrieval on the web. In its draft C & IT Strategy the UK Centre for Legal Education 2000 sought to promote the effective delivery and transformation of existing learning through the use of datasets and provide advice and assistance to the legal education community.

Computer-mediated education should not be accepted uncritically, and academic writers have already begun to reflect on the effectiveness and desirability of web-based learning. A substantial study by Alexander and McKenzie in 1998 and quoted by Robinson (2001) found that outcomes were affected by a range of factors whose weighting and combination were shaped by particular contexts of use. They concluded, 'The most important factor in determining successful project outcomes was the design of the student's learning experience. Clearly evaluation is of paramount importance, providing qualitative feedback on new learning environments, which are breaking down barriers and continue to challenge traditional teaching boundaries, generating issues of accountability and ownership.

Where are we now?

A recent trawl of the CILIP website indicated no obvious links to virtual learning environments or web-based learning as key headings, yet during the last ten years the authors experience has been that information professionals have embraced and applied the new learning technologies efficiently and effectively. The evolving framework for both the efficient provision of academic learning resources and the acquisition of the necessary competencies to utilise them, would seem to have acquired a maturity which owes itself in someway to the opportunities afforded by the VLE. The SCONUL (1999) task force further defined the objectives and provided a refocus for e-literacy (Martin and Rader, 2003) as a synthesising concept involving 'awareness, skills, understandings and reflective-evaluative approaches that are necessary for an individual to operate comfortably in information-rich and IT-supported environments'.

References

Armstrong, C. and Lonsdale, R., 2000. Scholarly monographs: why would I want publish electronically? *The Electronic Library,* 18 (1), 21–28.

Atton, C., 1996. Towards a critical practice for the academic library, *New Library World*, 97, 4–11.

British and Irish Legal Education Technology Association (BILETA), 1991. *Report of Inquiry into the provision of information technology in UK law schools.* University of Warwick.

British and Irish Legal Education Technology Association (BILETA), 1996. *Second BILETA Report into information technology and legal education.* University of Warwick, CTI Centre.

Broad, M., Matthews, M., and Shephard K., 2003. Audit and control of the use of the Internet for learning and teaching: Issues for stakeholders in higher education. *Managerial Auditing Journal,* 18 (3), 244–253.

Broad, M. and Matthews, M., 2004. Accounting education through an online-supported virtual learning environment. *Active Learning in Higher Education*, 5 (2), 135–152.

D'Esposito, J.E., and Gardner, R.M., 1999. University students' perceptions of the Internet: an exploratory study. *The Journal of Academic Librarianship,* 25 (6), 456–461.

Doring, A., 2002. Challenges to the academic role of change agent. *Journal of Further and Higher Education*, 26 (2), 139–148.

Edwards, R., 1997. *Changing places, flexibility, lifelong learning and a learning society.* London: Routledge.

Ferarri, E. and Thuraisingham, B., 2000. Secure database systems. *In* M. Piattini, and Diaz, O., *Advanced database technology and design.* 353–402.

Held, D., 1995. *Democracy and global order.* Cambridge: Polity Press.

Jones, R. and Scully, J., 1998. Effective web teaching and learning of law on the web. *Web Journal of Current Legal Issues*, 2.

Kennedy, D., 1997. *Academic duty.* Massachusetts: Harvard University Press.

Krause, M., 1993. Look beyond Lexis and Westlaw: other computer applications in the practice of Law. *Law Library Journal*, 85, 575–582.

Landoni, M. et al., 2000. From the visual book to the web book: the importance of design. *The Electronic Library* (18) 6, 407–419.

Laurillard, D., 1993. *Rethinking university teaching. A framework for the effective use of educational technologies.* London: Routledge.

Laurillard, D., 2002. *Rethinking university teaching. A conversational framework for the effective use of learning technologies.* 2nd ed. London: Routledge.

Marfleet, J. and Kelly, C., 1999. Leading the field: the role of the information professional in the next century. *The Electronic Library*, 19 (6), 359–364.

Martin, A., and Rader, H., 2003. *Information and IT Literacy, enabling learning in the 21st century.* London: Facet.

Morgan, E., 2000. Ebooks, libraries and ownership. *Information World Review*. Dec, 52–54.

Naylor, B. (1999) Collection management for the twenty-first century. *In* Jenkins, C. and M. Morley, *Collection management in academic libraries.* Aldershot.Gower, pp. 257–283.

Neufeld, M. and Corrog, M., 1986. Database History. *Journal of American Society of Information Science* 37 (4) l 183– 190.

Nielsen, J., 1993. *Usability engineering.* London: Academic Press.

National Committee of Inquiry into Higher Education (NCIHE), 1997. *Higher education in the learning society* [online]. Available from: http://www.leeds.ac.uk/educol/ncihe/ [Accessed 11 November 2004].

Ormes, S., 2001. *An E-Book primer.* UKOLN, on behalf of EARL, The Library Association and UKOLN. Available from http://www.earl.org.uk/policy/issuepapers/ebook.htm [Accessed on 4 April 2004].

Pack, T., 2000. E Publishing revolution. *E Content*. April/May, 52–56.

Piattini, M., and Diaz, O. (eds), 2000. *Advanced database technology and design.* London: Artech House.

Rieger, O. et al., 2004. Linking course web sites to library collections and services. *The Journal of Academic Librarianship*, 30 (5), 205–211.

Robinson, B., 2001. Innovation in open and distance learning: some lessons from experience and research. *In* F. Lockwood and A. Gooley, (eds), *Innovation in open and distance learning.* London: Kogan Page, pp. 15–27.

Rothkopf, E., 1971. Incidental memory for location of information in text. *Journal of Verbal Learning and Verbal Behaviour*, 10 (6), 608–13.

Rutter, L. and Matthews, M., 2002. InfoSkills: a holistic approach to on-line user education. *The Electronic Library*, 20 (1), 29–43.

Schon, D., 1983. *The reflective practitioner: how professionals think in action.* London: Temple Smith

Tennant, M., 1997. *Psychology and adult learning.* 2nd ed. London: Routledge.

Chapter 7

Changing Relationships in the University

Kerry Shephard and Marian Matthews

Introduction

We should consider first the nature of change in the university; particularly lest we appear as opposed to change, or in some way frightened of change. As described in other chapters in this book, change is a constant feature of life in the university and we are all fairly well adapted to it. But that is not to say that all change is good or that less change is better. We should be aware of what changes are occurring, be prepared to adapt to them, and do our best to ensure that changes are by and large beneficial. One important aspect of change is that it is very rarely localised, particularly in non-hierarchical higher education. Be sure that a significant change in my job is going to affect you and your job in one way or another. This chapter attempts to describe some of the changing relationships that are occurring in our universities that impact on librarians and others who support learners and researchers. It will start by identifying some of the pressures that are contributing to the changes that are occurring now. It will then describe some illustrative studies that identify some of the changing relationships that concern us. It then attempts to summarise the key groups that are involved in these changes and finally it makes a case for teamwork, while accepting that the allocation of responsibility within the academic environment has not traditionally rewarded team player qualities.

Pressures for change and indicators of change

Changing communication strategies: coping with the attention economy

Learning, teaching and research are all about communication. Listening, talking, writing, reading. We are experts at this. But there is little doubt that communication processes are changing, even in the university. In particular e-mail is replacing internal and external conventional mail and even the telephone in some circumstances. Although texting seems to have passed by the over-30s (or is that just us?), a range of web-enabled communications such as instant messaging and chatting are having an impact on how we communicate. Perhaps most pervasive of all is the webpage. No longer do we have to send an individual copy of a publication, memo or letter to each intended recipient. Now we can 'post' it to a website and send an e-mail to each intended recipient inviting, or requiring them to read it (or view it or listen to it). Sociologists are having a fine time analysing the impact of changing communication processes on social and work interactions (see for examples Kanfer, 1999; and Danet, 2001) but here we would like to focus briefly on just one. Inviting or requiring; which do you do, and to whom do you do it, and how is this changing as you rely less on the postman to make contact and more on your computer to avoid contact? Lankshear and Knobel (2003) argue that new economies are developing where resources and information are in oversupply and taken for granted while attempts to gain and maintain attention dominate. Is the most scarce and valuable commodity in this new age becoming our attention? As processes of communication become easier, faster and operate without consideration for distance do we all respond by attempting to communicate more than we used to? More than we need to? And do we then respond to the excesses of delivered communications by ignoring them or at the very least by prioritising them?

So, who do you listen to? One of us admits that e-mails from the Vice Chancellor, rare as they are, sometimes probably fail to penetrate the spam filter. What hope has an e-mail from a librarian, e-learning advisor or departmental manager? If the mechanical filter allows at least some e-mails through, we all have acquired highly sophisticated organic filters that allow us to separate out the junk and ignore the unwelcome. So the technology has influenced who we choose to listen to. It has also probably changed who we attempt to get to listen to us and what procedures and formalities we are prepared to adopt. Some years ago a subject librarian who wished to send a message to all staff in a department would have sent a memo to the head of department or to the departmental secretary, in the hope of having it brought to attention in a staff meeting. Nowadays that same librarian would have few qualms about sending an e-mail to all members of a department, copied to the head and secretary. The danger, of course, is in the assumption that the modern process is more likely to receive attention than the older process. The change, and what makes communication strategies so important to this chapter, is that the modern message is very likely to be ignored by everyone. What constitutes effective communication in Lankshear and Knobel's attention economy, and in our universities, is changing. If you want our attention you had better be sure that you are offering something that we need but please do not assume that you know what we need.

Quality assurance

It would be silly to deny that teachers in higher education have had to confront a huge range of externally and internally applied quality assurance 'processes' in recent years. Of course all of this has been necessary to ensure that public money is well spent and that students are well supported. The language has evolved from primarily quality-assurance to primarily quality-enhancement, but these have been and continue to be significant causes for change. Leaving aside the inputs of the QAA (Quality Assurance Agency) and HEFCE (Higher Education Funding Council for England), the current emphasis, as we write this chapter, is on the development of national professional standards in teaching and learning in HE. The new Higher Education Academy will develop a framework model to include distinct levels through which HE professionals will pass through teaching-related promotion, incremental progression or specific award. An important consideration here is that 'The Higher Education Academy is concerned with every aspect of the student experience' (HE Academy, 2004). The framework will attempt to address the input of a wide range of HE professionals who contribute to student learning. Change on this scale, initiated in the name of 'quality' is not new to HE professionals, but change that involves so many professional groups probably is.

Online learning resources and e-learning

Let us expand on a theme examined in Chapter 4. Subject librarians research and develop online learning resources. They often find themselves 'the acknowledged expert' in the use of these resources to support learning, particularly as a result of participating in research and development projects supported, for example, by FDTL or TLTP programmes. Subject librarians are also often enthusiastic about teaching and frequently have been among the first to join the ILT, ILTHE and HEA. Where teaching staff, in many institutions, have been reluctant to embrace the learning technologies, many subject librarians have not. Without imposing a 'value judgement' here, it is probably fair to say that many librarians find themselves given the opportunity to make significant contributions to student learning, often in areas that teaching staff find difficult or unappealing. They are also frequently actively involved in departmental and institutional programmes of change, contributing to both policy and strategy for the implementation of e-learning. So things are changing and librarians, along with many other professional groups, are actively involved in promoting this change.

Accessibility, flexibility and participation

There is also a trend in higher education towards inclusivity and a trend towards legislation to enforce it. Of particular significance is the imposition, for example in the UK, of legislation and substantial authoritative guidelines that seek equitable accessibility (Special Education Needs and Disability in Education Act, 2001), the broader application of e-Learning (Department for Education and Skills, 2003) and widening participation (HEFCE 2005; and OFFA, 2004). Universities seeking to ensure compliance with these instruments are finding the additional workload for academic staff to be problematic, particularly in research-active universities.

Students as customers

We do not want to overemphasise the nature of the changes that are currently occurring, supposedly as a result of students having more choice and having to pay more directly for higher educational 'services'. One of us had had many years experience of teaching mature students, primarily 'adult returners', and the other has been a mature student. Mature students have always been demanding customers. Students who have had to leave their employment, take out huge loans, or who have to do multiple jobs, have always been vociferous critics of those whom they regard as lazy or unsupportive teachers. Many staff in many institutions have responded and adapted to student customers. Others are just starting on this journey.

Some studies to illustrate changing relationships

In this section we intend to explore some specific claims in some detail. There is a slight emphasis here on innovations in higher education learning and teaching, on developments related to e-learning and on information skills. This is partly because this is where our personal experience is located but also, we suspect, because these areas are where development in higher education is most obvious and where changing relationships commensurate with these developments is most likely to be seen. Nevertheless, it does seem unlikely to us that more traditional areas of higher education, if indeed such still exist, will be immune from similar change.

Teaching and learning dualities in the 21st century

One of us attended a lecture, in 1999, delivered by Howard Newby, then Vice Chancellor of the University of Southampton. The lecture was on 'Higher Education in the twenty-first century' (Newby, 1999) and for those in the audience who do not embrace change, it must have been scary. The lecture is particularly relevant to this chapter because its presenter, now Sir Howard, is currently Chief Executive of the UK's Higher Education Funding Council and presumably in a position to guide us all towards some of his predictions from the last century. In 1999, Newby emphasised globalisation, changes in the mission of UK HE towards aiding economic competitiveness and promoting social inclusion, and supporting changes in the 'academic profession'. Newby described the activities of the University of Phoenix and how this 'online institution' apparently estimated 'that the entire US higher education system could be supported by around 250,000 course assistants (as opposed to 750,000 fully tenured professors at the present time) with bought-in performances from 1,000 star performers' – the leading researchers and teachers who actually appear in front of camera'. Newby suggested that

> ... it would be difficult to envisage a move to this extreme in the UK (or in the US for that matter), but an important rhetorical point remains, nevertheless, namely that the changes in higher education now rendered possible by developments in ICT and digital broadcasting could have profound implications for the structure and function of the academic profession. Failure to adapt to these challenges could lead to the profession being outflanked by institutions like the University of Phoenix ....

Clearly we would not wish to be outflanked in this way but the lecture at least emphasised the extent of the dichotomy that was opening in higher education between the highly-respected research-active professor and just about all others whose role could be relegated to that of course assistant. An analysis on these lines suggests that changing relationships within universities in the future will be extreme and will involve not just the relationship between academics and academic-support groups but changing relationships within the academic profession.

Closely related to this duality is the research/teaching divide that has engaged our interests, certainly for the latter half of the last century. It does seem inevitable that the current discussions in the UK on the granting of degree-awarding powers to 'teaching-only institutions' and the increased focus of research funding on a small, select group of research universities will widen this divide.

So the emphasis here is on specialisation and on the development of institutions, groups and individuals with specialist functions. Those who already thought that the 'typical academic' was both narrow-minded and out of touch may not find the prospect of increasing specialisation particularly promising but there is little doubt that relationships within institutions, between institutions and between institutions and the wider world will have to change.

Learning objects, repositories, intellectual property and inter-university co-operation

The nature of e-learning is that it is evolving rapidly. As a consequence, many of its concepts and processes are changing continuously and are therefore difficult to define. This certainly applies to learning objects but many would regard them as online resources or activities that relate to specific and identifiable learning outcomes. So an online lecture with an associated moderated discussion board linked to a specific learning outcome would be considered by many to be a learning object. A book would not; because it is not online. A streamed lecture would not; unless it is associated with a specific learning outcome. The key idea is that the learning object is reusable and portable. Once developed it should be possible to reuse it next year in the same module or next week in another module altogether. Perhaps you can sell it or give it away as a Christmas present. These ideas are innovative and useful for some but indicative of the 'dumbing down' of education for others. Yet others wonder what the fuss is about and suggest that lecturers have always used their lectures in this way. For some of us the learning is not defined by the content of the lecture or of the learning object. The UK's JISC (Joint Information Systems Committee) has another viewpoint;

UK Higher and Further Education institutions have invested substantial effort and resources in creating and acquiring e-learning content. To secure the long-term future of this investment, effort must now be put into ensuring that e-learning content can be retained in a usable state as long as it is pedagogically relevant. There is an increasing need to consider how the maintenance and re-use of e-learning materials can be maximised cost-effectively, and systems developed and implemented that can support easy portability and maintenance over time' (JISC, 2004).

Librarians who also consider themselves to be information scientists are intimately associated with these discussions and indeed with the development, cataloguing and use of learning objects. A significant 'industry' has developed that attempts to identify educational technology standards (see for example CETIS, 2005), to promote interoperability (to ensure, for example, that learning objects developed in one place will work in another), to store learning objects in repositories that will enable authorised access; and to describe learning objects using metadata (to ensure, for example, that the learning object will do what you hope it will do). The 'industry' is also having to get to grips with the copyright and intellectual property rights issues that learning objects have raised. Some academic teachers seem happy to share (see for example, the MERLOT repository; 'MERLOT is a free and open resource designed primarily for faculty and students of higher education. Links to online learning materials are collected here along with annotations such as peer reviews and assignments.' MERLOT, 2005). Other teachers are happy to share but find that their liberality is restricted by their employers who are concerned, rightly or wrongly, about the generosity of their employees. In many cases uncertainty about intellectual property rights is unnecessarily restricting open access to learning objects. Some appear to assume that if the situation is not clear, we should not share. Copyright legislation is itself complex, changing and poorly defined for academic purposes (Broad, Matthews and Shephard, 2003).

We can only hope that information scientists are enjoying the intellectual challenges involved in this large project because the educational literature and our own experience suggests that the use of online learning objects in education, particularly evaluated use, is not keeping up with their development and the activities of the 'industry' that surrounds them. Writing in 2003, Friesen, an acknowledged enthusiast for learning objects and related technologies concludes that 'there have been no in-depth studies of the pedagogical consequences of these systems and ways of thinking, and no examinations of their epistemological and ideological implications. On a more practical level, others have noted a general lack of adoption of these technologies by both practitioners and vendors' (Friesen, 2003, p.1). A year on, Downes, another acknowledged enthusiast, offered a more optimistic outlook

The full benefits of learning objects may take another five years to realize, as we move through the second phase of the transition. Once learning objects are widely available and widely used, the traditional thinking surrounding the organization of learning will be increasingly questioned. People will begin to ask why learning resources must be organized by hand by a designer before they can be used by students. Systems will emerge that allow students to be their own designers. Instead of viewing learning design as some sort of script in which students are actors, following directions, we will begin to see a model where students are players, following no script at all ' (Downes, 2004, p2).

What strikes us in all of this is the focus on learning resources as something separate from learners, teachers and the processes involved in learning and teaching. It is almost as if the ranks of the librarians have been suddenly swollen by the addition of instructional designers, IT technicians, cataloguers, metadata experts and archivists intent on constantly updating 'learning' and improving access to resources without concern for whether or not learners are actually using these resources. And indeed this does seem to be the case. Teachers cannot look on with complete indifference as their ranks have also been disrupted by a wide range of professions intent on supporting students and 'improving the student experience'. Perhaps both groups await the arrival of students who really believe in the concept of student-centred learning and who make student-centred demands on learning resources, teachers and institutions. These students are already here but educators, and their supporters, do not necessarily recognise them. What is clear is that the working relationships between those who teach with learning resources and those who support these processes is changing.

Information skills: who has them, who needs them and who teaches them?

Information skills are those needed to find and make use of books, references and online resources. When information has been found and used, information skills allow the user to communicate to others where the information came from and how it helped. Information skills involve evaluating the usefulness of information and consideration of appropriate uses. They are needed, to various degrees, by all who learn, teach and research. Most teachers and researchers learn information skills on the job. Most students who come to higher education already have received instruction and practice in many information skills as part of their schoolwork (see for example *Curriculum 2000* in the UK, Learning and Skills Development Agency, 2005). Specialist information skills are then often integrated into programmes of study or addressed in specific units or modules.

So what's new? In recent years the range of information skills needed by students has increased dramatically. Evaluating web content, using search engines effectively and avoiding plagiarism are particular examples. Information skills merge into new IT skills and study skills. They overlap with academic skills, key skills and transferable skills. Perhaps because information skills are so varied and perhaps because so many academic teaching staff feel that most students already have them, or perhaps because teachers regard information skills as just skills rather than knowledge or understanding, higher education often delegates their support to information skill specialists.

One consequence of this is that information skills, at one time successfully integrated within subject teaching, are in danger of becoming more isolated and separate from the subject to which they apply. Separate, taught elsewhere, not assessed, not important.

Another consequence is the extent to which a student's lack of information skills is not noticed by academic departments. This becomes particularly acute for information skills that overlap with IT skills and for students who do not have long-term educational experience with computers. Some mature students find it difficult to use online catalogues, to enrol online, to remember their password and their floppy disc. They find it difficult and embarrassing to ask for help online, or to work with online support, no matter how well intended. Most of all they lack the resourcefulness to overcome the inevitable problems of broken weblinks or non-functional printers.

These situations require higher education professionals to interact in imaginative and unplanned-for ways. Learners need our support. Some need it more than others and some need particular support.

Who else is involved? A case for teams, or not

It is an interesting exercise to compare the aspirations of an institution's learning and teaching, or research, strategy with its 'wherewithal' to succeed. Naturally such strategies propose visions that are there to aspire to, not necessarily achieve and we all accept this distinction to a point. Some elements of each strategy, however, become more concrete objectives with targets, deliverables and milestones. Here we would expect to see close correlation between what is proposed and the means to achieve it. One such comparison was made by Shephard (2004) in an attempt to relate what university teachers need to do to establish a significant e-learning 'presence', with the support that the institution needs to make available so as to achieve a successful outcome. The paper suggests that institutions often underestimate how much work is involved in meeting even modest e-learning objectives, and in the process described a continuum of support. At one end of the continuum lurk 'hypothetical' institutions that consider their primary role is to 'help teachers to help themselves'. The issue is one of continuing professional development. Academic teachers can do it all themselves as long as they are given time and resources to learn how to. And academics in these institutions, by and large, are in control of their own time. At the other end of the continuum are institutions who support their teaching staff in a different way. Rather than requiring their staff to acquire the skills needed to do the job, they consider it their role to provide support staff with these roles. From experience we would suggest that all institutions actually occupy space on this continuum somewhere between these extremes. Here we want to elaborate on the various support roles that exist and that are developing and that require changing relationships in higher education.

Many sources stress the need for new areas of expertise and new working relationships. Inglis, Ling and Joosten (1999), for example, identify zones of expertise; expertise in information technologies, expertise in instructional design as well as subject expertise but also note that 'Different roles have different emphases but the boundaries overlap and each specialist requires the contribution of the others....' (Inglis et al., 1999 p. 86). Their analysis accepts the need for all individuals in 'zones of expertise' to undertake professional development to facilitate integration with others. The prime need is for teamwork with different members of the team contributing different areas of expertise. Although the concept of a team to develop and deliver educational units of study and their learning resources is not new (it has been a fundamental feature of the UK's Open University (Daniel, 1996), and is broadly accepted in many distance-learning settings) it is not common in traditional universities. Recent trends towards such teamwork have been identified by Shephard (2004) who draws, in particular, on the results of research and development projects that have contributed to the development, operation and evaluation of innovative learning and teaching. Typically these have made use of a range of 'expert consultants'. It is not uncommon to find a wide range of non-academic partners involved in these projects with particular skills in learning resources, professional development, educational evaluation, project management, information skills and assessment. Many of these projects have been extensively evaluated and demonstrate potential for the success of this team-based approach in a project setting (see for example, projects from the UK by the NCTeam, 2003). Many universities are now embedding the results of this institutional research and development into institutional practice (TELRI, 2003). The range of direct-support available for many academic staff is now very broad and it seems likely that at least some of these team-based projects will gradually change the way that institutions operate. The team-based approach may lead to a substantial realignment of the traditional 'division of labour' alongside a redistribution of resources and responsibility. In particular it promises to place the 'principle academic talents at the centre of the curriculum' as emphasised by Daniel (1996, p. 130).

So who are these 'new' team members, what relationship will they have with traditional teachers and researchers and can they really deliver? Here is a 'light-hearted' analysis.

Administrators and managers and the academic-related catch-all

Many universities are managing the increasing complexity of their operations by employing non-academic managers who undertake activities previously within the academic domain and the responsibility of an 'academic board'. Sometimes they take over responsibility for something as discrete as 'admissions' but in other cases they assume responsibility for all aspects of programme management. In some cases this raises the profile of the traditional departmental secretary, while in others it fundamentally changes the nature of staff/student interactions. It will be difficult to keep members of this new 'academic-related profession' away from developing teams. It is their job to be in them. We understand that in some situations their role has been informally described as an essential bottleneck (that is, they regulate the flow of information to some predetermined minimum).

Educational developers

This benign name for a group of academic-related staff hides the nature of their current activities in educational *development*. Gosling, for example, surveyed members of the Heads of Educational Development Group in the UK in 2001. He reports, 'all the respondents agreed that it was their role to encourage innovation and change in teaching and learning' (Gosling and D'Andrea, 2002). If you let an educational developer into your team, beware; she or he will consider it their role to change what you do and how you do it (continuously).

Student support specialists

Teaching teams cannot survive without access to a specialist, or two, in equal opportunities, disability legislation, dyslexia and counselling.

Learning resources specialists

At last, a proper role for subject librarians! Real team members with valued skills in: finding learning resources; helping students acquire information skills; developing resources; evaluating resources; supporting online activity; and supervising research projects and other tasks traditionally the reserve of academic staff.

Learning technologists

Learning technologists struggle to identify what this new group does (Oliver, 2002) but you will almost certainly need one to enable you to communicate with the IT experts who are not members of your team but who do dictate what your team and students can actually achieve.

Bringing them all together: teamwork but are they all team players?

What is a team and how do teams work?

It is probably fair to say that the term *team* is used too liberally here. Perhaps slaves in the Roman galley, or chain gangs, were considered teams by some; but presumably they operated differently from Manchester United FC or the teaching team responsible to the first year module on Calculus for Nurses. Important considerations in team operation are the hierarchy of management, rewards and recognition for team members, individual and group responsibilities, common ownership of goals. The list of course goes on and is well within the jurisdiction of management science. We are clearly just dabbling.

Teamwork from another perspective

'So let's get this right. You want me to continue to be responsible for this module, for now. I have to continue to give the lectures, organise the tutorials, and ensure that my post-docs and postgraduates are available to help teach it. I have to write all the course documentation and attend to all assignments. I have to write the examination and mark it. I also have to ensure that the module goes through its quality assurance processes and that it is reviewed every five years. OK, I have been doing all of that. That is my job. But then the changes come in you say? You need me to write the same course in another format suitable for distance learning. And you want me to ensure that all of my course document make sense online and can contribute to learning even if the students can't get to my lectures. But you're going to give me access to an e-learning adviser who is going to help me. They know all about what learning activities work best online and there is every hope that learning works better that way. There is also a specialist in the library who is going to make sure all of the students can access all the learning resources online. Then you will ensure that there is a computer-assisted assessment officer available to help me put all of my assignments online and even run the examination online. Alongside all this there is a special student support officer who will ensure that everything I produce all works OK for students with disabilities and learning difficulties. Now all of this is going to operate in a virtual learning environment and I'm going to be given some special privileges to enable me to communicate effectively with my students. Oh, no, sorry. I got that wrong. The department is going to employ teaching assistants to do the online bit, that is to communicate with the students. So all you really need from me are the original materials and then the team will do the rest. Well I guess that will allow me to get on my research. What's that? But I thought those rumours about the teaching only university were just gossip! Wow, you departmental managers are good!'

References

Broad, M., Matthews, M., and Shepard, K.L., 2003. Audit and control of the use of the Internet for learning and teaching: issues for stakeholders in higher education. *Management Accounting Journal*. 18 (3), 244–253.

CETIS, 2005. The centre for educational technology interoperability standards [online]. Available from: http://www.cetis.ac.uk/static/about.html [Accessed 16 January 2005].

Danet, B., 2001. *Cyberpl@y: Communicating online*. Oxford: Berg Publishers.

Daniel, J.S., 1996. *Mega-universities and knowledge media*. London: Kogan Page.

Downes, S., 2004. The rise of learning objects – editorial [online]. *International Journal of Instructional Technology and Distance Learning*. Available from: http://www.itdl.org/Journal/Mar_04/editor.htm [Accessed 16 January 2005].

Friesen, N., 2003. *Three objections to learning objects and e-learning standards* [online]. Available from: http://www.learningspaces.org/n/papers/objections.html [Accessed 16 January 2005].

Gosling, D. and D'Andrea, V. 2002. How educational development/Learning and Teaching Centres help higher education institutions manage change [online]. *Educational Developments* 3 (2). Available from: http://www.seda.ac.uk/ed.devs/vol3/Gosling.doc [Accessed 27 March 2006].

Higher Education Academy, 2004. Higher Education Academy-interim website[online]. Available from: http://www.sjp.ac.lk/careers/educForm/uk_reform/highereducationacademy.htm [Accessed 27 March 2006].

Higher Education Funding Council for England (HEFCE), 2005. *Widening participation* [online]. Available from: http://www.hefce.ac.uk/widen/ [Accessed 16 January 2005].

Inglis, A., Ling, P., and Joosten, V., 1999. Delivered digitally: Managing the transition to the knowledge media. London: Kogan Page.

Joint Information Systems Committee (JISC), 2004. *Long-term retention and reuse of e-learning objects and materials* [online]. Available from: http://www.jisc.ac.uk/index.cfm?name=project_elo [Accessed 16 January 2005].

Kanfer, A., 1999. *It's a thin world: the association between e-mail use and patterns of communication and relationships*. Available from: http://archive.ncsa.uiuc.edu/edu/trg/info_society.html [Accessed 14 January 2005].

Lankshear, C., and Knobel, M., 2003. *New Literacies*. Buckingham: Oxford University Press.

Learning and Skills Development Agency, 2005. *Curriculum 2000* [online]. Available from: http://www.lsda.org.uk/curriculum2000/ [Accessed 16 January 2005].

Merlot, 2005. *Multimedia educational resource for learning and online teaching* [online]. Available from: http://www.merlot.org/Home.po [Accessed 16 January 2005].

National Coordination Team (NCTeam), 2003. Available from: http://www.ncteam.ac.uk/projects/index.htm [Accessed 16 January 2005].

Newby, H., 1999. Higher education in the twenty-first century [online]. *Southampton University – New Reporter,* 16 (14).

Available from: http://www.soton.ac.uk/~newrep/vol16/no14future.html [Accessed 16 January 2005].

Office for Fair Access (OFFA), 2004. Office for fair access home page http://www.offa.org.uk/news/ [Accessed 16 January 2005]. Shephard, K.L., 2004. The role of educational developers in the expansion of educational technology. *International Journal for Academic Development*, 9 (1), 67–83.

Technology Enhanced Learning in Research-Led Institutions (TELRI), 2003. Exploring institutional approaches to embedding ICT in teaching and learning: A review and analysis of generic national projects. Available from: http://www.telri.ac.uk/Transfer/ltsngc/ltsngc.htm [Accessed 16 January 2005].

PART II
Serving Different Constituencies

Chapter 8

Serving Different Constituencies: Undergraduates

Jenny Campbell and Pete Maggs

Introduction – the Newcastle experience

This case study describes the specific efforts of Newcastle University Library in devising, introducing, delivering and evaluating a coherent programme of information literacy training for undergraduate students, during each stage of their course. It accurately presents what happened and how problems were dealt with as they arose, with varying degrees of success.

Context – external and internal

The context in which Universities in UK Higher Education now operate is one of unprecedented change. Current Government projections are that, by the end of the decade, 50 per cent of all 18-year-olds will be in HE (Department for Education and Skills, 2003). Put another way, this 'massification' (Chan, 2004) means an increase of approximately 240, 000 full-time equivalent students – the same as the creation of 16 new universities – by 2010 (Baker, 2004). Coupled with this is:

- The introduction of top-up fees, with resultant changes in expectations of service level provision. Undergraduates are now more aware of themselves as 'customers', and increasingly make demands for value for money in all aspects of their education, including library services – where they can have unreasonably high expectations of the resources available.
- A changing student profile with the ongoing rise in non-traditional students (for example, part-time, mature, distance learners or learners with disabilities) and their differing teaching and learning needs.
- The blurring of the boundaries between higher education and further education (Department for Education and Skills, 2003) achieved mainly through work-focused foundation degrees and flexible courses designed to meet the needs of a more diverse student body.
- The adoption of strategies to widen participation in higher education for students from the state school sector, for example through Newcastle

University's Partners initiative (University of Newcastle, 2005a)
* Increased competition between higher education institutions for undergraduate students. This competition is encouraging Newcastle University to develop a unique curriculum brand as part of an overall marketing strategy, particularly the concept of the degree 'plus' – including, for example, a focus on aspects such as 'employability'; encompassing the Library's information literacy programme.
* Growing uncertainty about the future of the block grant from government resulting in a rise in the number of non-UK-based students.

Although not a comprehensive list, it does illustrate the pressing need for library services that, as far as possible, meet the requirements of the undergraduate constituency. Relatively recent changes to the Quality Assurance Agency review process (Quality Assurance Agency for Higher Education, 2005) have been implemented, a theme that will be returned to later, but experience indicates (at time of writing) that the quality of the student learning experience will be at the very heart of the process.

Previous practice

Previously, while the vast majority of undergraduates received a standardised induction to library services, only a minority received formally timetabled specific training in using the information resources available to them. Although information skills training was offered to all undergraduates via their Degree Programme Director or module leader, the actual take-up of library-based sessions remained relatively low.

The needs of these students were often met instead through individual, personalised help – offered at the point of need (for example, when a student realised they required assistance and asked for help at a library information desk). This was one of the most staff intensive tasks facing Liaison Librarians; ensuring that those students who did not receive organised information skills training as part of their course were not significantly disadvantaged.

A lot of staff effort went into the provision of assistance and creation of a variety of print and online resources necessary for bridging the information gap – between those students who received formal library based training and those who did not.

Many of the timetabled information skills sessions were workshop based, accommodating relatively small numbers of students and involved a presentation or demonstration of a resource, followed by a hands-on, practical session. Most sessions taught students how to use a particular information resource timed to coincide with submission of a specific piece of course work. Again, this method of delivery was extremely staff intensive.

Faculty Liaison Librarians recognised that alternative methods of information skills teaching were needed. As transferable skills gained a higher profile within the institution, demand for information skills training grew accordingly. In order to offer an equitable service to all students, it was acknowledged that the delivery method for all information skills teaching needed to be reviewed. The days of the small-scale practical hands-on workshop were numbered.

In effect an information skills lottery existed – depending entirely on the library awareness of a particular academic and their willingness to involve the library in adequate teaching of information literacy to their students. Clearly this was no longer a scaleable, effective or efficient strategy given all the factors impacting on the changing profile of the undergraduate cohort outlined above.

Developing new structures

Clear understanding of the implications of the organisational objectives at Newcastle University (that is, delivering customer-focused programmes firmly anchored in appropriate performance monitoring and evaluation of pedagogic rigour) meant that the library recognised the changing needs and capabilities of undergraduate users and had to prioritise elements of its service delivery to satisfy them. Alongside, and in many ways because of, the shifting profile of the undergraduate cohort has been an increasing emphasis on student-led learning. This has implications for the ways in which students study and the skills they need in order to become effective learners. Undergraduates need to be both self-motivated and capable of adapting to the challenges of working independently.

The library at Newcastle University regarded the need to enter into an ongoing long-term relationship with undergraduates during their time at the University as imperative. From induction to dissertation and all points in between, timely support would be delivered through a co-ordinated programme of;

- induction
- supporting publications in both printed and electronic formats
- information literacy sessions
- one-to-one help.

Such student-led learning assumes a level of information-handling skills amongst new undergraduates which practical experience has shown is not always there – although often there is the automatic and incorrect assumption, by both students and educators, that they are. Do school leavers have the skills necessary to become independent learners to make a successful transition from school to university? If not, whose responsibility is it to tackle this skills 'gap'? The contention is that it falls to librarians to close it; managing these sometimes conflicting pressures. It is vital libraries have a well-defined strategy, an information literacy strategy if you like (SCONUL, 2000), in place, to do this.

Whilst beyond the remit of this chapter, there is a growing body of evidence of the need for basic information skills to be embedded in the Learning Resources Strategies of secondary schools. With the potential future development of a 16+

baccalaureate, there should be a dialogue between schools and Universities to ensure the requisite skills are covered in the school curriculum and are being developed at that stage. Currently there is some evidence (Barrett and Danks, 2003) that the assessment culture in schools is producing students who have difficulty in adapting to the demands of the student-led learning and teaching methods prevalent in UK higher education.

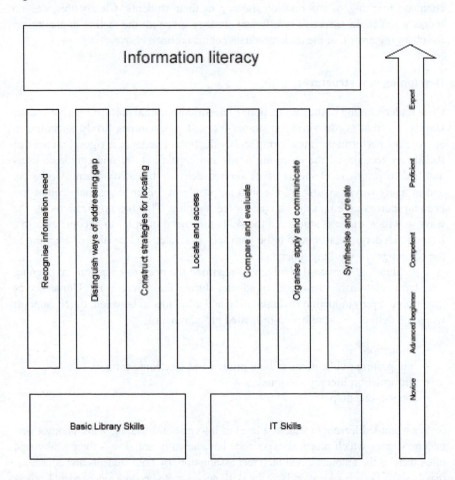

Figure 8.1 Seven Pillars of Information Literacy model
Published with the permission of SCONUL (SCONUL, 2000)

While the existing body of literature on the development of a structured information skills programme was of some help in informing our thinking, for example Big Blue (JISC, 2004) and the American Library Association information literacy gateway (American Library Association, 2004), it became apparent that attempts to meet the University's objective of providing '… excellence in our learning and teaching activities, meeting internationally competitive standards…[and]…a more systematic delivery of study skills provision' (University of Newcastle, 2004) required the library to employ fresh thinking in its approach, developed in close association with academic staff from all Schools in the University, with which to engage the students.

After lengthy investigation, it was ultimately decided to structure the new Programme on the seven headline skills framework identified in the Society of College, National & University Libraries' position paper (SCONUL, 2000), seeking to encourage the '… adoption of appropriate information behaviour to identify, through whatever channel or medium, information well fitted to information needs, leading to wise and ethical use of information …' (SCONUL, 2000).

The ability to recognise a need for information

This step covers introduction to (and location of) library resources at the University. The process does not necessarily begin with Freshers' Induction week but often starts before that with Open Days for prospective students. The library now plays a vital role in this, as the competition for student numbers intensifies. At Newcastle University, parents have proved particularly interested in the library and consequently it is always included in Open Days programmes, having to field questions along the lines of – how many computers are there? How many copies of key texts (per student) are held? How many electronic journals are subscribed to? Is your library wireless network enabled? This kind of interest will undoubtedly rise with the implementation of top-up fees.

At a pre-undergraduate level, basic information skills sessions have been increasingly embedded in the library events on pre-course English language sessions for international students and, as a credit bearing module, on the Partners' Widening Participation programme.

After offering staff-led library tours for a number of years, concerns about the economy and effectiveness of this approach to library induction prompted a change in practice – after consultation with academic Schools. Students are now given a self-guided tour booklet including a quiz (with prize draw for all correct responses) and feedback form. Library induction sessions for new students are still timetabled in conjunction with academic Schools, and students are required to attend.

For the new undergraduate cohort, a range of activities is offered during induction week, intended to suit a wide range of learning styles. A library film, focusing on the services and resources that are crucial to new students, is streamed via the library's webpages (in fact this continues throughout the year). An introductory presentation about using the library is also available directly from the library's web pages (University of Newcastle Library, 2005). A printed Library Guide containing basic information about resources and services is supplied to all new students.

Library induction concentrates squarely on identifying and locating typical resources required by a new undergraduate student; that is, categories of reading list material.

The ability to distinguish ways in which the information 'gap' may be addressed

A strong emphasis is placed on the central importance of the library as the key resource for locating material of an academically appropriate standard. Obviously familiarity with library resources beginning with the steps outlined above is crucial for students.

The full portfolio of library resources is available via the library website (redesigned in 2004) as well as via a range of print publications. With over 200 bibliographic databases, approximately 10, 000 electronic journals and an increasing number of electronic books, the library service recognises it is vital to teach students how to identify the appropriate resources.

The ability to construct strategies for locating information

Library policy is to request that all students have information skills training embedded into their taught modules at a relevant time, for example – as the need for information becomes apparent when a major essay or project is due for submission. Experience has long been that the most successful way of ensuring students participate in library-based information skills training is to embed the sessions formally in the curriculum so they recognise their value. This helps develops students' transferable planning and time-management skills, resulting in fewer desperate last-minute requests for information on useful sources.

There are strong reservations amongst subject liaison staff regarding the provision of information skills simply as an arbitrary 'bolt-on' session to an existing taught module. These staff, during regular dialogue with academic Schools, consistently emphasise the need not only to have information skills training embedded as an integral part of a module, but wherever possible to make this component formally assessed with a specific element of the final assignment focussing on the skills acquired. This further reinforces the value of our sessions to the students and forces them to apply their learning practically. Many of Newcastle's stage 2 undergraduates are now required to prepare an assessed sample bibliography (and critical evaluation of their search strategy) as part of their dissertation proposals.

The ability to locate and access information

As already discussed, bibliographic instruction in the use of specific information resources has been practised at Newcastle University for many years, although these sessions are now considered as a component of a broader information skills programme. Detailed instruction in the use of the individual resources is still important and new methods of offering such assistance are constantly being trialled. A portfolio of tutorials authored using the INFORMS tutorial software (University of Newcastle Library, 2005c) have been extensively used in the past year as a means of re-enforcing the learning from class-based teaching sessions. They provide customised, subject-specific guidance to e-resources ranging from the library catalogue, to bibliographic databases, current awareness services and full-text electronic journals, available 24/7.

The ability to compare and evaluate information obtained from different sources

The library endeavours to teach all undergraduates how to evaluate information. Many high quality externally authored resources (such as Net tutor, TONIC (Netskills), Resource Discovery Network Virtual Training Suite and Internet Detective already exist and are freely available on the Web. This aspect of critical evaluation is perhaps more important than ever before, as the number of information resources proliferate, and this forms a substantial part of the library's Information Skills teaching.

The ability to organise, apply and communicate information to others in ways appropriate to the situation

In addition to literature searching, increasingly emphasis is placed on the whole literature review process, (from carrying out the search, locating, analysing and evaluating the information found and preparing an accurate bibliography). As the profile of plagiarism-detection increases, so library teaching explicitly considers the need for accurate citation, emphasising the importance of academic integrity, ensuring both that a student cannot be accused of cheating (or plagiarism) and that he or she knows how to protect their own work. Again the library based sessions exploit high quality resources that already exist in support of this, such as Academic Integrity at Princeton (Princeton University, 2003).

As the University develops a more proactive policy for tackling plagiarism, it is constantly examining its own role in the process. The library also has a responsibility for explaining the importance of ensuring academic integrity through accurate and full citation. Students need to be taught how and why they must cite references accurately. Use is made of resources such as Online! (Harnack and Kleppinger, 2003) a reference guide to using Internet resources, 'Cite them Right' (Pears and Shields, 2004), Guide to Harvard Referencing (Leeds Metropolitan University Library, 1996).

At Newcastle University, the library plays a major role in the user support of bibliographic software across the institution. EndNote workshops (which demonstrate how the software can be used to store bibliographic information and assist with the creation of accurate and consistent bibliographies) are run as frequent drop-in sessions as well as being built into undergraduate research skills modules. Demand has increased dramatically and drop-in workshops are now run monthly. The library also provides one-to-one assistance with individual EndNote queries, although more technical queries are referred to the University's Information Systems and Services section.

The ability to synthesise and build upon existing information, contributing to the creation of new knowledge

When considering skills at the top end of the SCONUL model, the library is working primarily with a small number of final year undergraduates and all postgraduate students, in a one-to-one or small group context. The contention is that these skills are less frequently required at an undergraduate level, but remain crucial to students planning to progress on to postgraduate study. Structured support is available via the library's ResIN (Research Information at Newcastle) web site, particularly in areas such as scholarly communication, primary sources, and the institutions special collections (University of Newcastle Library, 2005d).

Monitoring outcomes and quality assurance

At Newcastle University, the library continues to play an integral part in the development of learning resource strategies with many of the academic Schools, to give focus to the provision and development of learning resources over the next three to five years. This approach must be informed by – and firmly embedded within –the broader mission and strategic plans of both the School concerned and the library. Specific priorities for the planning period and immediate tasks to be undertaken need to be identified – and then fully costed, developed, implemented and monitored effectively.

Such an approach must be a continuous process, needing to be regularly reviewed and updated. It has to take into account the academic School's wider educational and information strategies and also informed by University-wide directives. It is of *direct* concern to all those who are involved in the teaching, learning and administration that take place in the University. Excellence in learning and teaching must be supported by well-funded, high quality learning resources. They must be managed, maintained and updated to reflect the changing nature of subject curricula and the opportunities being offered by new educational learning technology.

In order to maintain the appropriate level of academic rigour and pedagogic effectiveness, the library has to be seen to take full account of, and respond to, the new 'light touch' developmental engagements or subject reviews, as a precursor to the University's Institutional Audit. This makes clear the need for effective information skills programmes to be more of an integral part of the undergraduate curriculum than ever before. Quality Assurance Agency panels expect this as part of the portfolio of teaching provided for undergraduates; as already said, it can no longer simply be viewed as an optional extra bolted onto a taught course at the whim of a lecturer. Developing and maintaining quality standards through audits, surveys and research/review is critical, while not hampering individuality or setting unreasonable targets.

In addition, it includes scrutiny not only at the institutional level but also by sampling at the discipline level. This is achieved by means of a number of Discipline

Audit Trails. These will enable the auditors to see how University policies and procedures work in practice. The library is required to produce a self-evaluation document for institutional audit but will also be able to use recent internal subject review reports where these are available. Particular attention must be paid to processes such as annual monitoring and review, consideration of external examiners' reports and student feedback.

In summary, experience of the new subject reviews so far has been that the library service is increasingly expected to be both:

- at the heart of the student learning experience, in terms of the formal teaching of information literacy and therefore
- to be able to demonstrate internal quality assurance processes as part of that teaching – measuring quality at the point of delivery to improve standards and efficiency, so that the fullest range of skills possible is being delivered to as many students as possible; increasingly important as student numbers and class sizes grow.

As outlined in the previous section, the Library is mindful of the need to be clear about what it is to assess – to understand exactly what the students are learning from us.

An Honours graduate will have developed an understanding of a complex body of knowledge, some of it at the current boundaries of an academic discipline … [and] … the ability to manage their own learning, making use of scholarly reviews and primary sources (e.g., refereed research articles and/or original materials appropriate to the discipline). (Quality Assurance Agency for Higher Education, 2005).

The library employs as many communication channels as possible in order to get feedback/evaluation from users on the effectiveness and relevance of the information skills training that is delivered *and*, crucially, then use it to re-design subsequent course material(s) and teaching programmes. For example, feedback on the self-guided tours (from both staff and students) has been very positive but following a request from certain academic Schools, a customisable version of the self-guided tour booklet was produced – so that they could produce their own version tailored to subject-specific interests.

A number of strategies are used to get feedback – no one way is ideal but it has been found that a combination of these approaches does give a plentiful supply of comments from users:

- a suggestions board (available in the library and online via our "Tell us what you think" facility)
- session feedback forms *(formative assessment* – gathered as the information skills class is ongoing)
- module outline forms with specific question(s) on library resources/skills component (*summative assessment*)

- formally assessed assignments (in part based on the information skills classes) – requiring students to apply the knowledge acquired (again – summative assessment);

Increased emphasis on the quality of the student learning experience is at the heart of the new developmental engagements, but has only served to emphasise even further that the needs and expectations of students are met as fully as possible, if the University is to compete successfully for undergraduate "customers".

Another key outcome of the process is the management of user expectations, both in a qualitative and quantitative sense. The former is rooted in the students' increasing expectations that as they are paying fees they will expect unreasonable levels of provision (such as numerous multiple copies of key text books) and the latter is due to the need to maximise usage of the full portfolio of high quality information resources that have been identified by academic staff and paid for by the library from hard pressed budgets and need to earn their keep. It is vital to encourage students to see that there is no one textbook to read that will give them all the answers but that they need to engage more fully with the existing (and forthcoming) literature on their subject. This is an increasingly difficult area, where the increasing cost of textbooks – resulting in unwillingness on the part of some students to purchase their own copies – coupled with the very prescriptive nature of some learning styles familiar to overseas students, can cause enormous pressure on a relatively small number of essential texts. It is a process of education – both for the students, in encouraging them to use the full range of information sources available to them, and for the lecturers, in asking them to emphasise the need for students to read broadly and not limit their information sources to too narrow a base.

The future

At Newcastle University, the shift towards independent learning is being supported by the use of the Blackboard Virtual Learning Environment, enabling teaching staff to tailor their teaching styles to the needs of a larger audience. Blackboard opens up new opportunities for libraries and librarians to become more integrated into undergraduate courses, enabling seamless linking of the mainstream curriculum with the provision of key information skills training resources and activities. An additional benefit of which is that the library based programme is seen sitting under the same 'umbrella' alongside the rest of the module.

New technologies, such as SFX and Metalib, are revolutionising the information retrieval process at Newcastle University, enabling cross searching of library resources and easier linking between e-resources. It both simplifies the retrieval process for students new to the concept of literature searching and improves the usage of expensive library resources. However, although such cross-searching technologies increase the accessibility of e-materials, students will need highly developed skills in the critical evaluation of the information they retrieve and the relevance of this material to their work.

There needs to be continual re-evaluation of why and how undergraduates use the library. Amongst the issues recognised at Newcastle University were:

- Increased emphasis on transferable 'employability' skills as a key component of the student learning experience: for example, the ability to work in groups to complete a project and, in some cases, formally evaluate the contribution of other group members towards achieving successful outcomes.
- Requirement for 24/7 access to e-resources; to course materials through a virtual learning environment, along with other relevant online catalogues, e-journals and archives, databases, other media, as student familiarity with e-resources increases over time.
- With students coming from increasingly varied backgrounds, different learning styles have to be supported, as far as resources allow.
- Rising student expectations; premium fee-paying students have premium service level expectations and this is not always reflected in the budget allocated to the library. As resources are stretched increasingly thinly, it becomes more crucial that students are able to recognise;
  - when there is a need for information, and then,
  - how to identify, locate, manage and use it appropriately for problem solving, decision making and research.
- Pressure on resources such as academic staff time and library facilities from a growing number of students mean improvements in teaching and learning support strategies have to be devised to maintain the effectiveness of the service provided by the library.

Conclusion

Although the SCONUL model was chosen as a starting point or framework on which to build the information literacy strategy at Newcastle, there is a recognition of the need for this to be an iterative process, continually updating the information skills programmes to suit individual user needs (identified through close dialogue with academic staff) to ensure that the programme retains a close relevance to identified teaching and learning outcomes. Where this has happened, the experience at Newcastle University has been that the results are very encouraging. Wherever possible, the library has sought to identify current best practice elsewhere and use that as a benchmark for its own service provision. However, the intention has always been to draw on the very best available resources, whether they be locally or externally authored.

The over-riding concern is the provision of an information skills programme that is relevant to the needs of students. No such programme can ever assume the 'one-size fits all' approach, as clearly it will never work. Even at Newcastle

University, differing approaches are adopted to address the fact that the information skills needs of a cohort of undergraduate engineers differs significantly from those of a corresponding group of fine art students. In order to keep pace with the rate of change in teaching and learning in higher education, it is important that whatever model or structure is adopted, to remain aware of the need to review, evaluate and modify our approach to the delivery of key information skills.

Experience has shown that the SCONUL model provides an intellectual framework that effectively underpins an information skills programme – ensuring that whilst not sacrificing consistency of approach across the undergraduate cohort, it is possible to remain flexible enough in terms of approach to be relevant to the vast majority of undergraduate needs.

Without doubt, balancing increasing student numbers, increasing service level expectations and matching support to appropriate learning styles is very challenging. The task at Newcastle has been to devise an information literacy programme that is both sensitive to the needs of different subject disciplines (See Appendix to this chapter) and recognises diverse learning styles. This enables us to deliver efficient and effective customer-focused teaching – which also incorporate transferable life-long 'employability' skills – to an ever-growing and more diversified cohort of undergraduates.

The authors contend that a long-term relationship must be developed between undergraduates, their academic Schools and Liaison Librarians, demanding new behaviours on the part of all

There must be a clear recognition on the part of everyone of the need for this and a willingness to exploit all available tools (such as virtual learning environments and externally authored resources) in order to achieve it; thus maximising the efficiency and effectiveness of information literacy strategies.

There are major staff skills training and resourcing issues that libraries must address. Rolling out such an increased portfolio of teaching (and accompanying assessed work that subsequently requires marking by library staff) to an expanding proportion of the undergraduate cohort, has huge implications for the workload of library staff.

There is a need to deploy as wide a variety of teaching strategies as possible to help students, within existing resource constraints.

While existing thinking proved useful up a degree it did not provide a ready-made solution. Moving away from a 'one size fits all' approach, thinking needs to be much more focused, flexible but more academically rigorous, for example, in terms of exploiting multiple delivery mechanisms).

If government plans to blur even more the boundaries between further and higher education become reality, then we need to keep on developing, adapting and refining our strategies. Higher education library services must be prepared to re-invent their approach as pressure on resources increases, top-up fees are introduced and the hybridised library is developed.

If libraries choose to ignore the need to continually re-engineer and re-focus the services we deliver then they risk becoming little more than an anachronism in the 21st-century university landscape.

Appendix A

Examples from Subject Benchmark statements:

a. *Town and Country Planning*; ... "make effective use of evidence and information sources."

b. *Engineering*; ... "Research for information to develop ideas further ... [and] ... can consider given information, extract that which is pertinent to a routine problem and use it in the solution of the problem."

c. *Politics*; ... "Research methods and methodologies in Politics and International Relations include the use of information retrieval techniques, quantitative methods, research design and the use of IT. Their weight and character cannot be prescribed except to say that *these should be determined in the light of requirements of the particular curriculum being taught* (author's italics)."

Full information can be found on the QAA website.

References

American Library Association, 2004. Information Literacy Gateway [online]. *ALA Official Home Page*. Available from: http://www.ala.org/ala/acrl/acrlissues/acrlinfolit/informationliteracy.htm [Accessed 14 February 2005].

Baker, M., 2004. *Demand for Universities to soar* [online]. *BBC News – Education* Available from: http://news.bbc.co.uk/1/low/education/3701767.stm [Accessed 31 January 2005].

Barrett, L., and Danks, M., 2003. Information literacy: a crucial role for schools [online]. *Library and Information Update*, May. Available from: http://www.cilip.org.uk/update/issues/may03/article3may.html [Accessed 9 September 2004].

Chan, W., 2004. International cooperation in higher education: theory and practice. *Journal of Studies in International Education*, 8 (1), 32–55.

Department for Education and Skills (DfES). 2003. *The Future of Higher Education* [online] (Cmnd.5735, 2003). Norwich, Stationery Office. Available from: http://www.dfes.gov.uk/hegateway/uploads/White%20Pape.pdf [Accessed 31 January 2005].

Harnack, A., and Kleppinger, E., 2003. *Online! A Reference Guide to Using Internet Resources* [online]. New York: Bedford/St. Martin's. [Internet], Available from: http://www.bedfordstmartins.com/online/index.html [Accessed 31 January 2005].

Joint Information Systems Committee (JISC), 2004. Manchester Metropolitan University Library and Leeds University Library – The Big Blue – information skills for students [online]. *MMU Library Home Page*. Available at: http://www.

library.mmu.ac.uk/bigblue/bigblue.html [Accessed 14 February 2005].

Leeds Metropolitan University Library, 1996. *A Guide to Harvard Referencing* [online]. Available from: http://www.leedsmet.ac.uk/lskills/open/sfl/content/harvard/index.html [Accessed 4 March 2005].

Pears, R., and Shields, G., 2004. *Cite Them Right: Referencing Made Easy.* Newcastle, Northumbria University Press.

Princeton University, 2003. *Academic Integrity at Princeton* [online]. Princeton University Home Page. Available from: http://www.princeton.edu/pr/pub/integrity/pages/original.html [Accessed 31 January 2005].

Quality Assurance Agency for Higher Education (QAA), 2005. *QAA Official Home Page* [online]. Available from: http://www.qaa.ac.uk/ [Accessed 31 January 2005].

Society of College, National & University Libraries (SCONUL), 2000. *Information Skills in Higher Education: a SCONUL Position Paper* [online]. SCONUL Official Home Page. Available from: http://www.sconul.ac.uk/activities/inf_lit/papers/Seven_pillars.html [Accessed 14 February 2005].

University of Newcastle, 2004. Corporate Planning Statement 2003/4 [online]. *University of Newcastle Home Page,* Available from: http://www.ncl.ac.uk/documents/planning_statement.pdf [Accessed 14 February 2005].

University of Newcastle Library, 2005a. *Partners Home Page.* [online]. Available from: http://www.ncl.ac.uk/partners/ [Accessed 31 January 2005].

University of Newcastle Library, 2005b. *Introduction to the Library* [online]. *University Library Home Page,* Available from: http://www.ncl.ac.uk/library/welcome.php [Accessed 14 February 2005].

University of Newcastle Library, 2005c. *Finding Information –Informs Tutorials* [online]. *University Library Home Page.* Available from: http://www.ncl.ac.uk/library/info_skills_finding.php [Accessed 31 January 2005].

University of Newcastle Library, 2005d. *ResIN* [online]. University Library Home Page. Available from: http://www.ncl.ac.uk/library/resin [Accessed 14 February 2005].

Chapter 9

Serving Different Constituencies: Asynchronous Learners

Janet Peters

Introduction

University students increasingly come from varying backgrounds, often with existing family or work commitments. Part time students form 40 per cent of the total (SCONUL, 2004b), and full time students often work during term time to finance their studies. The luxury of full time, focused study, normally based on a university campus, is no longer available to many students. One indicator of this is that university libraries are reporting drops in the number of visits (SCONUL, 2004c). At the same time, it is becoming apparent that students use a range of libraries for their work (Mynott et al., 2001; Nankivell and Eve, 2002); internet availability in the home or room is expanding (70 per cent of students owned PCs in 2002/3 and over 55 per cent of universities provide Internet access from their halls of residence (UCISA, 2004)); the use of electronic resources is increasing (SCONUL, 2004c). All of these changes are having a dramatic impact on the way in which Subject Librarians can support students.

During recent years there has also been new legislation such as the Special Educational Needs and Disability Act, 2001 (SENDA) and the Race Relations (Amendment) Act 2000, both of which require adjustments to be made to policies, procedures and buildings to enable all students (and staff) working in higher education to have an equal opportunity to benefit from the experience. Government initiatives to widen participation in higher education (DfES, 2003) are also encouraging universities to enroll students who do not necessarily have a recent academic background, or who come from areas with historically low levels of entry into higher education. Sometimes these students need a different kind of support from that which libraries have traditionally offered. At the same time, staffing levels are decreasing in relation to the number of students served (SCONUL, 2004c) and so new ways of offering support need to be explored for economic reasons also.

Asynchronous learning may offer a partial solution to these issues. It is defined at least in computing dictionaries as: 'The use of media in DISTANCE LEARNING which does not impose a REAL TIME interaction between the student and the teacher. Examples of such media include EMAIL, CONFERENCING SOFTWARE, and NEWSGROUPS.' (Ince, 2001).

A more academic definition highlights the benefits: '(1) the ability to deliver instruction anytime and any place, thus increasing access for learners who could otherwise not be served, and (2) the ability to create an environment that allows for knowledge building based on collaborative and reflective learning' (Moller et al., 2003, p. 140).

However, for this chapter I am adopting a broader definition: 'asynchronous learning occurs where the primary method of teaching is not dependent on traditional contact time on campus'.

It can include courses offered by distance learning, either in full or in part, or alternative delivery methods which some students may adopt by choice. These are likely to be electronic, but could also include self-study workbooks, for example. It could even be argued that libraries have always allowed students to undertake a form of asynchronous learning in that they may visit at times unrelated to their formal studies. The fact that students demand this is shown by the increasing trend for 24/7 access to learning resources, both on and off-campus.

The role of Subject Librarians is to work with their academic course teams to ensure that the learning resources they need are also provided in a flexible way. It may often be the case that online information provision will precede the electronic delivery of course materials, providing a test-bed for academic staff of its popularity and effectiveness. This chapter will explore the implications, particularly for Subject Librarians, of these developments.

Political imperatives

From the publication of the Dearing report (NCIHE, 1997), widening access to higher education, particularly for students from non-traditional backgrounds, has been part of the political agenda. More recently, an ambitious target of 50 per cent of 18–30 ear-olds experiencing higher education by 2010 has been set by the Government for England (DfES, 2003). This has inevitably involved increased marketing activity to schools and within communities to encourage those who would previously not have considered a university education to enrol as students. Since many of these students are mature (over 25), they often have financial and/or domestic commitments, which make the traditional concept of full-time study impossible. As providers of library services, we need to be responsive and sympathetic to the needs of these customers, otherwise they are likely to be the first to 'drop out', not only contributing negatively to the university's reputation, but, more significantly, suffering a major blow to their confidence as learners. This flexibility is often achieved by delivering learning resources electronically.

Providing the opportunity for students to work at their own pace and in a location of their choice can contribute to their ability to stay the course – provided that the provision of electronic resources is not seen as a complete panacea. Face to face contact is probably even more important with these learners, and it is no coincidence that many library services still operate busy enquiry desks, and some are enhancing this service by providing study skills support in a broad sense (see the case study of Newport). Sheffield Hallam University has a well-developed support service for distance learning students, but is finding that its Learning Centre on campus is busier than ever, especially for group work (Moore and Aspden, 2004). Where students study at a distance, this kind of social interaction is clearly necessary; it is notable that the Open University, delivering distance learning to over 200, 000 students per year, still includes a summer school for many of its courses and offers local tutorials for groups of students. Moller et al., (2003) argue that the concept of 'community' is critical to asynchronous learners; students need to be encouraged by their tutors to communicate with their peers on a social level so that they can provide mutual support. Ideally this would be done face-to-face at some point in the course, but can be done electronically. The point is that it needs to be considered as part of the course delivery package, in which libraries may well have a role to play.

Case study 1: University of Wales, Newport

Located on two main campuses, one in Newport and the other on its outskirts at Caerleon, the university teaches in all subject areas except medicine. The six Schools are divided between the campuses, but the administrative headquarters is at Caerleon. Recently, a branch of the Community University of the Valleys (East) has been established in Tredegar, through which many of the university's outreach programmes are operated, enabling the achievement of its mission 'to bring learning to the heart of our communities'. Approximately a third of the university's 9, 500 students are based in Further Education Colleges throughout Wales and overseas.

Newport is unusual in its high proportion of part-time students (over 50 per cent) and in the overall age profile, with only 10 per cent under 20 and 50 per cent over 30 years of age. The largest subject areas are in art, media and design, teacher education (particularly primary) and business studies. The university prides itself on its supportive approach to students, offering extensive tutorial and welfare services alongside varied learning environments in libraries and computer suites operated by the department of Library and Information Services. Study Zones, offering one-to-one help with study skills, are provided as part of Library and Information Services, and Information Librarians deliver an expanding programme of information literacy sessions to all Schools.

Over the last three years, the number of visits to the libraries has reduced slightly, but the use of electronic resources has increased by nearly 23 per cent and continues to grow, indicating that students are not necessarily visiting the library to obtain their information, although they are using its facilities remotely. Another benefit of providing resources electronically is that they can be actively marketed to the university's students in the FE Partner Colleges via their College Librarians. One of the Information Librarians at Newport has the role of keeping in touch with her colleagues in the Colleges, and provides a support service by means of e-mail; there is also an annual conference which brings together the librarians from all of the HE providers and their FE Partners in Wales for an exchange of experience. Another

Information Librarian leads the Library's work in providing specific support for students with disabilities.

The case study illustrates the wider geographical and demographic spread of students using the resources of any one university, and indicates some of the ways in which the roles of library staff are changing to meet these needs.

Learners using multiple access points for information

It has long been the case that students will use libraries which are most convenient for them, not just the one at the university where they are enrolled. The *People Flows Project* (Mynott et al., 2001) discovered that over two thirds of college and university students also use other libraries, and that almost one third of these other libraries are public libraries. Both this project and an earlier one in Birmingham in 1998 (Mulvaney and Lewis) found that students were not always welcomed by other academic libraries. In the last few years, however, there has been a flurry of activity in developing new schemes which enable students to use other academic and public libraries. Many of these are at a regional level, but the scope of national schemes is increasing all the time. The notable national schemes (in 2004) are:

- UK Libraries Plus
- SCONUL Research eXtra
- CURL
- INSPIRE (England)

There are also many regional schemes are listed on the UK Libraries Plus site.

These schemes allow certain learners to use other university libraries where this is more convenient for them, or where the resources are not available locally. UK Libraries Plus permits part-time and distance learning students in member libraries to borrow resources from up to three member libraries in the UK. The scheme has been a great success, with more than 5600 students using the scheme in 2003 (Edwards, 2004).

SCONUL Research eXtra and CURL (Consortium of University and Research Libraries) both allow researchers and academic staff to borrow from other member libraries, maximizing the use of unique research collections. These facilities are to be augmented in the next few years by the Research Libraries Network (RLN) which will develop electronic resource collections for use by all researchers in the UK.

INSPIRE (England) has established the principal of free managed access between public and HE libraries. It has also made it easier for university students to use the British Library in London. Various projects are being undertaken in the English regions to promote cross-usage of libraries. In Scotland there are many initiatives which are improving access between higher education and public libraries, most of which are coordinated by SCURL (Scottish Confederation of University and

Research Libraries); similarly in Wales WHELF (Wales Higher Education Libraries Forum), supports its members in the development of cross-sectoral schemes.

A slightly different approach to providing access to information is provided by the UK Ask a Librarian service. This allows members of the public to e-mail their requests for information at any time of the day or night and to receive a response within 2 days. The enquiries are answered by a rota of librarians from both public and academic libraries.

The other major way in which learners obtain information is via the Internet. Now that universities are well-equipped with IT, inevitably the Internet is the first port of call. Unfortunately the search engines are far more popular than the academically quality-assured gateways (Spink et al., 2003), leading to information overload and the use of relatively poor quality information for assignments. One of the most important roles of Subject Librarians is to explain the context of information and teach evaluation skills if students are to use appropriate resources for their work. Another key role is to evaluate the resources now available electronically and to consider their viability compared with their print alternatives. This will be discussed in a later section.

Information literacy

Hand in hand with increasing access to other libraries and other types of learning resources for students is the requirement for students to understand the nature of the information they are seeking and to be able to make best use of it when they find it. The increasing use of Internet sources requires students to develop a degree of information literacy, which is defined thus: 'To be information literate, a person must be able to recognize when information is needed and have the ability to locate, evaluate and use effectively the needed information' (American Library Association, 1989). SCONUL (1999) also offers a more detailed breakdown of the steps involved in its 'Seven Pillars' model.

In the context of supporting asynchronous learning, Subject Librarians need to teach students not only how to use their 'home' library, but also how to use information wherever it is located, whether in printed or electronic form. This requires a deeper level of understanding than many of us have achieved in library tours and 'user education' sessions in the past, and is particularly important for students working at a distance. Most universities are now actively developing their provision of information literacy, with some successfully integrating this into the mainstream curriculum. Edgehill University College is a good example of adopting a team-working approach with academic staff (Martin and Williamson, 2003) but there are many others. To help students working off-campus, several university libraries are developing information literacy tutorials which are provided through the university's Virtual Learning Environment, and some of these are available for others to use; for example INFORMS, and the subject-based tutorials in using Internet resources provided by the Resource Discovery Network. The Open University offers a module in Information Literacy called Mosaic which may be taken as a stand-alone module by any student, or which universities may be able to license for use with their own electronic resources. There are active e-mail lists of information workers involved in this on JISCMail, which provide a wealth of useful information about what already exists so that Subject Librarians can avoid re-inventing wheels. A useful list of sources of information about information literacy is provided by the Advisory Committee on Information Literacy on the SCONUL web site.

Increasingly, Subject Librarians are being encouraged to integrate their information literacy work into the curriculum by developing formal learning outcomes and devising forms of assessment. A plethora of publications have been written about the increasingly academic role of Subject Librarians, which is discussed further in chapters 4 and 7.

Electronic resources for asynchronous learning

In addition to widening participation, the government is seeking to promote e-learning throughout the whole of the education system. Its consultation paper *Towards a unified e-learning strategy* (DfES, 2003a) encourages the development of ICT skills in people of all ages as a means of increasing participation in learning. As Charles Clarke states in the foreword (p.2): 'E-learning has the power to transform the way we learn, and to bring high quality, accessible learning to everyone – so that every learner can achieve his or her full potential.' The strategy suggests that the widespread use of e-learning will facilitate progression between educational levels (such as from school to university) and into employment, which will foster a culture of lifelong learning in the workplace. One of its main benefits is perceived to be the flexibility of time or place of study.

With the increase in numbers of students choosing to study remotely or to use e-learning, it becomes more important that the resources they need are provided in an accessible way. This often means providing them electronically, and in some subject areas, notably the sciences, a reasonable proportion of the available journals can now be purchased in electronic form. In other subject areas the coverage is less comprehensive, so a mixed economy is likely to be necessary for some time. However, Subject Librarians may utilise services such as HERON (Higher Education Resources Online) to provide copyright cleared extracts from books or journals electronically for their students. Although a charge is made for each item, this needs to be balanced against the 24/7 access from anywhere which providing this service offers for the students. It is quite likely, following a recent parliamentary inquiry (House of Commons Science and Technology Committee, 2004) that electronic publishing may become more prevalent, which will provide further scope for offering resources to asynchronous learners online. Additional advantages are that the information is complete, pristine, and does not need to be borrowed, returned (nor shelved!).

Attracting new learners into HE

As part of the government's drive to increase the participation rate in higher education, universities have been extending their marketing activities into new areas. School children from the age of 14 are now targeted for attention, and summer taster sessions or sports activities are all designed to encourage them to visit a university campus and begin to aspire to a university course. However, successful economies require high levels of skilled employees, who can re-learn throughout their career. The need for constant re-skilling is driving the agenda for lifelong learning in documents such as the government white paper, *The future of higher education* (DfESb, 2003). Universities are therefore trying to encourage people to undertake courses later in life, often to improve their career prospects, but also to allow them to play enhanced roles as citizens in their local communities. The high proportion of students over the age of 30 in the Newport case study demonstrates that this can be an effective strategy. Work-based learning is another growth area, especially with the support of the government for the development of Foundation degrees. This has the advantage (at least for employers) that the employee does not leave the workplace and can customise their project work to meet the needs of the organisation. Asynchronous learning clearly benefits these students in that they can fit their studies into their working timetable (Bridgland and Blanchard, 2001).

Universities which aim to increase participation in higher education from areas where there have been few precedents are changing the way learning is delivered even where campus attendance is required. Attendance times are often adjusted to fit in with school hours, or after work, or even at weekends to enable people to attend who have other commitments. But, to offer complete flexibility of study time, in Australia – as in the UK – flexible learning (usually offered online) is allowing students to participate in learning activities without 'the tyranny imposed by distance and time, the difficulties in arranging a course of study around a full-time occupation, and restrictions imposed by formal learning programs' (Bridgland and Blanchard, 2001, p. 181). Subject Librarians need to be able to contribute to the development of such asynchronous learning if library resources are to remain relevant, both by developing their own information literacy curriculum, which can be delivered asynchronously, and also by working with academic staff on embedding the use of online as well as printed learning resources into the curriculum. The LTSN (Learning Technology Support Network) has produced a range of useful guides on e-learning aimed at different groups of staff, one of which encourages support staff to get involved in the development of curricula by becoming 'learning intermediaries' (Core, 2003).

Subject Librarians will also, along with academic staff, need to acquire new skills. Web design, including interactivity and self-assessment tools, the creation of images, videos and animations are now all tools of the educational trade (Bridgland and Blanchard, 2001), which enable asynchronous learning to take place. Some have even experimented with online chat services to respond to student enquiries (Hinton and McGill, 2001).

Ironically it is the students in disadvantaged areas who are currently being encouraged to use asynchronous learning to provide the flexibility to fit their studies into their lifestyles. Yet these students are the least familiar with academic study and its conventions and need the most support (Hull, 2001). Some initiatives are exploring the best mix between providing taster sessions for learners in community venues and online provision of course materials.

Case study 2: Community University of the Valleys (East)

The Community University of the Valleys Partnership (CUV-East) is in the eastern part of the Welsh Valleys, in the counties of Blaenau Gwent, Torfaen and Caerphilly. It has obtained European funding to establish local community centres where learners can be encouraged to take short courses. The catchment area for this outreach activity has a total population of over 300, 000 (based on 1991 census data). Progression is offered to higher education courses which are either delivered locally or via nearby universities.

Jones (2003, p.3) describes how the CUV-East operates:

> The majority of the provision has been offered during the day and is supported by crèche facilities. Learners have the choice of attending one module at a time or multiple modules within the framework of the Certificate of Higher Education (Combined Studies). Undoubtedly the European funding has enabled the CUV-East to develop a particular style of working which includes resources for recruitment and levels of support for learners, which have not been available at the campus.

The paper goes on to describe how people who were alienated from school, often many years before, are being given the confidence to demonstrate their ability to succeed at academic work. This is being achieved by the high level of support offered by the tutors, the learner-friendly opening hours and the short length of the individual modules. This allows students to gain early feedback on their work and inspires them to take further modules in a building block approach to gaining an award.

Students in the CUV-East are encouraged to develop their IT skills and to use a virtual learning environment. They are given an e-mail account and the opportunity to attend workshops or to download tutorials in using IT from the Web. Although many may not yet have Internet access at home, they can come to the community venues and use the IT facilities there (or their local public libraries), which provides them with reasonable flexibility. Although the courses are not delivered completely asynchronously, they are timetabled around their target group's availability and staff are available at other times to support them.

Experience at Sheffield Hallam (Moore and Aspden, 2004) has also demonstrated the enthusiasm of students to master ICT skills where these are essential for their learning. Subject Librarians will need to find ways of promoting library resources to learners like these, who they may never see, and who are often supported by a different 'arm' of a university. Taking book boxes out to community venues and organising visits to university libraries have been tried, but the involvement needs to be more continuous. One solution may be to incorporate direct links to electronic library materials via the virtual learning environments the students use for their courses. It is important that we volunteer our involvement in initiatives such as these to make sure that students are encouraged to use high quality resources rather than just what is available on the Internet. We may also need to adapt our library procedures to allow for enrolments for a term at a time, and delivery of materials to off-campus venues. Unless these learners are supported effectively by library staff, they will not receive their full entitlement as university students, and, more importantly, may progress to higher levels of study without understanding how to use information effectively.

Assisting learners with special needs

The government's drive to widen access to higher education is not only aiming to attract students from disadvantaged communities but also to encourage people with disabilities to apply to universities and colleges. With an integrated school approach to including pupils with disabilities in mainstream classes (DfES, 2001) more students with disabilities are entering higher education. The proportion is conservatively estimated at 4 per cent, with disabilities in the population in general estimated to be between 12 and 20 per cent. (SCONUL, 2002, p. 11).

Many of these learners will have greater difficulty in using on-campus facilities than others, preferring to use their own computer equipment in their room, or to work from home if they live locally. Asynchronous learning may in these cases be more of a necessity than a choice but universities need to ensure that 'students with disabilities should have access to a learning experience comparable with their non-disabled peers' (QAA, 1999).

Subject Librarians will need to adapt services to meet the needs of students with disabilities. For example, guides to subject literature should be available in alternative formats (such as online, large print, audio, Braille), shelving layouts may need to be adjusted to accommodate wheelchairs; they may need to be familiar with various forms of assistive technology; and they need to be able to adjust services to meet specific needs. Valuable guidance on the kinds of support which libraries should be offering is provided by SCONUL (2002). Self-help groups such as CLAUD are also important to enable us to keep up to date and to do as the legislation requires, to anticipate needs. The CLAUD website has a wealth of useful information for library staff, and organises an annual conference. There is also a range of advice on the technical issues available from the JISC TechDis site. Information on the accessibility of buildings is provided by organisations such as the Joint Mobility Unit who will carry out access audits. General advice on providing support for students with disabilities is available from SKILL, the National Bureau for Students With Disabilities.

Other groups of students who may need bespoke services are those from overseas or from ethnic minority backgrounds. Consideration should be given to providing guides in languages other than English where this is consistent with university policy. Some libraries offer English language support delivered by qualified staff as part of their support service.

It is a moot point whether a library should provide 'special' services for these groups, with designated staff to support them, or whether such support should be part of everyone's role. The decision will depend on each library's circumstances, but the key is that a consistent response should be offered, with all staff trained in how to advise appropriately (SCONUL, 2002). In many cases, reflection on how services may be delivered effectively for those with particular needs may well improve the service for everyone.

The future

How will all of this affect the role of libraries and Subject Librarians? Will learners still need to visit us, or shall we be transmitting our resources directly to them? Will the existing buildings become redundant, or will they need a new face? Will they become social meeting places where students who have worked together electronically make the most of the opportunity to work in groups (Moore and Aspden, 2004)? Some universities are already developing the concept of the Learning Café, such as Glasgow Caledonian and 'approachable buildings' (Oyston, 2003). Will stock be moved into the background, and the emphasis be placed on IT facilities? Will human assistance be provided face to face, or will more support be provided by electronic reference services? Will items need to be catalogued, or digitized so that they are automatically searchable?

The future could be radically different as technology changes the use of information further. The libraries cooperative OCLC, in an Environmental Scan (Wilson, 2003), proposes: 'We need to stop looking at things from a library point-of-view and focus on the user's view. Librarians cannot change user behaviour and so need to meet the user' (p. 13). Just as we cannot fight the use of mobile phones, we should exploit them by using them to communicate with our users; we cannot prevent students from using search engines, so need to ensure that the information provided by libraries uses similar technology; we cannot force students to turn up for lectures or to come into the library, but we can ensure that they have alternative ways of obtaining the materials if they wish.

Higher education libraries are at a turning point, where the opportunities to adopt asynchronous learning already exist; collectively most of us are either unwilling to take the plunge to rely completely on electronic resources, or cannot afford to, or are unable to persuade our university colleagues that this is a preferred course of action. With increasing competition from non-university providers of electronic courseware, we need to be sure that we are meeting our users' needs, otherwise they may go elsewhere. As we have seen, students already use other libraries and the internet if they are more convenient. In addition to market research and user surveys to find out how students want information to be provided for them, there is scope for much more research into the pedagogy of online learning, effective support mechanisms for asynchronous learning by universities (not just libraries), into evaluating learner behaviour, and into learning styles, particularly for the 'new' categories of students. We should grasp every opportunity to participate in these discussions, especially with the changes taking place in electronic publishing. It is up to us as librarians, particularly Subject Librarians to exploit our strengths in providing information and in teaching people how to use it, regardless of the context. Whether asynchronous learning is the solution, or whether hybrid educational systems and hybrid libraries are here to stay for a little longer is unimportant; what matters is that we contribute to and influence the debate.

References

American Library Association. Presidential Committee on Information Literacy, 1989. *Final report* [online]. Available from: http://www.ala.org/acrl/nili/ilit1st. html [Accessed 2 April 2005].

Bridgland, A. and Blanchard, P., 2001. Flexible Delivery/Flexible Learning. Does it Make a Difference? *Australian Academic and Research Libraries,* 32 (3), 177–191.

Core, J., Rothery, A. and Walton, G., 2003. *A guide for support staff,* York: Learning and Teaching Support Network.

Department for Education and Skills (DfES), 2001. *Special Educational Needs: code of practice*, Annesley: Department for Education and Skills.

Department for Education and Skills (DfES), 2003a. *Towards a unified e-learning strategy* [online]. Available from: http://www.dfes.gov.uk/consultations/ conResults.cfm?consultationId=774 [Accessed 2004, September/09].

Department for Education and Skills (DfES), 2003b. *The future of higher education*, Norwich: The Stationery Office.

Edwards, A., 2004. *UK Libraries Plus statistics* [online]. Available from: http:// www.uklibrariesplus.ac.uk/libraries/statistics.htm [Accessed 2 April 2005].

Hinton, D. and McGill, L., 2001. Chat to a librarian : 21st century reference for distance learners. *Vine,* 122, 59–64.

House of Commons. Science and Technology Committee, 2004). *Scientific publications: free for all?*, London: The Stationery Office.

Hull, B., 2001. Libraries and lifelong learning. *Adults Learning,* 12 (6), 20–22.

Ince, D., 2003. *A Dictionary of the Internet* [online]. Available from: http://www. oxfordreference.com [Accessed 02 April 2005].

Jones, C. (2003), Apprehension and achievement – twin poles of the adult learning experience, Newport: University of Wales, Newport.

Martin, L. and Williamson, S., 2003. Integrating information literacy into higher education. *In* A. Martin and H. Rader, (eds), *Information and IT literacy: enabling learning in the 21st century*. London: Facet.

Moller, L.A., Harvey, D., Downs, M. and Godshalk, V.M., 2003. Identifying factors that affect learning community development and performance in asynchronous distance education. *Educational Media and Technology Yearbook,* 28, 139–151.

Moore, K., and Aspden, L., 2004. Coping, adapting, evolving: the student experience of e-learning. *Library + Information Update,* 3 (4), 22–24.

Mulvaney, T.K. and Lewis, E., 1998. Analysis of library services for distance learning students at the University of Birmingham. *Education Libraries Journal,* 41 (1), 29–34.

Mynott, G., Nankivell, C., Foster, W., and Elkin, J., 2001. *People flows: an investigation of the cross-use of publicly-funded libraries,* Birmingham: University of Central England.

Nankivell, C., and Eve, J., 2002. Public libraries matter. *In* P. Brophy, S. Fisher and Z. Clarke (eds.) *Libraries without walls 4: the delivery of library services to distant users,* London: Facet.

National Committee of Inquiry into Higher Education (NCIHE), 1997, *Higher education in the learning society,* Norwich: HMSO.

Oyston, E., (ed.), 2003. Centered on learning: academic case studies on learning centre development, Aldershot: Ashgate.

Quality Assurance Agency (QAA), 1999. *Code of practice for the assurance of academic quality and standards in higher education Section 3: Students with disabilities* [online]. Available from: http://www.qaa.ac.uk/academicinfrastructure/ codeOfPractice/ [Accessed 04 April 2005].

Society of College, National and University Libraries (SCONUL), 1999. *Seven Pillars of Information Literacy* [online]. Available from: http://www.sconul. ac.uk/activities/inf_lit/seven_pillars.html [Accessed 04 April 2005].

Society of College, National and University Libraries (SCONUL), 2002. *Access for users with disabilities.* London: SCONUL.

Society of College, National and University Libraries (SCONUL), 2004a. *Annual Library Statistics 2002–2003.* London: SCONUL.

Society of College, National and University Libraries (SCONUL), 2004b. *SCONUL Library Statistics: trend analysis to 2002–03.* London: SCONUL.

Society of College, National and University Libraries (SCONUL). 2004c, *UK Higher Education Library Management Statistics 2002–2003,* London: SCONUL.

Spink, S., Thomas, R. and Yeoman, A., 2003. *JUSTEIS: JISC usage surveys: trends in electronic information services. Executive summary final report – 2002/2003 cycle 4* [online]. Available: http://www.justeis.info/Executive per cent20Summary per cent204.htm [Accessed 04 April 2005].

Universities & Colleges Informations Systems Association (UCISA), 2004, *HEITS statistical return 200 –2003* [online]. Available from: http://www.ucisa.ac.uk/ activities/stats/stats03.htm [Accessed 04 April 2005].

Websites

CLAUD [http://www.bris.ac.uk/claud/welcome.html].
INFORMS [http://informs.hud.ac.uk/cgi-bin/informs.pl].

INSPIRE [http://www.sconul.ac.uk/use_lib/inspire.html].

HERON: Higher Education Resources Online [http://www.heron.ingenta.com].

JISCMail [http://www.jiscmail.ac.uk]

JISC TechDis [http://www.techdis.ac.uk].

Joint Mobility Unit Access Partnership [http://www.jmuaccess.org.uk/].

Learning Café, Glasgow Caledonian University [http://www.realcaledonian.ac.uk/learningcafe.html].

Mosaic [http://www.open.ac.uk].

Resource Discovery Network [http://www.vts.rdn.ac.uk].

SCONUL – Advisory Committee on Information Literacy [http://www.sconul.ac.uk/activities/inf_lit].

SCURL: Scottish Confederation of University and Research Libraries [http://scurl.ac.uk].

Skill: National Bureau for Students With Disabilities [http://www.skill.org.uk].

UK Ask a Librarian service [http://www.ask-a-librarian.org.uk].

UKLibraries Plus – National Regional and Local Access Schemes [http://www.uklibrariesplus.ac.uk/libraries/sconul.htm].

WHELF: Wales Higher Education Libraries Forum [http://whelf.ac.uk].

Chapter 10

Serving Different Constituencies: Researchers

Matt Holland

Introduction

The past decade from 1992 has been formative in shaping the support for and delivery of research degree programmes. A number of initiatives are now in place which promise a coherent national strategy to underpin developments for at least the next five years. This chapter of necessity contains a considerable amount of background information, in part because this is now a good moment to reflect on the journey from Follett to the Research Libraries Network (RLN) but also because understanding the future direction of support for researchers requires an understanding of how we got to this point.

The broader context

The United Kingdom higher education infrastructure comprises elite research institutions, commonly but not exclusively defined as the Russell Group of 19 research-led institutions, and mass higher education institutions. Mass higher education universities include the redbrick universities founded in the post-war era and 'new universities' created post-1992 from former polytechnics. The elite universities with a heritage of scientific and technical research retain their dominance of research but keep a significant stake in undergraduate teaching. The mass higher education institutions provide courses for graduates mainly in professional and vocational areas, and in new subjects such as the apocryphal 'meeja studies' much derided by the media. They retain, however, an interest in research. This system creates a number of tensions, between learning and teaching, between elite universities and mass education universities, and in competition for funding. Government funding attempts to ensure that excellence is adequately rewarded wherever it is found, while at the same time supporting the expensive scientific and technical research of the elite universities. Funding for research is delivered in two streams, known as the dual funding system, through Higher Education Funding Council for England (HEFCE) awards to departments judged excellent in the Research Assessment Exercise (RAE) and through the Arts and Humanities Research Board (AHRB)/Research Councils.

In recent years the Office of Science and Technology has provided additional money for a number of special initiatives.

Two recent initiatives, the White Paper *The Future of Higher Education* (2003) and the Roberts Review (2003) of the RAE have set the climate for research that will prevail at least until 2008. The title of the White Paper's chapter on research, 'Research Excellence – building on our strengths' sets the tone of government strategy to focus resources on institutions with an existing research capability. It embraces a broad view of research to include social sciences, arts and humanities, giving examples of topics normally found in new universities, such as tourism, design and performing arts, and committed to the creation of an Arts and Humanities Research Council, established in April 2005. However, the White Paper explicitly questions the link between teaching and research, suggesting that the prestige perceived to be gained from having a research capability might equally be gained by excellent teaching-only institutions. Although this argument was criticised at the time of the release of the White Paper, and now has less prominence, the changes to the support structure for research mean in effect that those institutions which do not already have a research profile with high RAE ratings will find it difficult to establish one. More money is to go to the top 25 institutions through the RAE with the creation of an additional higher tier. Support will be directed at institutions that work together in consortia to deliver a research capability. The funding for research has moved to a more expensive 'economic cost model' and the standards set for PhD programmes require an appropriate research environment in which research at a high level is already being carried out. Institutions, in order to secure funding for PhDs, will also have to meet the more rigorous conditions for research training set down by Research Councils.

The RAE assesses research on the basis of the outputs of research active staff across a range of approximately 70 subject areas awarding scores from 1 (very poor) to 5* (of international standing). The RAEs have previously been conducted in 1986, 1991, 1996 and 2001. Those with scores of 3a/4 or above receive additional funding. The RAE was recently reviewed by the HEFCE sponsored Roberts Review (Roberts 2003). The RAE process was endorsed by both the review and HEFCE and will continue with modifications to the panel structure that assesses submissions and to the scoring structure. The next review due in December 2008 and will continue in a six year cycle thereafter.

The RAE and the White Paper have implications for Subject Librarians. The White Paper and the accumulation of other initiatives and policies addressed in the rest of the chapter have in effect drawn a line in the sand. Those institutions not involved in research at higher levels are unlikely to expand their research activities and may take the strategic choice in the direction of excellence in teaching and learning. Those who are have a stake in the RAE have begun to plan for 2008, directing resources either to achieve higher ratings or to support existing excellent ratings which will have knock-on effects for Subject Librarians who support these areas.

Access to research libraries

The Joint Funding Council's Libraries Review Group (1993) chaired by Professor Brian Follett devoted a chapter to 'Libraries and the Researcher'. This chapter and recommendations made by the Follett Report set in motion a series of initiatives that have had a lasting and beneficial effect on research libraries, in particular creating rational systems for resource discovery and access. Follett supported funding for the development of the Consortium of University Research Libraries (CURL) database into a national Online Public Access Catalogue, which evolved into CURL OPAC (COPAC). Many recommendations directed funding at resources for Social Sciences and Humanities which Follett recognised as making greater use both of library resources and librarians than other disciplines. The Follett Report set out the principles to guide further policy making including local autonomy in provision, but also (where possible) co-operation between libraries and special support for the social sciences and humanities. In particular Follett set up a second Review Group on a National Strategy for Library Provision for Researchers, chaired by Professor Michael Anderson.

The Anderson Report (*Joint Funding Council's Library Review Group*, 1996) set out the six broad principles of a strategy for library provision for researchers: (1) provide a means to locate material with reasonable ease; (2) long term preservation of material of importance to the national heritage; (3) operate fairly for individuals and institutions (4) work economically; (5) be flexible and not undermine existing good practice; (6) draw on existing strengths. Anderson recommended that a guiding principle of access should be that researchers go to collections and not vice versa and that researchers should begin with their own library and only use major national and research libraries as a last resort.

Anderson made 18 recommendations, but an area of great concern was the cost imposed on major research libraries by visiting researchers. A third report was commissioned from Coopers and Lybrand, *Funding Councils study of the level and costs of use of higher education libraries by external researchers* (1997). The report concludes that most external researchers concentrate on about 20 university libraries costing somewhere between £6 million and £10 million and that visiting researchers consume more resources because they make more requests for assistance from Library staff.

The Funding Councils responded to the need for more financial support for research libraries with the Research Support Libraries Programme (RSLP), investing £30 million of funding over three years, 1999–2002. The funding, delivered in three streams, reflected the conclusions of Anderson and Follett, supporting the Humanities and Social Sciences, collaborative collection management and a resource description framework to aid resource discovery. In a second initiative Funding Councils set up the Research Support Libraries Group (RSLG) in 2001 chaired by Brian Follett. The key recommendation of the RSLG report in 2003 was the establishment of a high profile strategic body to oversee research libraries, the Research Libraries Network (RLN), comprising National Libraries and Funding Councils. The RLN is currently being created at the British Library. The press release announcing the creation of the RLN promises a 'joined up' library service for researchers in the United Kingdom, focusing on three areas:

- provide strategic leadership for collaboration between publicly-funded research information providers and their users – to develop effective, efficient and integrated information resources and services to support UK research;
- co-ordinate action to propose and specify solutions to meet researchers' changing needs – building on the earlier studies into UK researchers' needs carried out by the RSLG;
- act as a high-level advocate for research information, across the UK and internationally (HEFCE, 2004).

A number of related initiatives have contributed to enhanced access to research libraries. The UK Archives Hub, developed by CURL and funded by the Joint Information Systems Committee (JISC) provides information on archival and special collections in universities and colleges. Institutions from across the sector have contributed archival descriptions to the hub. The Archives Hub supports researchers, librarians and archivists in the Arts and Humanities but has the benefit of raising awareness across the higher education sector for other users of the richness of university and college collections.

Responding to concerns about supporting visiting Scholars, an issue of particular concern to Anderson, SCONUL have instituted SCONUL Research Extra, a widely supported scheme with 157 participating libraries, to provide a coherent system allowing researchers to visit other libraries. Beginning operations in 2003, the statistics for researches registering with the scheme provide for the first time a statistical picture of how many researchers use other libraries. Registration in the first year was 2417 staff and 3484 students, with the majority of activity centered on the major research universities as predicted by the Coopers and Lybrand study.

The decade from Follett to the RLN has perhaps asked more questions than provided answers. The future, however, looks promising, with the prospect of a national strategy, supported by the considerable financial and political weight of the Funding Councils and informed by the needs of researchers.

Research training

Issues relating to research training are addressed in a number of government, Funding Council and Research Council reports as part of a general concern with the quality, delivery and funding of research degree programmes. Three consistent themes emerge in the discussion of research training: (1) the relevance of skills acquired by research students to employment in industry; (2) how research students get access to research training, and (3) developing guidelines and codes of practice for research training and the mechanisms through which quality can be assured.

What are variously termed information skills, information retrieval or bibliographic skills are bundled in with skills related to employment and research management. The following briefly reviews the discussion of research training reflected in published reports from the White Paper, *Realising our potential: a strategy for science, engineering and technology* (Chancellor of the Duchy of Lancaster, 1993), to the current HEFCE review *Improving standards in postgraduate research degree programmes* (2003).

The White Paper endorsed the view that research training should include such transferable skills as communication and management of resources. The mechanism identified to deliver research training to students was the Master's degree forming the first stage of PhD. Successful pilots led to the creation of Master's of Research (MRes) programmes to prepare students for PhDs. A search of the Prospects database identifies over 150 MRes courses currently offered in the UK. The White Paper also identified examples of good practice by Research Councils, including the publication by Economic and Social Research Council (ESRC) of Postgraduate training guidelines (ESRC, 1991) which set out the research training that institutions had to provide to qualify for ESRC support, a model that is now widely accepted.

In 1996 Prof. Martin Harris published a *Review of postgraduate education* (HEFCE, 1996b) conducted on behalf of HEFCE, The Committee of Vice-Chancellors and Principals (CVCP) and the Standing Conference of Principals (SCOP). The Harris Review recommended that a code of practice be drawn up to cover, among other things, infrastructure and environment including learning resources. It commended the work of the Higher Education Quality Council (HEQC) which issued *Guidelines on quality assurance for research degrees* in 1996 (HEQC, 1996). The Harris Review recommended that postgraduate research be brought within the remit of the planned Quality Assurance Agency (QAA). This recommendation was accepted and implemented by HEFCE and endorsed a year later by Professor Ron Dearing's report into Higher Education in the Learning Society. Dearing also made a specific recommendation that higher education institutions (HEIs) review postgraduate research training with the aim of ensuring that it not only included training in research but employment-related skills – 'the development of professional skills, such as communication, self-management and planning.' (NCIHE, 1997).

The Roberts Review, commissioned by the Treasury, Department of Trade and Industry and the Department for Education and Skills, appeared as *SET for success: The supply of people with science, technology, engineering and mathematics skills* (H.M. Treasury, 2002) and addressed postgraduate education as one part of an all-embracing review of education from school to post doctoral research. A key conclusion was that '… PhDs do not prepare people adequately for careers in business or academia. In particular, there is insufficient access to training in interpersonal and communication skills, management and commercial awareness.' (H.M. Treasury, 2002 p. 111). The Government has provided £150 million to implement the recommendations of the Roberts Review with some money being allocated to research training for Research Council funded students. The minimum expectation is that students will attend a two-week UK GRAD Course from 2005 in the second or third year of their studies. Universities are invited to pool funds to support the delivery of in-house programmes.

The Government White Paper, *The future of higher education* (DfES 2003), makes specific reference to the training of PhD students, with concerns about quality standards, supervision and providing students with transferable skills. Meeting these concerns inevitably raises the costs of providing PhD training. It might be that smaller Graduate Schools are not able to meet the increased cost of research training, with a trend towards larger better financed programmes that attract a critical mass of funded PhD candidates. The White Paper directed HEFCE to review standards and for research training, prompting the HEFCE sponsored consultation on Improving standards in postgraduate research degree programmes (HEFCE 2003). This initial document recommends that facilities including Library and IT should reach national standards, and that research training be provided to a level consistent with the AHRB/Joint Research Councils Skills Training Requirements for Research Students. The review also raised concerns that multiple standards might be created where one standard issued by the QAA in 1999 already existed. In response the funding councils asked the QAA to revise their code in the light of the review. QAA issued the revised code in September 2004 for implementation in 2005/6.

Guidelines and codes

The guidelines and codes of practice for research training require institutions to demonstrate to Research and Funding Councils that programmes have been delivered with evidence of student satisfaction. Where Subject Librarians have not been invited to participate in research training the guidelines and codes represent an opportunity to argue for their inclusion. Their language is very general creating scope for a broad interpretation of what information skills are allowing them to be tailored to specific institutional and subject contexts.

The QAA published the *Code of Practice for the Assurance of Academic Quality and Standards in Higher Education: Postgraduate Research Programmes* (1999). Under the category of employment-related skills, information retrieval skills are specifically identified 'general and employment-related skills including, for example, interpersonal and team working skills; project management, information retrieval and database management, written and oral presentational'. (QAA, 1999 p. 10).

The ESRC published the third edition of the *Postgraduate training guidelines* (2001) setting out the standards they require to be met for recognition. Only institutions recognised by the ERSC are able to received ESRC funded studentships. The ESRC has adopted a '1+3' model with one year funding for research training and three years funding for the PhD element. The guidelines are specific in relation to bibliographic and computing skills:

> ... these are likely to include: the identification of library resources and how to use them; training in other bibliographic sources and methods; techniques for keeping track of the literature; the use of annals, theses, journals and conference proceedings; the maintenance

of a personal research bibliography; word-processing; other basic computing skills including spreadsheets and database management; and procedures for the evaluation of research, including refereeing and book reviews (ESRC, 2001 Section D2.1).

In October 2002 the AHRB/Joint Research Councils produced a statement setting out the *Skills Training Requirements for Research Students* (Joint Statements of the Research Councils and AHRB, 2002) in seven specific areas. Under research management, students are expected to 'identify and access appropriate bibliographical resources, archives, and other sources of relevant information.'

Building on the same joint statement the AHRB have set out a framework for research training to be applied from 2004. Departments applying for funding will have to demonstrate that they can provide research training that meets with the framework in order to receive AHRB funded studentships. Among the core skills required by the framework are 'bibliographical skills and contextualising practice-based research; identifying and using web-based resources; record-keeping and record management.' (AHRB, 2003 p. 3).

The revised QAA *Code of practice for postgraduate research programmes* (2004) identifies 27 precepts that underpin quality. Precept 5 requires that institutions 'only accept students into an environment that provides support for doing and learning about research and where high quality research is occurring', this includes 'adequate learning and research tools including access to IT equipment, *library and electronic publications*' (QAA, 2004, p. 8). Precept 10 requires institutions to provide a comprehensive induction programme which includes 'a summary of the facilities that will be made available to the student, *including the learning support infrastructure*.' (QAA, 2004, p. 13) The code, following the lead of the White Paper leaves the door open to bi-lateral or regional co-operation to provide 'opportunities for skills development' (QAA, 2004, p. 20).

The cumulative effect of the guidelines and codes is to provide a base line for support for postgraduate research degrees supported by QAA and by the requirements for funding of the AHRB/Joint Funding Councils. Encompassed within these is an explicit commitment to provide resources, information skills training and support which can be validated as part of a quality assurance regime.

Delivery of research training

Research training and the information skills component build on students' experiences in undergraduate and master's programmes. Typical PhD candidates will have good undergraduate degrees and a relevant master's degrees. They are likely to have been exposed to information skills teaching at both levels and have sufficient skills to have completed an undergraduate dissertation or project and a master's thesis. Research training programmes are delivered as part of a generic Graduate School programme or alternatively by a single department or faculty. Students preparing for postgraduate research may be required to complete a Master's of Research as a condition for proceeding to a PhD. Research supervisors advise students on research techniques and share their experiences of searching for information and using information resources. Subject Librarians should be aware of researchers in their area and offer one to one subject support. PhD students also have access to the national UK GRAD Programme, previous known as the Research Councils' Graduate Schools Programme, which offers national residential programmes and supports a regional network of hubs that provide courses and support.

However, not all research students fit a typical profile. A significant number of PhD candidates are from overseas. Although they may take a master's degree in the UK their experience of undergraduate education will be very different from that of British students. Another significant group is part-time PhD candidates who may be working, teaching or live remotely from their 'home' institution. The diversity of the range of subjects together with a growth in postgraduate research students presents problems that mirror those of undergraduate students. As we will see later in this chapter, there is plenty of evidence from recent research that students do not feel that they have the skills they need.

The UK Council for Graduate Education (UKCGE) has conducted three studies on research training in specific contexts, the Humanities (2000), Creative and Performing Arts and Design (2001) and the Healthcare Professions (2003). UKCGE has developed a four-part needs based model. The model is described as a framework with four dimensions: (a) Desired outcomes of doctoral research; (b) Preparation and development – achievement and evaluation; (c) Levels of requirement – knowledge, understanding and skills; (d) Types and levels of knowledge, understanding and skills. Bibliographic skills are included in (d). The purpose is to provide a basis from which the individual needs of the student can be assessed, rather than to outline a programme of training. The UKCGE make a number of points that are echoed in wider discussions of research training. The studies found that there is a tension between generic university-wide courses and courses specific to student's research. Students prefer department or faculty courses that are sympathetic to their area of study. However, students working in small departments can feel isolated. In some areas and in smaller institutions it is difficult to get a critical mass of research students to form a community of like-minded researchers.

Studies of researchers' use of libraries and information services

There have been two major cross-sector, cross-disciplinary surveys of researcher use of libraries in the period following Follett. The Social and Community Planning Research (SCPR) was responsible for a 1995 survey which repeated an earlier survey in 1989 (Erens, 1996) and a survey was also commissioned by the Research Support Libraries Group (RSLG) (Carpenter et al., 2003). In addition, there are a number of surveys looking at behaviour in single institutions: Sussex University (Jacobs, 1998), Leeds Metropolitan (Hewitson, 2000), Glasgow Caledonian (Ferguson and Crawford, 2001) and consortia activities (Bloor, 2001). Taking a different perspective, Eti Herman in a series of articles (2001a, 2001b, 2004a, 2004b) looks at information needs and information seeking behaviours from the perspective of individual researchers.

The surveys reveal a user community under pressure. The burden of teaching and administrative activities reducing the time available to spend on purely research activities is a persistent theme. Services that save time, in particular access to electronic information resources over the web, are highly valued. Hewitson and Carpenter et al. find evidence for what is now known as the 'Google factor', a preference for using generic search engines to locate information, bypassing library websites which provide access to bibliographic and full text databases. Carpenter et al. also note the very low rating for the use of the Research Discovery Network (RDN) Gateways and an even lower awareness of electronic resources created outside higher education, commenting that 'archive services will be disappointed to see how low their profile is with researchers, even in Art and Humanities' (p. 20).

Researchers are, however, reluctant to engage in training to improve information skills, citing lack of time as one reason. Carpenter et al., in a focus group on training, found participants reluctant to admit to training needs and with an aversion even to the word training, although it was apparent that participants demonstrated an incomplete range of information skills. Researchers participating in the Carpenter study did show agreement across disciplines about areas where they would like more information. These included:

- specialised online search skills;
- ways of keeping up-to-date with what is available;
- locating high-quality information sources;
- how to filter online information effectively;
- how to find/create online archives;
- how to find out what resources are available through their own university.

This brings us to the question about what is different and unique about the researcher outside the framework provided by taught courses or programmes. Here the progress through a programme is generally predictable, marked out by the curriculum and assessment deadlines. For researchers, the only common point of departure, where a group session or workshop might be appropriate or perceived to be useful, is at the beginning of the research process. Institutions may choose to start researchers at a given date and deliver an induction course to support new researchers. They may, however, run courses periodically directed at researchers who have started to study but not received training. The former is preferable to the later as research is a very personal activity. Researchers tend to focus only on what can be proved to be effective and useful to their very specific research area. Their negative attitude towards training reflects similar issues raised about broader research training, that researchers are reluctant to engage with activities that they perceive are generic or not specifically sympathetic to their own area of research.

Different discipline areas have different approaches to research. The natural habitat of the scientist is the laboratory, research projects are often driven by practical considerations, such as setting up and conduct experiments or tests. Scientists, because of the scale of scientific research, often work in teams or in close collaboration with colleagues. Social Scientists may work within a broader research group but tend towards the more individualistic subject analysis of the arts or humanities researcher, who generally work alone on a single project. Programmes which support researchers have to show awareness and sympathy with the particular scholarly research process to the point that, just as when undergraduate information needs can often be deduced from knowing the course year and unit, the researchers' information needs can be broadly identified from a description of where they are in their own research process.

Researchers are exposed to a wide range of external influences. These include supervisors based in their home institution but also in other institutions with a different experience of information access and use. Communication is likely to be two-way, with supervisors both giving advice and in turn learning from the knowledge of new resources encountered by researchers. Knowing who is supervising research is useful. Supervisors are one channel through which information about new and useful resources can be directed. There are a number of times in the life-cycle of a PhD. When research is presented to a wider audience: a proposal to a research committee, at the point of transfer from MPhil to PhD, at research seminars and workshops and as papers at conferences. At each point the information base of the research is tested and provokes questions that require further research and clarification. It is often at these points that research students are in most frequent contact with Librarians.

All surveys reveal disciplinary differences among researchers in a spectrum from the sciences to the arts, supporting the sketch Follett included in his initial report. Science and technology researchers focus on journals, value currency of information, and are likely to make use of large bibliographic databases and inter-library loan services. Researchers in the humanities and social sciences require access to long journal runs, make more use of monographs and require access to primary texts. These conclusions are supported by the subsequent research reported by Erens and Carpenter et al. A division emerges, however, with those students who make more use of physical resources being slightly less satisfied with provision now than ten years ago, noting for example the cancellation of journals, a result of the increasing financial pressure on libraries. Students studying disciplines such as medicine, who make extensive use of electronic resources have a more positive view of the provision of resources and their ease of use. As Eti Herman points out (2001a) the flow of information is slowly, and in some discipline areas, rapidly changing direction. The information in other words flows to the researcher and the researcher no longer goes to the information. Ferguson and Crawford and Carpenter et al. suggest that for some groups the need for physical access to the Library is declining but researchers increasingly value *services* provided by the Library, such as inter-library loan, access to databases and catalogues and the advice of Subject Librarians. Arts and humanities remain the most wedded to physical collections, especially to book and monograph collections. We might speculate that this makes a virtue out of necessity, with electronic access to journals widespread but the emergence of electronic books lagging behind (although catching up). In other words, will researchers in arts and humanities follow the trajectory of scientific colleagues once a critical mass of book material is available in electronic form?

Research support

Ferguson and Crawford (2001) discover that researchers are able to identify their Academic Liaison Librarian to whom questions can be directed. Similarly Jacobs (1998) concludes that the support which is most effective is that which is closest to the end users. The Subject Librarian who has a broad knowledge of the organisational context in which research is undertaken, who combines this with knowledge of the information sources in the appropriate subject domain and who is skilled in one to one consultations is well placed to provide the informed individual support that researchers need.

A survey by Harrison and Hughes (2001) of Librarians involved in research support reveals a diversity of approaches to research support. Some dedicated posts were funded for specific projects and a small number of institutions provide dedicated Research Support Librarians. Manchester Metropolitan University have provided a dedicated Research Support Librarian since 1995. The post has evolved from one that worked directly with researchers, to one that seeks to promote the effective use of electronic resources and library services directly to researchers and working in partnership with Subject Librarians. Generally research support is provided by Subject Librarians, or Subject Teams as part of a broad responsibility to provide support for a school or faculty. In institutions that have a Graduate School, as is the case at Bournemouth University, the responsibility for issues specifically generated by the Graduate School have been delegated as an additional task for one Subject Librarian, while support for individual researchers is delivered by Subject Teams.

Research support includes providing information skills teaching. In recent years information skills has been absorbed into the wider concept of information literacy. This is as an idea that is still in the early stages of development in the UK: the Chartered Institute of Library and Information Professionals (CILIP) is currently developing a definition of information literacy. There exist already a number of national and international definitions of information literacy skills. The definition designed for higher education in the United Kingdom is the SCONUL Seven Pillars Model (see also Chapter 8). A scheme modelled on this structure for undergraduate programmes is now used at South Bank University (Goodwin, 2003).

Information professionals working to design and deliver information literacy skills face the challenge of incorporating a national initiative from the QAA, the Framework for Higher Education Qualifications (FHEQ) (QAA, 2001). The FHEQ is a five level structure that defines the skills and capabilities students should be able to demonstrate at the end of each level. Undergraduates progress through three levels from Level C (Certificate), to Level I (Intermediate) to the final year at Level H (Honours). Masters are Level M, and postgraduate research students Level D.

Bournemouth University, along with many others in UK HE is putting together a local framework that defines what skills an information literate student should have at each level using the Seven Pillars Model. The ability to assess students' skills against a framework has advantages. It allows students to see where they are and how far they have to progress to achieve competencies appropriate for their level and it provides an opportunity for individualised help to bring students to a point where they can engage with colleagues who have achieved higher levels of information literacy skills.

A definition of what information literacy skills might be at Level D is challenging since any student who achieves entry to a research degree programme should have a broad range of skills in their researcher's tool kit. In addition with the 1+3 model for research degree programmes the information literacy skills delivery that underpins D Level is likely to be delivered at M Level as a Master's or Master's of Research qualification. However, using surveys of researchers, the requirements of guides and codes, and current practice it is possible to make an informed statement of postgraduate information literacy skills using the Seven Pillars Model. This example leaves out the first level skill, 'Understanding the need to use information', which perhaps can be assumed at this level.

- **Information Literacy Skill 2. Packaging of information and choosing suitable sources for research**
  - sound knowledge of the range of resources available with the ability to select resources appropriate resource(s) for the task.
- **Information Literacy Skill 3. Search tools and the need for a search strategy**
  - confident in the use of advanced search skills, for example Citation Searching, and in the use of significant bibliographic databases.
- **Information Literacy Skill 4. Locating and accessing information**
  - knowledge of research resources both in higher education and outside higher education, including archives, special collections and other significant depositories or organizations;
  - the ability to assess with confidence the current state of research in any area, using published and unpublished sources, such theses or journals, and electronic sources such as websites.
- **Information Literacy Skill 5. Comparing and evaluating information**
  - the ability to pursue an argument, theory or model through the published literature, to identify and critically evaluate significant contributions and place them in an appropriate context.
- **Information Literacy Skill 6.** Organising, applying and communicating information sources to others;
  - the ability to manage bibliographic data including using a personal bibliographic software package to search, retrieve and store information;
  - an awareness of the research landscape in the UK and the ability to identify and network with research colleagues working in similar areas;

- a knowledge of the scholarly communication process, and the ability to make informed judgements in selecting appropriate channels for communication;
- an understanding of intellectual property and fair use of copyrighted material, and ensures that text, data and images are obtained and disseminated legally.
- **Information Literacy Skill 7. Keeping up to date and contributing to new information**
  - ability to keep up to date, to find and filter information using electronic current awareness services.

Good practice in research support

There are examples of good practice in this sector that point the way to providing timely information, online support and delivery into research training programmes. This is a rapidly developing area of practice, however, this can only be indicative of work currently undertaken in UK higher education.

Researchers Weekly Bulletin – Manchester Metropolitan University

The Research Support Librarian compiles and distributes an e-mail based bulletin to Research Directors and individual researchers who have asked to be on the mailing list. The *Researchers' Weekly Bulletin* contains announcements of new electronic resources acquired by the Library (for example, databases and journals), news of new websites, trials of web-based databases, announcements of forthcoming conferences and other information of interest to researchers. [http://www.library.mmu.ac.uk/rwb/index.html] (Harrison and Hughes, 2001).

Researcher's Companion – University of Surrey and University of Roehampton

The *Researcher's Companion* was developed to address the information needs of doctoral students at the then Federated University of Surrey (the Universities of Surrey and of Roehampton). It was designed to be used either as a series of modules to be worked through in a linear fashion or by a researcher selecting individual topics of interest in any order. It comprises guidance in literature searching, citing references, copyright and plagiarism, evaluating resources and other items of interest to researchers [http://www.federalsurrey.ac.uk/researcherscompanion] (Rumsey, 2004).

ResIN – Researcher Information Network – Newcastle University

The Researcher Information Network is based on a review of existing services, a survey of user needs and a review of best practice in other institutions. The ResIN webpages were published on October 2001 to provide a coherent point of access to services and information. The ResIN is regularly updated, and fully integrated into the Libraries' web presence, while retaining a distinctive identity. The Research Support Project that underpins ResIN is now an established part of the Library [http://www.ncl.ac.uk/library/resin/] (Bent, 2004).

Conclusion

After a period of rapid change post-1992, research in higher education is entering a consolidation phase. Those institutions at the margins of research activity have the opportunity to invest in the run up to the RAE in 2008 or choose a strategic withdrawal. Following a similar trajectory, the research libraries and the British Library have moved after a decade of reports, policy and funding initiatives to a point where a new national strategy is possible. This can only be positive in creating an infrastructure that meets the needs of future researchers. Research Training encompasses transferable skills, including information skills and library support for research. This has gained a place on the national policy agenda which will have important implications for libraries in delivering support to researchers, including drawing the provision into the realm of quality audit. The guidelines and codes from Research Councils and QAA place a responsibility on library services to be explicit about support for researchers, perhaps pointing in the direction of Subject Librarians dedicated to research support or at least being able to demonstrate that such support is delivered at an appropriate level from existing Subject Librarians. Researchers require support that is sensitive to their situation, and relevant to the broad subject of their research and reject support perceived as being generic or unfocused. Researchers are reluctant to engage in 'training' but in many cases lack adequate information skills. They prefer support that is individual, informed, timely and sensitive to the research lifecycle. They may make more or less use of the library as a physical entity depending on their disciplinary approach but increasingly value services delivered by the library and Subject Librarians. In addition to an awareness of some electronic resources, there are gaps in knowledge of resources away from home institutions and outside higher education. The emphasis on collaboration and co-operation among institutions may point the way for Subject Librarians in particular regions or within subject disciplines to join together and share ideas, support and training materials.

References

Arts and Humanities Research Board (AHRB), 2003. *The AHRB's framework of research training requirements* [online]. Available from: http://www.ahrb.ac.uk/

ahrb/website/images/4_93947.pdf [Accessed 11 November 2004].

Bent, M., 2004. ResIN: Research Information at Newcastle University Library. *SCONUL Focus,* 32, 28–30.

Bloor, I., 2001. CORSALL: Collaboration in Research Support by Academic Libraries in Leicestershire, De Montfort University.

Carpenter, J. et al., 2001. Discovering research resources: researchers' use of libraries and other information sources. *Cultural Trends,* 43/44, 3–22.

Chancellor of the Duchy of Lancaster, 1993. *Realising our potential: a strategy for science, engineering and technology/presented to Parliament by the Chancellor of the Duchy of Lancaster by Command of Her Majesty, May 1993.* London: HMSO.

Coopers and Lybrand, 1997. *Funding Councils study of the level and costs of use of higher education libraries by external researchers: Final Report.* London: Coopers and Lybrand.

Department for Education and Skills (DFES), 2003. *The Future of Higher Education* [online]. Available from: http://www.dfes.gov.uk/hegateway/uploads/White%20Pape.pdf [Accessed 11 November 2004].

Economic and Social Research Council (ESRC), 1991. *Postgraduate training guidelines.* London: ESRC.

Economic and Social Research Council (ESRC), 2001. *Postgraduate training guidelines* [online]. Available from: http://www.esrc.ac.uk/esrccontent/postgradfunding/POSTGRADUATE_TRAINING_GUIDELINES_2001.asp [Accessed 11 November 2004].

Erens, B., 1996. How recent developments in university libraries affect research. *Library Management,* 17 (8), 5–16.

Ferguson, R., and Crawford, J., 2001. The use of library and information resources by research staff at Glasgow University. *Library and Information Research News,* 25 (70), 31–38.

Goodwin, P., 2003. Information literacy, but at what level? *In* Martin, A., and H. Rader, (eds), *Information and IT Literacy: Enabling learning in the 21st century.* London: Facet.

Harrison, M.K. and Hughes, F., 2001. Supporting researchers' information needs: the experience of the Manchester Metropolitan University Library. *New Review of Academic Librarianship,* 7, 67–86.

Herman, E., 2001a. End-users in academia: meeting the information needs of university researchers in an electronic age. *ASLIB Proceedings,* 53 (10), 431–457.

Herman, E., 2001b. End-users in academia: meeting the information needs of university researchers in an electronic age. Part 1. *ASLIB Proceedings,* 53 (9), 387–401.

Herman, E., 2003a. Research in progress: some preliminary and key insights into the information needs of the contemporary academic researcher. *ASLIB Proceedings,* 56 (1), 34–47.

Herman, E., 2004b. Research in Progress. Part 2 – some preliminary insights into the information needs of the contemporary academic researcher. *ASLIB Proceedings*, 56 (2), 118–131.

Hewitson, A., 2000. The use and awareness of electronic information services by academic staff at Leeds Metropolitan University. *Library and Information Research News*, 24 (78), 17–22.

Higher Education Funding Council for England (HEFCE), 1993. *Joint Funding Councils' Libraries Review Group: report.* Bristol: HEFCE.

Higher Education Funding Council for England (HEFCE), 1996a. *Guidelines on the quality assurance of research degrees.* London: Higher Education Quality Council.

Higher Education Funding Council for England (HEFCE), 1996b. *Review of postgraduate education.* Bristol: HEFCE.

Higer Education Funding Council for England (HEFCE), 2003. *Improving standards in postgraduate research degree programmes* [online]. Available from: http://www.hefce.ac.uk/pubs/hefce/2003/03_23.htm [Accessed 11 November 2004].

Higher Education Funding Council for England (HEFCE), 2004. *£3 million national framework for UK research information announced: Research Libraries Network promises UK researchers 'joined-up' services* [online]. Available from: http://www.hefce.ac.uk/news/hefce/2004/rln.asp [Accessed 11 November 2004].

Higher Education Quality Council (HEQC), 1996. Guidelines on the *quality assurance of research degrees.* London: Higher Education Quality Council.

H.M. Treasury, 2002. *SET for success: The supply of people with science, technology, engineering and mathematics skills. The report of Sir Gareth Roberts' Review* [online]. Available from: http://www.hmtreasury.gov.uk/Documents/Enterprise_and_Productivity/Research_and_Enterprise/ent_res_roberts.cfm [Accessed 11 November 2004].

Jacobs, H., 1998. Academic Researcher's use of the Internet, and their consequent support requirements. *Library and Information Research News*, 22 (70), 30–34.

Joint Funding Councils' Library Review Group, 1993. *A Summary of* the *Report on Libraries prepared for the HEFCE, SHEFC, HEFCW, and DENI.* Bristol: HEFCE.

Joint Funding Council's Library Review Group 1996. *Joint Funding Council's Library Review: Report of the Group on a National/ Regional Strategy for Library Provision for Researchers* [online]. Available from: http://www.ukoln. ac.uk/services/elib/papers/other/anderson/ [Accessed 11 November 2004].

Joint Statement of the Research Councils' and AHRB 2002. *Skills Training Requirements for Research Students* [online]. Available from: http://www.grad. ac.uk/downloads/rdp_report/rdp_framework_report.pdf [Accessed 11 November 2004].

Library service provision for researchers: proceedings of the Anderson Report seminar organised by LINC & SCONUL, 10 and 11 December 1996. *Cranfield University.*

Markland, M., 2003. Embedding online information resources in Virtual Learning Environments: some implications for lecturers and librarians of the move towards delivering teaching in the online environment. *Information Research* [online], 8 (4). Available from: http://informationr.net/ir/8-4/paper158.html

National Committee of Inquiry into Higher Education (NCIHE), 1997. *Higher education in the learning society* [online]. Available from: http://www.leeds. ac.uk/educol/ncihe/ [Accessed 11 November 2004].

Quality Assurance Agency (QAA), 1999. *Code of Practice for the Assurance of Academic Quality and Standards in higher education: postgraduate research programmes* [online]. Gloucester: QAA. Available from: http://www.qaa.ac.uk/ public/COP/cop99/COP_postgrad.pdf [Accessed 07 February 2005].

Quality Assurance Agency (QAA), 2001. The framework for higher education qualifications in England, Wales and Northern Ireland [online]. Gloucester: QAA. Available from: http://www.qaa.ac.uk/crntwork/nqf/ewni2001/contents. htm [Accessed 07 February 2005].

Quality Assurance Agency (QAA), 2004. *Code of practice for the assurance of academic quality and standards in higher education: Section 1: Postgraduate research programmes* [online]. Gloucester: QAA. Available from: http://www. qaa.ac.uk/public/COP/cop/contents.htm [Accessed 11 November 2004].

Research Support Libraries Group (RSLP), 2001. *Research Support Libraries Group* [online]. Available from: http://www.rslg.ac.uk [Accessed 11 November 2004].

Research Support Libraries Group (RSLP), 2002. *Research Support Libraries Programme* [online]. Available from: http://www.rslp.ac.uk [Accessed 11 November 2004].

Roberts, G., 2003. *Review of research assessment: Report by Sir Gareth Roberts to the UK funding bodies, issued for consultation May 2003* [online]. Available from: http://www.rareview.ac.uk/reports/roberts.asp [Accessed 11 November 2004].

Rumsey, S. 2004. The researcher's companion: enhanced library support for postgraduates. *New Review of Information Networking*, 10 (1), 91–95.

Russell Group, 2004. *The Russell Group* [online]. Available from: http://www. russellgroup.ac.uk [Accessed 11 November 2004].

UK Council for Graduate Education (UKCGE), 2000. *Research training in the humanities for postgraduate students* [online]. Available from: http://www.ukcge. ac.uk/filesup/Humanities.pdf [Accessed 11 November 2004].

UK Council for Graduate Education (UKCGE), 2001. *Research training in the creative & performing arts & design* [online]. Available from: http://www.ukcge. ac.uk/filesup/CPAD.pdf [Accessed 11 November 2004].

UK Council for Graduate Education (UKCGE), 2003. *Research training in the healthcare professions* [online]. Available from: http://www.ukcge.ac.uk/filesup/ Healthcare%20Book.pdf [Accessed 11 November 2004].

UK Council for Graduate Education (UKCGE), 2003. *UK Council for Graduate Education* [online]. Available from: http://www.ukcge.ac.uk/ [Accessed 11 November 2004].

Chapter 11

Serving Different Constituencies: International Students

Frank Trew

Introduction

According to UKCOSA: The Council for International Education, for the year 2002/03 there were some 275,000 international students within the UK higher education system, making up 11 per cent of the total student body. It is this body of students that library personnel have taken an interest in and reported on in a spate of articles from the 1970s onwards. My intention here is to review the main themes that emerge from this literature and to offer some suggestions for further research.

The modern library – the library as alien

For most students academic library is a different world, but for international students the library as we know it in the UK or US is an alien world. Focus groups at the University of Alabama revealed that many minority and international students found the library overwhelming (Norlin, 2001 p. 60), and this is borne out by Meredith at Ohio State University who had a student complain about how complicated the library had become' (1999 p. 20). This is because use of the library in their own country was either not required or the library was a place for study and reference, not for information gathering. Cynthia Helms is not the only researcher who found that 'international students are overwhelmed by the quantity of books and periodicals and the multiplicity of automated tools' (1995 p. 296). The concept of independent library research is also an unfamiliar one (Wayman, 1984 p. 339), and McSwiney, writing about Asian students in Australia, reports the experience of one individual from Indonesia who previously had been used to standing outside the desk while the library officer tried to find the books he wanted, but now was confronted with a very different system, 'like supermarket', where he had to go and find the books himself (1995 p. 107). Hendricks remarks that the Japanese are more likely to buy the books they want than to borrow them from a library, and that reference services are generally unknown (1991 p. 222). Moeckel and Presnell write about the 'functional barriers' to library use experienced by international students: some foreign libraries do not enjoy open stacks; many developing nations have outdated collections; many foreign libraries serve simply as study halls; some libraries are staffed mostly with clerks who may not be helpful in locating information; many international students learn not to expect service and freedom of access in libraries (1995 p. 311). 'What is taken as a matter of course by some of the American students (knowledge of classification systems, alternative approaches to research topics, automation and electronic technologies) is totally unfamiliar territory to most or nearly all of the international students' (Burhans, 1991 p. 5). Mary Beth Allen, surveying international students at the University of Illinois to identify what features were different from libraries in their home countries, found computer database searching, the online catalogue and inter-library loan to be unfamiliar (1993 p. 327). Suzanne Irving writes specifically about the problems international students have with inter-library loan (1994). In addition, the literature identifies concepts such as open stacks, loan period, recall, book return, and self-service issue as being alien to the international student. Classification systems relying on numerical order and alphabetisation can be problematic (Brown, Downey and Race, 1997 p. 81; Liestman, 1992 p. 12; Meredith, 1999 p. 19; Wayman, 1984 p. 339), while some students often struggle with a system that goes from left-to-right and from top-to-bottom (Robertson, 1992 p. 43). Getting to grips with Library of Congress classification and subject headings can be troublesome (Liu, 1993 p. 28). Trying to work out the difference between forenames and surnames can be a source of confusion. Add to this the exposure to all the new information technology (Brown, Downey and Race, 1997 p. 81; McKenzie, 1995 p. 27; Robertson, 1992 p. 37) and the international student can be left floundering.

While some international students recognise the library's complexity (as mentioned by Meredith above), the majority of international students, with their former library experiences in mind, remain unaware of the range of services available in the modern UK or US library, and so rarely use them. It is the librarian's job to introduce them to these 'alien' features: 'if the library could make students aware of those services and the type of information they could provide, more students would use them' (McKenzie, 1995 p. 28). The danger, however, lies in overwhelming the students with too much new information and adding to the anxiety that international students already experience, as reported by Jiao and Onwuegbuzie in several articles on library anxiety (1996, 1997 and 1999). Wales and Harmon review other literature (Westbrook and Debecker and Gilton) that comes to the same conclusion: for many users the library is not a welcoming place and inspires feelings of anxiety. While all college students are subject to library anxiety, culture shock compounds the problem for international students (1998 p. 24). To combat the anxiety, it is imperative that libraries be made as attractive, as welcoming and as comfortable as possible and that all library staff be friendly and professional. Students must be made to feel in control of the library environment (Jiao, Onwuegbuzie and Lichtenstein, 1996 p. 159).

Language and culture – the librarian as communicator

However, there are further hurdles for the international student before they can feel totally in control of the library environment. All the literature comments on the communication difficulties they face, especially as, for many, English may not even be a second language, let alone their first. Natowitz (1995) reviewed 18 journal articles on international students use of US academic libraries and remarked that all the authors commented on the language barrier between librarians and students (p. 5), and Sarkodie. Mensah (1998) noted, 'there is hardly any study about international students in the US that does not mention language as the major problem' (p. 218). He goes on to say, 'language is among the highest criteria by which students are graded and treated in class. Sometimes the first uttered statement in a class will be an indication of the grade international students earn at the end of the semester' (p. 219). It is important that we do not fall into the trap of judging people on such a superficial basis. As Brown, Downey and Race put it: 'Don't interpret lack of English language skills as an indicator of lack of ability' (1997 p. 80). The literature offers suggestions on how to support students, though it is not always in agreement about what is best. Speak slowly is the accepted norm, but this is not always easy to do: 'what makes a foreign language sound so fast ... is that the words are run together [whereas] in class each word was learned separately' (Hendricks, 1991 p. 225). Speak clearly and enunciate the key words? Fine, as long as we do not treat the library patron as less intelligent: the me-Tarzan-you-Jane approach is not necessary (Ormondroyd, 1989 p. 157). Use simple or easy words is other advice, but using 'baby-talk' only further confuses the student and insinuates a low degree of intelligence (Moeckel and Presnell, 1995 p. 312). Staff members should understand that in spite of the simple language being used the students are actually quite sophisticated (Greenfield, Johnston and Williams, 1986 p. 230). Hendricks goes further and calls the simple-language approach dangerous advice. English as a Second Language is learned from textbooks and literature so 'everyday words used in family, among friends, when shopping ... may never have been encountered by a foreign student' (p. 225). Liestman makes a similar point when he states that 'overseas English classes usually emphasise reading and grammar over communication ...The objective of these classes is not so much to teach English as much as it is to pass college entrance exams' (1992 p. 11). McSwiney makes the same point when she states 'for many overseas students the English language within the learning experience may have been restricted to listening and reading (input). Thus their experience of speaking and writing (output) is often quite limited' (1995 p. 30). Rephrasing what you say can help, but do not repeat the same thing: if the listener did not understand the first time, saying a word or phrase over and over again is not going to make it any clearer (Ormondroyd, 1989 p. 157).

Further common advice is to avoid jargon, colloquialisms, and idioms because, while they may add colour and vitality to the language, 'international students occasionally struggle to comprehend the context and meaning of [these] in conversations' (Wang and Frank, 2002 p. 212). However, this is easier said than done, as the native speaker may not always be aware of using these idioms (Hendricks, 1991 p. 225). Watkins tells us not to make jokes unless the students are excellent speakers of English (1996 p. 77) and Liestman reiterates this point saying that jokes and allusions may not translate well (1992 p. 14).

Several authors comment on the difference between reading speeds and oral comprehension: overseas students read English at half the speed of British students

(Robertson, 1992 p. 47); an average Asian's reading speed is half that of the average American student (Wayman, 1984 p. 337). To help overcome this, the advice is to use visual aids to reinforce the spoken word because 'visual presentations are more easily comprehended than just audio...' (Philip Rappaport quoted by Liestman, 1992 p. 13; Spanfelner, 1991 p. 71). However, it should not be assumed that all international students are alike. Liestman reports on researchers at BYU-Hawaii who found that some ESL students respond better to written instruction than oral, while for others the reverse is true: Polynesians did better orally, Chinese and Koreans did better in written and reading assignments, the Japanese showed no significant difference (p. 12). As well as using visual aids, it may be necessary to ask the patron to write down any troublesome word or words (Wales and Harmon, 1998 p. 32) or write down yourself words that may not be familiar to the students (Watkins, 1996 p. 77; Brown, Downey and Race, 1997 p. 80).

Library staff should also be alert to some of the communication problems the students themselves might have. For example, the student may have mastered all the rules of grammar but be using words translated directly from their native language and so the English sense is difficult to fathom. Or some students may speak English words in non-standard ways, or may speak English with an accent that is occasionally unintelligible to others (Wang and Frank, 2002 p. 211), so much so that many college campuses [in the States] offer accent reduction training for all international students (Sarkodie-Mensah 1992, p. 221). Burhans makes a similar point stating that the language problem is likely to arise 'more from a dialect or non-standard English usage that middle-class, white, female librarians (the largest single personnel category in academic libraries) have not been exposed to' (1991 p. 5). The issue of accent, of course, works both ways: if it is difficult for native speakers sometimes to understand a strong Glaswegian or Liverpuddlian accent, how much more difficult for the non-native speaker. All of this highlights the fact that there is more to language communication than merely learning vocabulary: grammar, accent, intonation, the 'musical flow of words' all contribute to the exchange, and the international student may have difficulty with any or all of these.

If the spoken word is fraught with problems, there is also the added layer of non-verbal communication. How we stand, walk or gesture, and even the physical distance we place between themselves and our students, may convey an unintended meaning. For example, North Americans feel comfortable at a conversational distance approximately five feet apart while Arabs feel comfortable at two feet (Ball and Mahoney quoted by McKenzie, 1995 p. 9; Kflu and Loomba, 1990 p. 527). This may cause some staff to feel their personal space is being invaded when talking with students who approach too near, perhaps culminating in the comic scenario of the student getting closer and closer as the staff member retreats further and further until backed into a corner. The Japanese may nod and appear to indicate understanding when what they really mean is that they are listening (Moeckel and Presnell, 1995 p. 312). Looking someone in the eye, intended perhaps as a way of being attentive or offering encouragement, might be perceived by another culture as being defiant or too familiar, especially where the contact is between the female librarian and the male student (Liestman quoted by Maloy, 2000 p. 2; Robertson, 1992 p. 42; Wayman, 1984 p. 337): It is certainly considered discourteous and disrespectful in Japan (Meredith, 1999 p. 21). It is impolite to hand anything to a Muslim Arab with your left hand and an African student might easily misconstrue a librarian pointing as a command to go away (Robertson, 1992 p. 42). Chinese students may correlate 'correct posture' with respect for others. Middle Eastern students may view sitting with one leg crossed over the other as offensive (Wang and Frank, 2992 p. 212). The American 'okay' signal can be misinterpreted as vulgar or obscene in other countries (Meredith, 1999 p. 22), as recent HSBC advertising has made clear.

There can also be cultural misunderstandings regarding time-keeping, attitudes towards the sexes and attitudes towards authority. An English student running fifteen or twenty minutes late to an appointment with us may come in full of apologies. The Egyptian student may come in full of smiles (by way of greeting) with no conception that they are late. Obviously the definition of 'being on time' differs from one country to the next (Wayman, 1984 p. 337), with some cultures viewing appointment times as relative, not exact (Moeckel and Presnell, 1995 p. 313). A librarian's gender may influence the way an international student approaches them for example, Middle Eastern students, typically, may not respect or believe the advice of a female librarian (Robertson, 1992 p. 42, Wayman, 1984 p. 337). Other international students come from a more stratified society and may view the librarian as an inferior (Moeckel and Presnell, 1995 p. 313), and, viewing the librarian on the information desk as a lowly subordinate, may insist on speaking to a higher authority (Wayman, 1984 p. 337). Social class differences may make some students too embarrassed to admit they do not know something, or students from relatively privileged backgrounds may be used to having other people doing the running around for them and expect the librarian to do the same (Brown, Downey and Race, 1997 p. 79). The whole concept of self-sufficiency, which is the model in most UK academic libraries, may be alien to some of the international students.

The most common solution to overcome the language barrier is to provide plenty of handouts to students, amongst which there should be a glossary of library terms that need explanation. Of course, such a glossary would be beneficial to all students, not just the international ones, as student knowledge of library jargon is somewhat limited. When I replaced the phrase 'Library catalogue' with 'Library OPAC' on our library website I was rather taken aback when some students reported that they could no longer find books from the website. I thought they meant that the link was not working. Only after talking with them for a while did I realise they did not understand that the OPAC *was* the library catalogue. Similarly, Wang and Frank report on a student focus group where the term 'checking out books' was associated with paying for them, so the library staff changed 'Check Out Books' to 'Borrow Books' (p. 211). Marama's survey of international students in a Nigerian university reveals similar problems in the understanding of library terminology (1998 p. 94), so the problem seems to be a universal one. Pemberton and Fritzler's article (2004) sums up the whole issue: 'Don't let library lingo get in the way of learning'. Pemberton argues that, while students do not need to become little librarians, they do need to understand various concepts behind the terminology. She refers to five guides to library lingo at universities throughout the States (p. 155) and she herself plans on surveying students at the University of North Carolina-Wilmington to find out which library-related terms students there do not understand.

If library jargon can be confusing for native speakers, it is even more difficult for international students. Howze and Moore measured international students' understanding of concepts related to the use of library-based technology and concluded that 'language is enough of a barrier to the non-native speaker without the additional layers of jargon and the vocabulary of technology' (2003 p. 64). This is especially so if services such as database searching, inter-library loan and term paper consultation do not exist in their home libraries (Kflu and Loomba, 1990 p. 525). Obviously the guide is only really useful if it is well-constructed, so concise text, no complicated sentence structure, and even refraining from using all capital letters for titles or headings which might confuse students not familiar with the Roman alphabet, is the advice of Liestman (1992 p. 13). But if done well, producing the glossary helps not only with the language difficulties that students might have, but also as a means of publicising the services that are available. Ormondroyd (1989) reports that, after producing a library vocabulary for their international students at Cornell University, 'we found ourselves being asked more questions about the concepts we were trying to put across' (p. 153).

I think that the majority of people working with students, let alone international students, recognize the importance of producing handouts on library services and resources. The American College and Research Libraries' literacy standards explicitly state: 'Libraries should provide as many print and online aids as possible' (quoted in Baron and Strout-Dapaz, 2001 p. 319). Where there is less agreement is in the assumption made by several authors that, in producing these guides, they will not only provide an explanation of library terminology, but that they will also *translate* that terminology into the student's own language. The international students section of the Association of College and Research Libraries (ACRL-IS) has done just this and produced a multilingual glossary (http://ww.ala.org/ala/acrlbucket/publicationsacrl/ multilingual.htm) that translates English library-related terms into Chinese, Korean, Japanese, French and Spanish. Liu is not a lone voice in the recommendation that, in addition to the glossary, 'the library's basic rules and procedures should be written in the student's native languages as well as English' (1993 p. 29).

Sandra Marcus (2003) advocates 'Multilingualism at the reference desk', though this does not meet with overwhelming support. The main issue in the debate here seems to be whether we are doing the students a disservice by communicating in their native language, when their language of instruction is English. Some take the line that international students should not have chosen to study here in the UK unless they are fluent in English and fully understand the culture. Marcus, on the other hand, is on the side of providing multilingual help to students arguing that 'a few moments of native language conversation will do little to detract from the hours of English practice'. She remarks later that 'of course, we are not all multilingual and we cannot communicate in all the languages spoken by the students ... All we can do is attempt the best assistance we can for as many students as we are able to reach' (p. 336). We can see a similar strategy in society at large: my local health authority has just sent a letter that is translated into Albanian, Chinese, French, Polish, Portuguese, Spanish, Turkish, Somali, Vietnamese and Russian. Voting information is often produced in different languages, and which languages will depend on the ethnic mix of the target population and even street signs may be in different languages, as anyone who has walked through Soho's China Town or the East End's Brick Lane can testify. The same approach is being extended to the promotion of public libraries where a new site, Multikulti, provides a welcome in 11 languages in its mission 'to support citizenship through the delivery of culturally appropriate and accurately translated information'. Marcus would argue that doing what we can should not infer an injustice towards those whose language we cannot provide. At the same time we should be careful about treating international students as different from our home students (Pritchard, 2004 p. 36).

Within the library it quickly becomes apparent how pervasive an issue multilingualism is. The advent of the Internet, for example, raises issues about multilingual services for students, if only regarding the extent to which foreign-language characters are available on keyboards or browsers, particularly if students are being directed towards international newspapers on the Internet, where reading Chinese, Japanese or some Arabic scripts needs special support. We might also question whether hardcopy newspapers should be provided in the native language itself? Or whether the library should be purchasing materials to support the curricula in foreign languages? Do university tutors and professors accept foreign-language materials in the student's bibliography or works-cited list? Should the library provide recreational materials (novels, videos, DVDs) in foreign languages? Should there be special orientation sessions in native languages? And should this also apply to the library's information literacy classes?

The literature reports many university libraries responding to these issues: Chau (2002/03) at Oregon State Libraries describes the Helping Hands initiative there whose aim is to translate a two-page handout describing library services into different languages. Liestman and Wu (1990) describe library orientation for international students in their native languages at Rutgers University. Downing and Klein (2001) describe a multilingual virtual-tour for students at Baruch College, CUNY. Spanfelner (1991) writes about teaching a library-skills class to international students with an accompanying worksheet in French, Spanish and English. And Marcus, as mentioned above, writes about multilingualism at the reference desk. However, there is something of a shortage, as far as I am aware, of literature describing multilingual initiatives within the United Kingdom. Robertson (1992) mentions that Glasgow University library provides guides in Arabic and Chinese (p. 47). A recent e-mail on LIS-LINK enquired about the take-up of Chinese e-journals within academic libraries as the University of York sought to support their Chinese students (lis-link@jiscmail.ac.uk, 26 November 2004), and the e-mail referred readers to an article which discusses the take-up of Chinese e-journals at Loughborough University (Zhang and Rowland, 1996). A quick search of the top ten websites of the universities listed by

UKCOSA as having the most international students revealed only one with a special library guide for international students. This, from the University of Warwick, states that 'if English is not your first language and you find it difficult to understand the leaflets and guides or what the Library staff say, please tell us'. However, there is no indication of what help is available in such cases.

While language is an issue, this is by no means the only area of concern. Pellegrino's book (2005) looks at the problems faced by international students in expressing their personalities in a foreign language and culture. For example, we are told not to make jokes as international students may not understand them, but conversely, the international student renowned for wisecracking in their native country may come across as a very different type of person if language hinders him/her from expressing this side of their personality.

While language may dictate the personality of the student we encounter, this personality may also be the product of culture. Of course there is a danger of stereotyping the international student, and we are warned that this body of students is not as homogenous as we assume, but nevertheless, there are some characteristics that do seem to be common to certain nationalities. Asian students are 'perceived as more reserved or non-assertive … [and] place an emphasis on harmony and respect for authorities' (Wang and Frank, 2002 p. 210). Thai students pride themselves on being the most polite in the world (Robertson, 1992 p. 39; Moeckel and Presnell, 1995 p. 313). Chinese students are also notoriously polite and shy (Robertson, 1992 p. 39). For Japanese students conformity and unity are of great importance, mistakes are unacceptable and public ignorance is shameful (Hendricks, 1991 p. 222; Moeckel and Presnell, 1995 p. 313; Maloy, 2000 p. 3). Vietnamese students are very obedient in the classroom and, along with Japanese, Chinese and Middle Eastern students, are 'usually verbally passive in class, may respond only to direct questions and learn by observation and practice' (Wayman, 1984 p. 338). Joanne McClure (2001), working with postgraduate international students, comments that her 'experience of working in Asia has been that students are accustomed to sitting attentively and following the teacher's instructions, but when questions are directed at them, they are reluctant to reply in case their answer should be wrong' (p. 143). Indians tend to stress discipline, tact and openness. They value social restraint and self-control (Moeckel and Presnell, 1995 p. 313).

The reference desk – the librarian as helper

These characteristics have implications for us as library staff in many areas, and one of those areas is at the reference desk. Asking for assistance does not always come easy, even to native-born students. It is less easy when using a second language. And when the setting is also foreign it becomes an ordeal (Brigid Ballard (1991), quoted by McSwiney, 1994 p. 200). Coupled with the language difficulties may be the cultural differences just mentioned, so that the student, in the desire to save face, may hesitate to ask for help for fear of making a fool of themselves. All too often students 'approach a librarian with a problem, express it badly and come away with a useless reply because they are too polite to ask again, embarrassed at being thought inadequate, or because the librarian's response merely confused them more' (Robertson, 1992 p. 44). Sometimes the desire to save face makes the student acknowledge that they have understood the assistance being provided even when they have not (Wang and Frank, 2002 p. 212; Hendricks, 1991 p. 224). While the anticipation is that international students might be more reluctant to ask for help, research by Westbrook and Debecker suggests that this is an unfounded assumption, and that in fact both international and native students have trouble equally when it comes to asking for help (Wales and Harmon, 1998 p. 24–25). They might be reluctant to approach library staff because they do not want to disturb staff or the question seems too basic (Jiao, Onwuegbuzie and Lichtenstein, 1996 p. 151–152). However, when they do ask for help, they are, on the whole, pleased with the response that they get, finding staff to be helpful and polite. This, argue Wales and Harmon, heightens the importance of library staff offering assistance in a pro-active manner (p. 33). Meredith is quite blunt about this: 'Be proactive. Do not wait for the user to come to you. Go to the user... If I see someone browsing the shelves I will ask if they need help... Often the clients are grateful for this proactive approach' (p. 22). While appreciating that this is not always easy to do (for example, our own temperament may make us timid in approaching people) nevertheless we should try, even adopting a 'roving reference' approach where possible. At Stirling University 'librarians circulate in the library wearing colourful identity badges which prompt students to stop them and ask for help' (Robertson, 1992 p. 35). Hendricks too makes the point about library staff being the instigator: 'No one wants to ask a 'dumb question' but especially not the Japanese. It is therefore especially important for public service staff to approach the Japanese student to see whether help is needed' (p. 225). On occasion I observe students moving back and forth from the OPAC to the shelves, and with a more and more puzzled look on their faces. Instead of waiting for them to come to me, I approach them. In no case has my offer of help offended them. Occasionally they are happy to manage on their own, but in most cases, as with Meredith, the offer of help is gladly accepted. From an information literacy point of view, these encounters often prove fruitful in allowing the librarian a chance to educate the student on a particular matter. Meredith (1999) makes the point when she writes that the process of answering a request may involve teaching the workings of databases, [or] explaining information packaging (p. 18). Others are more blunt: 'Make every reference encounter an instructional encounter', urge Baron and Strout-Dapaz (2001 p. 319). It is important, however, that in such encounters the librarian uses the opportunity to educate the student, and does not just do the work for them. If the student goes through the process once with you they are more likely to be able to do it for themselves next time. If you do the search and the retrieval then the student is still as ignorant as when they first approached you. In the case of international students the temptation to do the work for them may be even greater: 'Frequently librarians opt to do the work for overseas students rather than struggle with language difficulties and cultural misconceptions. As a result the student does not learn how to complete the task, and the situation continues to occur' (Robertson, 1992 p. 43).

Orientation/Induction – the librarian as guide

While it is sometimes useful to use the reference encounter as an opportunity to educate students, there are more formal ways that are traditionally used. International students attend these, though, as the literature makes clear, not always successfully: 'We may feel a fine sense of a duty accomplished, but the students may leave the library more confused and, worse still, with discouraging impressions of our library systems' (So, 1994 p. 8). Liu (1993) remarks that a common complaint from international students was that 'they could not fully understand what the librarian said during orientation tours' (p. 27), and Moeckel and Presnell's paper (1995) 'grew out of a frustration with the lack of effectiveness of the traditional library tour, which never seemed to alleviate international students' library navigational problems' (p. 310). The solutions put forward generally consider language to be the main problem and so propose alternatives such as video presentations, foreign language guides and multilingual tours. Wayman states that, since listening to English can be a problem for international students, and the disembodied voice of a native speaker enhances the problem, a video with the speaker visible is more effective (p. 340). Robertson reports that Strathclyde has three videos covering welcome, the library catalogue and the world of information (p. 36). Given what was said above about international students use of language and how visual presentations are more easily comprehended, the video is a useful way of providing orientation, or as a supplement to the traditional tour so that those with language difficulties can learn at their own pace. A further means to aid the student learn at their own pace is by producing handouts, and in the student's native language if possible: 'think about providing user-guides in different languages, [or] alternatively, special help-sheets in different languages can be designed to help such groups of students to address particular problems' (Brown, Downey and Race, 1997 p. 80).

Liestman and Wu (1990) report on a native-language orientation programme developed at Rutgers University in Fall 1988 and offered in English, Chinese and Korean. This consisted of a ten-question pre-test, a forty-minute orientation supplemented with overhead transparencies, a ten-question post-test, and an optional tour of the library. While the English students showed a modest improvement in their scores, the programme produced dramatic improvements amongst the Chinese students, demonstrating the efficacy of native-language instruction for incoming international students. At Baruch College, City University of New York (CUNY, 2005) a web-based tour is offered in nine languages. Developing this tour was not easy: non-Roman character sets posed a considerable challenge, translators had to be found amongst the student body, and the translations then had to be reviewed, but the end result was worthwhile as 'all versions of the tour were visited more than 2,500 times in the four months since public release' (Downing and Klein, 2001

p. 502). Meanwhile the State University of New York at Buffalo recruits overseas students fluent in English who are willing to conduct library tours in their own language, accompanied by a librarian as back-up and to represent a friendly face from the library (Robertson, 1992 p. 46 summarising Lopez). The International Cultural Services programme at Oregon State University recruits international students as 'cultural ambassadors'. The library hopes to use these same students as Helping Hands translators (Chau, 2002/03 p. 388). Several initiatives, while not offering formal multilingual tours, try to involve returning international students in the orientation programme to act as guides or potential interpreters for the new students or as a source of information, experience and reassurance as happens at the University of Sunderland (Pritchard, 2004 p. 37). Others recommend offering special sessions for international students: 'conduct 'open houses' for international students' and 'organize formal orientation programmes that focus on the unique issues, needs, and concerns of international students' (Wang and Frank, 2002 p. 212). For these sessions to work well the advice is to keep the groups small: 'have four groups of ten rather than one group of forty' (Moeckel and Presnell, 1995 p. 316); orientation classes and tours can be an efficient method of education if they ... are conducted in small groups (Wayman, 1984 p. 340).

But in the same way that some people object to multilingualism at the reference desk, so some object to multilingual orientation sessions. Both issues are related to the larger issue of bilingual education, a subject dealt with in detail by Rosalie Porter in her book *Forked tongue: the politics of bilingual education*. However, as So (1994) points out, the purpose of library orientation and instruction programmes 'is not to enhance the English proficiency level of international students; rather it is to introduce, as effectively and early as possible, the ... library system' (p. 10). She goes on to say that English is difficult enough for international students. Imposing it to learn the library system, even when native language orientations may be readily available, places the students under great strain at a time when we should be aiming to make their time as stress-free as possible. Furthermore, we are making a great presumption if we think that we can influence the student's mastery of English and acculturation in a short orientation session. Even with native-born English-speaking students there is no guarantee of a successful orientation (p. 11).

Working for an international university where every student is an international student, there are no special sessions for this group in my own institution. Instead we have also abandoned the traditional guided tour, where there was no guarantee that students took much in, and we have abandoned the 30-minute Power-point presentation, which used to be run together with a 30-minute IT presentation. Instead students have to answer a short set of questions by physically moving around the library (to the areas we might have taken them to in the original tour), and they have to either read a poster about the services in that area (the poster containing the answer), or they have to do an actual search in the library OPAC, find an actual back-issue of a periodical, and log on to the library's e-journals page on the Internet. This system seems to have several advantages. By getting the students to do the work themselves it is hoped that information is absorbed in a more lasting way.

Students can work at their own pace but are also encouraged to work together in answering the questions, the rationale being that introducing them to the services is the purpose of the session so where they get the answer from is less important. Furthermore, myself and other library staff – and all library staff can be involved in this – are around to help students find the right answers. This fosters a better relationship between the library staff and the students because the students have actually spoken with a friendly face within the library. What we have found from this is that students will now come and ask library staff about many other issues to do with university orientation in general that they are confused with in those first few days. Of course there are ways in which we could improve our orientation, perhaps introduce a multilingual element, but on the whole the orientation sessions seem to work very well, encouraging both student activity and engendering a friendly rapport with library staff.

Although the initiatives outlined above are aimed to improve the experience for international students, they do not come cheaply: there are resource issues both in terms of personnel and budget. Producing multilingual guides and orientation can be time-consuming, and depends on having the staff and/or student help to provide the translations. The Helping Hands project found that, as they did not always have the same 'cultural ambassadors' every season, there was not always a student to translate a certain language. Another concern was the quality of the translations since the library staff were unable to verify the accuracy of all the translated guides (Chau, 2002/03 p. 391). Providing multilingual tours also requires staff or reliable students to conduct them, and we need to resolve whether providing a guide or orientation in, for example, Spanish, because the library happens to have a Spanish-speaking member of staff, is a disservice to other international students who are not offered a similar service. Likewise, if signs, instructions and other guides are translated, how many of them are translated, and in which languages? The literature tells us to find out the international make-up of the student body as a means to deciding what languages to offer, but what number of students makes all the investment of time, energy and resources worthwhile?

Information literacy instruction – the librarian as teacher

In addition to offering orientation or induction, many academic university libraries also offer training in information literacy. However, the literature that describes native-language instruction is usually referring to a one-off, 50-minute session that is often part of the induction process such as Deborah Spanfelner's library research skills class. In my own institution we run an 80-minute class each week for the first ten weeks of a semester, which all second-semester students are obliged to take. Trying to offer this amount of instruction in multiple languages is well-nigh impossible: we have a student body recruited from 94 different countries and we have neither enough language expertise within the library to provide instruction in every native language nor enough staff to deliver all the sessions that would be required.

Of more immediate concern within the classroom are the different experiences of education that students bring with them. Ward, Bochner and Furnham (2001) devote a chapter to international students as 'sojourners', and state:

> Two dimensions that exert strong influence on classroom communication and interactions are individualism-collectivism and power distance . In the broadest terms students from individualist cultures are more likely to want to 'stand out' in class, to ask questions, give answers and engage in debate. Students from collectivist cultures, in contrast, are more strongly motivated to 'fit in'. They are less likely to be verbally interactive in classes and are usually unwilling to draw attention to themselves. Collectivism is strongly related to power distance, and those students from high power distance cultures are also less likely to question and debate. This is generally seen as an inappropriate challenge to the teacher, which may result in loss of face. Students from high power distance cultures are more strongly motivated to show respect to teachers and to maintain formal and distant relationships with them' (Ward, Bochner and Furnham p. 156).

They continue, stating, 'from one perspective quiet but attentive collectivist students may be perceived as uninterested or withdrawn by individualist teachers. From another viewpoint, the relatively frequent interruptions to lectures by individualist students may be seen as rude and unmannered by their collectivist classmates' (p. 157). These sentiments are echoed in other literature: 'One of the biggest challenges is the classroom culture' (Sarkodie-Mensah, 1998 p. 216), and participating in class is a concept that is foreign to many international students. Many customs of Japanese society, and of Japanese higher education in particular, are diametrically opposed to American values, and presumably UK ones too. In Japan students are not expected to show initiative: 'they do what they are assigned, and they are not assigned creative or imaginative tasks' (Hendricks, 1991 p. 222). At Sheffield Hallam University, Diana Ridley (2004) writes about a small-scale research study into the teaching and learning experiences of international students and their tutors, and remarks that 'it is often the students who have not had similar language, literacy and learning experiences to those encountered in the higher education environment who do not have the cultural capital needed to succeed quickly and easily in the new domain' (p. 92). She concludes by asking us to consider 'whether dominant ideologies should be changed, and in what ways it is possible to learn from and build bridges with the different learning cultures students bring with them' (p. 105). Wang and Frank (2002) follow a similar line of thought urging us to become familiar with the learning styles of international students (p. 213), referring us to Paula Ladd's *Learning style and adjustment issues of international students* as a means to do so.

One of the specific issues that emerges with regard to learning styles is the difference in attitude towards the tutor. Whereas US and UK education encourages a familiar classroom interaction between student and tutor, Asian students, for example, see the teacher as the unquestioned authority and worthy of great respect. Sarkodie-Mensah (1998) writes about the lecture notes of the professor being the gospel truth for some international students (p. 216), so much so that they may find it difficult to engage in challenging academic discourses with their professor. McSwiney (1997) writes about this difference in the context of Asian students in Australia. Wayman (1984) observes that Vietnamese children are very obedient in class and the teacher's status may supersede even that of the father (p338), and an article in *The Economist* (1999) talks about China where 'class discussion and questioning the teacher are rare and often discouraged'. Burhans (1991) goes on to remark that the status accorded to teachers may make Asian students reticent about approaching [even] library staff (p. 4).

The respect for the tutor also leads to different classroom dynamics in terms of eliciting responses to questions within the class. Studies have found that teachers give less attention to the quiet, passive student of foreign cultures (Wayman, 1984 p. 338). Sometimes it is tempting to leave well alone and enjoy what appears to be a smooth running class. At other times the passivity is interpreted as a lack of interest which can irritate the tutor. But the real fact is that some international students feel uncomfortable answering or raising questions in class, either because they do not want to lose face by giving the wrong answer, or because they are not used to the informal rapport between student and teacher that Western education often encourages.

The Economist article about Chinese students observes that memorising and regurgitating texts matter a lot. Robertson (1992) makes a similar observation with regard to developing countries generally (p. 42) where there is a greater emphasis on memorization and recitation than on developing and applying original ideas. McSwiney (1994) reports on her experience with Indian students which involved adapting to copious note taking and much memorising (p. 199). And Ridley (2004) quotes two students (an Italian and a Nigerian) who both comment on the difficulty they have with independent thought: 'In my country students are not required to express their own opinions', says one, and 'I'm better at repeating what I already know,' says the other (p. 95). The emphasis on memory and recitation, and the respect for authority figures we have discussed, may mean that the student considers it impertinent to improve on the words of a teacher or author by rephrasing them, and this can lead to accusations of plagiarism (Brown, Downey and Race, 1997 p. 81). Liu (1993) encountered a similar problem in a survey of Asian students at the University of California, Berkeley, and reports similar findings by Sally Wayman and Dick Feldman (p. 29). Greenfield, Johnston and Williams (1986) remark that, while certain cultures view published materials as community property that can be used, borrowed or changed according to individual needs, this is a view which runs counter to Western copyright laws and the value attached to the ownership of printed works (p. 229). That intellectual property rights and issues of plagiarism are a particular area of confusion for international students is noted in the ACRL's Literacy Standards for International Students which recommend open communication about these ethical issues to help students avoid potential academic dishonesty issues.

Another difficulty is that, whereas in the US and UK independence is rewarded, for many Asian students group achievement is considered far more important. But the borderlines between what is regarded as collaboration and what is considered cheating can be interpreted differently, especially where students come from a culture that values the group above the individual, and where supporting one another is paramount, even to the point of sharing written assignments amongst each other. Wayman (1984) remarks on this and observes that the strong emphasis in the Middle and Near East on friendship as a great virtue makes cheating an occasional problem (p. 338).

Although collaboration amongst international students may give rise to accusations of cheating on occasion, there are generally benefits to be gained from turning to ones' peers. Much of the literature observes that international students would sooner go to a fellow compatriot for assistance over any other source, and they use their peers for help in navigating the library or in understanding the information literacy classes (Liestman, 1992 p. 12; Liu, 1993 p. 27; McSwiney, 1995 p. 128; Marama, 1998 p. 95; Sarkodie-Mensah, 1998 p. 217; Wang and Frank, 2002 p. 209; Wayman, 1984 p. 340). Of course, this only works properly if the compatriot they turn too is well informed; if not then both students remain ignorant or misinformed. But the librarian can use this predilection of international students to stick together to the library's advantage: if you can educate one international student then they will often do your job in educating their fellows (Meredith, 1999 p. 20).

Information literacy, as defined by the ACRL, embodies the ability to effectively plan research, to efficiently gather information, to critically evaluate information and sources, to properly use information, and to ethically acknowledge sources. These concepts are difficult enough to get across to native-born students, without the added dimension of cultural difference. We have noted some of the difficulties with regard to the ethics of plagiarism and copyright. When it comes to efficiently gathering information, Victoria Maloy reports on a 1995 study that showed that international students who had a more limited vocabulary had difficulties in creating search phrases that utilized plurals, synonyms and alternate words. The limited vocabulary used in their queries resulted in fewer successful searches (Maloy, 2000 p. 4). When you try to teach Boolean operators, truncation or proximity searching, the problems are compounded. As Beth Patton (2002) notes, some languages do not distinguish between singulars and plurals, which affects the student's ability to understand truncation, and in the case of Chinese dialects that neither use plurals nor use connectors such as *and*, truncation and Boolean searching are especially difficult concepts for these students to grasp (p. 35).

Patton makes an interesting, additional point when she states that 'researchers advise librarians to present a realistic model of research by not producing a demonstration in which all search strategies work the first time ... Perfect presentations imply that searching is easy' (p. 16). Instead, it is the process of research which should be important, so watching the librarian model a procedure of poor choices and making mistakes, and then succeeding through problem-solving and revision of search strategies will be a much better approach. Sitting with a student and researching with them allows them to see the different attempts that can be made before finding what seem the better options. This is fine pedagogically as an opportunity to show the student the 'hit-and-miss' nature of research. Within our information literacy classes my colleague and I try to stress that research can be a time-consuming process, and involves trials and errors and revisiting resources with new vocabulary in mind. Drawing student attention to where the alternative vocabulary may be found is an important dimension of our information literacy classes.

In the information literacy classes we also try to balance the introduction of resources (the tools of research) with the techniques for searching (the strategies or process). In introducing the resources we adopt the advice in the literature and reinforce what we are saying by getting the students to use equipment as 'students often learn better by a sustained hands-on approach' (Helms, 1995 p. 302; Hendricks, 1991 p. 225; Liestman, 1992 p. 13; Meredith, 1999 p. 20; Wales and Harmon, 1998 p. 33; Watkins, 1996 p. 77). Students value the hands-on approach and their reviews at the end of each course often ask for more time in class using the resources. Getting the students to think critically, however, is more difficult, and for international students the problems can be multiplied. 'When the titles *People* and *TESOL Quarterly* are equally unfamiliar, determining which periodical is appropriate for research takes on new difficulties' (Patton, 2002 p. 76). Librarians can help with some of these problems, as evidenced in the added instruction session described by Ormondroyd (1989). Students were asked to describe their research strategies, to talk about the resources they had found, and to discuss any problems they had encountered. The librarian would be there to help them with their problems, *and* to comment on their research process (p. 155). International students will benefit from this as well: we may just need more patience when providing the feedback.

Cultural awareness – the librarian as diplomat

The more exposed we are to diversity in any of its manifestations, (and this is obviously broader than just recognising differences in nationality, as disability, ethnicity, gender, and sexual orientation are all aspects of multicultural diversity), the easier it is to accommodate international students. Papangelis (2000), at Western Kentucky University, writes about sensitivity training in the academic library which covers racial minority groups, students with disabilities, and other non-traditional students, as well as international students. Helms (1998), addressing the ASDAL conference on the topic of developing multiculturalism in academic libraries, produced a checklist of what we can do as librarians to foster multiculturalism. Some of the suggestions we have encountered previously, such as avoiding stereotypes and generalizations, and appreciating a wide range of cognitive styles, and making international students feel comfortable on campus. To these may be added: developing a tolerance of other cultures, encouraging the understanding of cultural diversity in an academic setting, and becoming adept at cultural appraisal and empathy. This latter is particularly recommended by Kflu and Loomba (1990) in their article on the culturally diverse student population (p. 527) and Wang and Frank (2002) also claim 'it is important to be familiar with key differences and similarities of the various cultures and histories' (p. 209). But So (1994) turns the tables on those who place the onus on the international student: 'Instead of focusing on acculturation of others, we would do ourselves a far greater service by shifting our attitudes to what may be called the "crossculturation" process, a mutual acculturation process that goes both ways' (p. 14).

In the context of multicultural awareness, Baron and Strout-Dapaz's literature review identified two dominant themes: the necessity for staff-training, and inter-departmental collaboration (2001 p. 318). On the one hand some writers suggest hiring staff from different nationalities, both to increase the cultural profile of the library, and also to provide opportunities for the multilingual services that have been mentioned above (Helms, 1995 p. 302; Onwuegbuzie, Jiao and Daley, 1997 p. 11; Wang and Frank, 2002 p. 213). At the University of Arizona, for example, the Central Reference Department compiled a list of library staff members who could speak foreign languages and so could be called upon to act as interpreters (Greenfield, Johnston and Williams, 1986 p. 231). Nance-Mitchell's whole article (1996) is devoted to the issue of a multicultural library where she writes at some length about hiring minority librarians (p. 410), and the need to train faculty members to become more understanding of minority needs (p. 409). On the other hand the training of native-born staff is an important theme: 'proper staff training can provide an awareness of the implications of both cultural and language problems and will reduce tension and increase staff confidence when dealing with overseas students. It is therefore important to train *all* library staff, not just those involved in formal user-education' (Robertson, 1992 p. 44). Wayman (1984) recommends an in-service training programme that involves both non-professional and professional staff (p. 340), Ormondroyd (1989) writes about a one-day workshop to raise the consciousness of library staff (p. 52), and Greenfield, Johnston and Williams (1986) report on a programme training library staff to communicate effectively with international students, which incorporated a simulation game, BaFá BaFá, allowing participants to explore the emotions of culture shock (p. 228). Sarkodie-Mensah (1992) recommends librarians taking classes in order to understand languages and cultures, and argues that people would soon come to realize how tiresome speaking another language is, and how much effort is required. Librarians would grow more patient with, less frustrated at and more receptive to student users who may require more time at the desk or more help in the classroom. McSwiney (1994) echoes this sentiment, writing 'the value of a sensitive, enlightened staff can make a positive contribution to the experience of a student' (p. 200). Within the UK, Oliver Pritchard (2004), at the University of Sunderland, ensures that staff there have an awareness of cultural differences, and several staff have participated in Diversity Day training (p. 37).

Natowitz, in his review of literature back in 1995, mentions in passing 'the creation of new positions dedicated specifically to serving international students' (p. 14), and Liu (1993) wrote 'it is necessary that those institutions with a substantial number of foreign students have library staff with a special responsibility for foreign students' (p. 30). So (1994) suggests a member of library staff 'could be designated to act as the international student contact person' (p. 15) and she mentions libraries such as the University of California at Santa Cruz and the University of California at Irvine both of which have created the position of Multicultural Services Librarian. My own cursory search found only one institution in the UK, the University of Warwick, where someone has been given specific responsibility for international students.

The second theme identified by Baron and Strout-Dapaz (2001), collaboration between departments, is indeed a dominant one in the literature: close collaboration with academic staff would be the key (Robertson, 1992 p. 38); librarians and college officials should co-ordinate their efforts (Onwuegbuzie, Jiao and Daley, 1997 p. 11); co-operate with other units on the campus is essential to facilitate success for international students (Wang and Frank, 2002 p. 213); the common trend now is for campuses to establish formal and informal networks that meet regularly to address the needs of international students (Sarkodie-Mensah, 1998 p. 220). These informal networks can help library staff cultivate relations with students outside the library that may translate into a positive experience for the students when they do come in.

Cultural diversity also has implications for the librarian as teacher as we are urged to ditch a Eurocentric curriculum and present a broad array of cultural perspectives. Natowitz (1995) reports on research by Koehler and Swanson who found that 'the use of international materials in the practice research [within a library class] helped to keep students' interest' (p. 8). I understand this to mean not just using a variety of materials to keep students entertained, but using a range of materials that responds to the cultural mix of the class we are teaching. For myself, information literacy classes are a continuous test of my own multicultural awareness and sensitivity as I try to help students research either the Intifada, weddings in Hinduism or Judaism, or doing business in Korea.

However, being multiculturally aware also carries some dangers and this is where the librarian needs to employ the tact of the diplomat. Many students, warns Sarkodie-Mensah (1992), are proud of their countries and will defend them against any negative perceptions. Expressing interest in other countries is admirable, but 'librarians should refrain from volunteering knowledge about countries unless they can be certain that such communication will not jeopardize interactions' with the international student. Some students are offended by people pretending to know too much about their country or its customs, or by the question 'Where are you from?' when it means, for example, 'Are you from China or Taiwan?' Politics and religion can be other taboo subjects: what, for example, is the student's view of Salman Rushdie – a desecrator of Islam, or a champion of free speech? While *we* might freely lampoon royalty or politicians, international students may not appreciate comments made at the expense of their political or religious leaders.

Collection development – the librarian goes cultural shopping

There is relatively little in the literature about collection development for international students, but it is important, especially as materials may be needed to support the multiculturalism that we are asked to bring into our teaching. The literature talks about the library acquiring dictionaries, of course, and perhaps materials to help students improve their English. But collection development is much more than this. 'The dominance of a white, middle-class culture on campus may make minorities feel left out or adrift from any connection with their own heritage. Libraries can help mitigate this somewhat by acquiring popular print and non-print materials that provide a connection to that missing element' (Burhans, 1991 p. 6). While we might not agree about the dominance of a white, middle-class culture – I would hope that things have changed somewhat since 1991 – the idea of helping students make a connection with their own culture is important. McKenzie's survey (1995) revealed that 78.8 per cent of international students would like the library to contain more multicultural materials (p. 25). The type of materials most students would like were native newspapers, followed by native journals or magazines. Roy Ziegler's whole article (1997) focuses on providing international students with 'country of origin' news to ease the bouts of homesickness and provide a welcome resource, and many others support this (such as Baron and Strout-Dapaz, 2001 p. 320; Kflu and Loomba, 1990 p. 527; So, 1994 p. 15; Wales and Harmon, 1997 p. 29). The newspapers do not need to be in the native language (though we have discussed this issue above). Rather the students are interested in keeping up-to-date with issues relating to their own countries (Onwuegbuzie, Jiao and Daley, 197 p. 7). Wayman (1984) commented that 'a common complaint of foreign students is that libraries have a paucity of materials on their own countries' (p. 340), but goes further than just recommending newspapers. 'If a university is educating a large group of students from India, then its collection should have current materials on India' (p. 340), a sentiment echoed by Kflu and Loomba (1990 p. 527). While it is true that most of the library's collection development budget will be spent on purchasing materials to support the curriculum, there is an argument for some money to be put aside to acquire items that cater for international students, or increase our own multicultural awareness. Acquiring these materials is not just about making students feel welcome. Liu (1993) comments on the tendency for international students to pursue research topics rooted in their native country or culture (p. 29), and my own experience supports this observation. In fact, one of the assignments on our Principles of Writing course explicitly asks students to research an issue of social concern from their own country so I find myself having to purchase books on street children in Brazil, for example, or environmental problems in India, or post-traumatic stress in Serbia in the aftermath of the Balkan wars. In fact there is a specific onus for all our courses to have multicultural or multinational content wherever possible. In addition to providing materials that support student research, there is also scope for purchasing more recreational materials that reflect our multicultural world; for example, world cinema and world music are increasingly a feature of our daily lives, rather than being confined to an art-house cognoscenti. What are less readily available are the databases that are very multicultural in content. Instead they still tend to have a US or European focus, and I find myself almost apologising to students that our electronic newspaper database, while being an excellent source for international newspapers, nevertheless does not really cover the African continent or the Middle Eastern region.

Where do we go from here?

Having reviewed the literature there are certain emergent questions that might profit from further research. It was said that the library was an alien world to the international student, but does this still hold true today? Even if the academic library in other countries is very different from that in the UK, Europe or the US, are the international students *we recruit* so unfamiliar with the modern academic library? Do they suffer the culture shock that the literature talks about or are they, for example, coming from international schools where they may already have been exposed to a multicultural environment? The fees that are charged are generally high, so does this mean that the students coming to the UK need to be wealthy? If so, does this mean that their educational experiences back home have been privileged, and the schools they attended were well-equipped? Most students seem to be familiar with the Internet, even if not quite information literate, which would make me assume that students nowadays have easy access to information technology. However, there are still some students who report feeling initially intimidated by computers, and we have certainly had one student who needed a lot of coaching in using a computer. Is this technophobia a product of their status as an international student or something else? One area of research might be to investigate the characteristics and background of the international students we recruit today.

Language and communication have been explored at some length. But while the problems are mentioned many times in the literature, what would be interesting to know is what impact the proposed solutions have had. There are many examples of solutions from the US, but what is being done here in the UK? Do libraries produce multilingual glossaries or guides? What policies are in place regarding multilingualism generally? It would be useful to research initiatives in these areas, and perhaps present some of the guides to the wider community.

Likewise, it would be good to hear about orientation, induction or information literacy classes for international students. The University of York has a Widening Participation Officer who arranges a special induction programme for international students in which the library is involved. Reading University produced library induction guides for international students. I have reported on our own orientation and referred to our information literacy course here in Richmond. It would be useful to research what works in other institutions.

I have also mentioned the University of Warwick which has a librarian with specific responsibility for international students. It would be interesting to know if other libraries have someone with specific responsibility, what their job description entails, and whether this is their sole job, or whether it is taken on alongside their other duties.

Finally, do any staff receive training in cultural awareness or multicultural etiquette? In the light of this research I have approached some of our faculty to see if they could offer cultural awareness training here, and hope to set up a training session for library staff shortly. I have also just come across a book entitled *Working with international students: a cross-cultural training manual* by Colin Lago and Alison Barty which I hope to obtain for library staff to consult and glean ideas from. What initiatives are in place elsewhere? I think we could all benefit from sharing our experiences, the projects that have been undertaken, and the successes and failures we have encountered.

References

Allen, M. B., 1993. International students in academic libraries: a user survey. *College and Research Libraries*, 54 (4), 323–33.

Baron, S., and Strout-Dapaz, A., 2001. Communicating with and empowering international students with a library skills set. *Reference Services Review*, 29 (4), 314–326.

Brown, S., Downey, B., and Race, P., 1997. *500 tips for academic librarians*. London: Library Association Publishing.

Burhans, S., 1991. Serving the information needs of the international and minority students at a small college library. ERIC Document ED335714.

Chau, M.Y., 2002. Helping hands: serving and engaging international students. *The Reference Librarian*, 79/80, 383–393.

City University of New York (CUNY), 2005. William and Anita Newman Library Virtual Tour. Available from: http://newman.baruch.cuny.edu/about/v_ tour [Accessed 31 March 2005].

Downing, A., and Klein, L.R., 2001. A multilingual virtual tour for international students. *College and Research Libraries News*, 62 (5), 500–501.

Economist, The 2003. Western promise, Chinese students. 29 March. 2003.

Greenfield, L., Johnston, S., and Williams, K., 1986. Educating the world: training library staff to communicate effectively with international students. *Journal of Academic Librarianship*, 12 (4), 227–231.

Helms, C. M., 1998. Developing multiculturalism in academic libraries [online]. *ASDAL 18th Annual Conference minutes* 24 June 1998. Available from: http:// www.asdal.org/minutes/helms.html [Accessed 31 March 2005].

Helms, C. M., 1995. Reaching out to the international students through bibliographic instruction. *The Reference Librarian*, 51/52, 295–307.

Hendricks, Y., 1991. The Japanese as library patrons. *College and Research Libraries News*, 52 (4), 221–225.

Hofstede, G., 2001. *Culture's consequences: comparing values, behaviors, institutions and organizations across nations*. 2nd ed. London: Sage.

Howze, P.C., and Moore, D.M., 2003. Measuring international students' understanding of concepts related to the use of library-based technology. *Research Strategies*,

19 (1), 57–74.

Irving, S., 1994. Addressing the special needs of international students in interlibrary loan: some considerations. *Reference Librarian,* 45/46, 111–17.

Jiao, Q.G., Onwuegbuzie, A.J., and Lichtenstein, A.A., 1996. Library anxiety: characteristics of 'at-risk' college students. *Library and Information Science Research* 18 (2),151–163.

Jiao, Q.G., and Onwuegbuzie, A.J., 2001. Library anxiety among international students. Paper presented at the annual meeting of the Mid-South Educational Research Association (MSERA), Point Clear, Alabama, November 1999. Reprinted in *Urban Library Journal,* 11 (1), 16–27.

Kflu, T. and Loomba, M.A., 1990. Academic libraries and the culturally diverse student population. *College and Research Libraries News,* 51 (6), 524, 526–7.

Ladd, P.D., and Ruby, R. Jr., 1999. Learning style and adjustment issues of international students. *Journal of Education for Business,* 74 (6), 363–367.

Lago, C.and Barty, A., 2003. Working with international students: a cross-cultural training manual. 2nd ed. London: UKCOSA, 2003.

Liestman, D., 1992. Implementing library instruction for international students. *PNLA Quarterly,* 56, 11–14.

Liestman, D. and Wu, C. 1990. Library orientation for international students in their own language. *Research Strategies,* 8.(4), 191–196.

Liu, Z., 1993. Difficulties and characteristics of students from developing countries in using American libraries. *College and Research Libraries,* 54 (1), 25–31.

McClure, J., 2001.Developing language skills and learner autonomy in international postgraduates. *ELT Journal* 55 (2), 142–148.

McKenzie, D.E., 1995. Survey of library and information needs of the international students at Kent State University. ERIC Document ED369403.

McSwiney, C., 1994. Academic library needs of students from non-English speaking backgrounds in Australia: a position paper and select bibliography. *Australian Library Journal,* 43 (3), 197–217.

McSwiney, C., 1995. *Essential understandings: international students learning libraries.* Adelaide: Auslib Press.

Maloy, V., 2000. *International students and academic libraries* [online]. Available from:http://mingo.info-science.uiowa.edu/~maloy/papers/biblinte.html [Accessed 31 March 2005].

Marama, I.D., 1998. Use of the technological university library by international students. *International Information and Library Review,* 30 (2), 87–96.

Marcus, S., 2003. Multilingualism at the reference desk: keeping students connected. *College and Research Libraries,* 64 (5), 322–323, 336.

Meredith, M., 1999. Confronting the styles and needs of an international clientele. *Information Outlook,* 3 (6), 18–23.

Moeckel, N., and Presnell, J., 1995. Recognizing, understanding and responding: a program model of library instruction for international students. *Reference Librarian,* 51/52, 309–325.

Multikulti: information, advice, guidance and learning materials in community languages. 2005. Available from: http://www.multikulti.org.uk [Accessed 31 March 2005].

Nance-Mitchell, V.E., 1996. A multicultural library: strategies for the twenty-first century. *College and Research Libraries,* 57 (5), 405–413.

Natowitz, A., 1995. International students in US academic libraries: recent concerns and trends. *Research Strategies,* 13 (1), 4–16.

Norlin, E., 2001. University goes back to basics to reach minority students. *American Libraries*, 32 (7), 60–2.

Onwuegbuzie, A.J., Jiao, Q.G. and Daley, C.E., 1997. The experience of non-native English-speaking students in academic libraries in the United States. *MSERA Conference November 1997*. Available from: http://www.msstate.edu/org/msera/ arc1997.htm [Accessed: 31 March 2005].

Ormondroyd, J., 1989. The international student and course-integrated instruction: the librarian's perspective. *Research Strategies*, 7 (4), 148–158.

Papangelis, P., 2004. Leading Ideas 12: Sensitivity training in academic library public services. Washington D.C.: Association of Research Libraries. Available from: http://www.arl.org/diversity/leading/issue12/papangelis.html [Accessed 31 March 2005].

Patton, B.A., 2002. *International students and the American university library*. La Mirada, California: Biola University.

Pellegrino, A.V., 2005. *Study abroad and second language use: constructing the self*. Cambridge: Cambridge University Press.

Pemberton, A. and Fritzler, P., 2004. The language barrier: don't let library lingo get in the way of learning. *College and Research Libraries News*, 65 (3), 154–155.

Porter, R., 1991. *Forked tongue: the politics of bilingual education*. New York, NY: Basic Books.

Pritchard, O., 2004. Are you an international university library? *CILIP Update*, 3 (2), 36–37.

Ridley, D., 2004. Puzzling experiences in higher education: critical moments for conversation. *Studies in Higher Education*, 29 (1), 91–107.

Robertson, J.E., 1992. User education for overseas students in higher education in Scotland. *Journal of Librarianship and Information Science*, 24 (1), 33–51.

Sarkodie-Mensah, K., 1992. Dealing with international students in a multicultural era. *Journal of Academic Librarianship*, 18 (4) 214–216.

Sarkodie-Mensah, K., 1998. International students in the US: trends, cultural adjustments and solutions for a better experience. *Journal of Education for Library and Information Science*, 39(3), 214–222.

SO, S.Y., 1994. *International students and American academic libraries: an empowering relation*. ERIC Document ED369403.

Spanfelner, D.L., 1991. Teaching library skills to international students. *Community and Junior College Libraries*, 7 (2), 69–76.

UKCOSA, 2005. *Higher education statistics*. Available from: http://www.ukcosa. org.uk/pages/hestats.htm [Accessed 31 March 2005].

Wales, B., and Harmon, H., 1998. A comparison of two user groups: international and US students in an academic library. *Public and Access Services Quarterly* 2 (4), 17–37.

Wang, J., and Frank, D.G., 2002. Cross-cultural communication: implications for effective information services in academic libraries. *Portal: Libraries and the Academy*, 2 (2), 207–216.

Ward, C., Bochner, S.. and Furnham, A., 2001. *The psychology of culture shock,* 2nd ed. Hove: Routledge.

Watkins, N., 1996. A case in point: individual library instruction for international students. *North Carolina Libraries* 54 (2), 76–79.

Wayman, S.G., 1984. The international student in the academic library. *Journal of Academic Librarianship*, 9 (6), 336–341.

Zhang, X. and Rowland, F., 1996. Chinese electronic journals. *62nd IFLA General Conference – Conference Proceedings – August 25–31, 1996*. Available from: http://www.ifla.org/IV/ifla62/62-zhax.htm [Accessed 31 March 2005].

Ziegler, R.A., 1997. International students and country of origin news. *Serials Review*, 23(1), 33–46.

PART III
International Perspectives

A Review of International Trends in Library Faculty Support in Higher Education: A Special Focus on Southern African University Libraries

Buhle Mbambo

Introduction

The role of the library in higher education has been well discussed in the literature. It is a commonly held view that the library is central to learning and research in higher education. However, the model of practice of librarianship varies from institution to institution. While some have moved on to provide subject specialist support to faculty some continue to use functionalist models. Are the two equally effective? Does it matter to clients? Are there social and cultural determinants of the support to faculty?

The first part of this chapter reviews literature trends on the forms and types of library support in academic institutions in Africa, Asia and Australia. It excludes a survey of the literature in the US except where it is used in comparison with other countries. The second part specifically investigates the types of library faculty support in Southern African countries. It reports on a survey done in 2004 to elicit views of librarians on the form of service they provided to faculty. The survey seeks to provide a basis from which to answer questions of current concern in Southern African academic libraries. Are the varied models each successful and effective? Is the subject specialist model more successful than the functionalist model in Southern Africa? The question of administrative costs in relation to the type of support, of concern to the author, is also discussed. This chapter looks at what has worked effectively in library faculty support and what may be best practice.

Definitions

In this chapter higher education is broadly defined as post-secondary education, sometimes referred to as tertiary education.

There are a number of possible definitions of faculty/subject librarianship. Miller (1977, 213) gives a very narrow definition as 'a formal, structured activity in which professional library staff systematically meet with teaching faculty to discuss stratagems for directly supporting their instructional needs and those of their students'. Suresh, Ryans and Zhang (1995) broadly define subject/faculty librarianship as a programme that involves library and academic departmental faculty jointly in the collection development process to foster communication between the library and the academic community and to enhance the patron-oriented image of the library. In this chapter, the broader view of Suresh, Ryans and Zhang is adopted. The term subject librarian is used to embrace faculty librarian, subject specialists or any other term used to describe a librarian who offers public service to a faculty.

Review of the literature

This literature review examines subject librarianship or faculty librarianship in a number of countries in Asia, Africa and Australia. Countries in Southern Africa are given particular prominence. While the literature on the practice of faculty support in Southern Africa is limited, that which is available was included. Documented examples are limited to two institutions, one in Botswana and another in South Africa. This chapter is, therefore, a major contributor to the body of literature on subject librarianship in Southern Africa.

Kotter (1999) asserts that for the library to remain viable in academic support, it is imperative that library-faculty relations are mutually beneficial. Kotter further highlights that good relations between the library and faculty lead to:

• faculty support of library programmes;
• faculty effectively utilising library services;
• improved support from librarians for researchers.

Jenda (1994) concurs with Kotter (1999), citing that establishment of close collaboration between the library and faculty enhances mutually beneficial service. The literature highlights the dependent nature of the relationship between the library and faculty. It further indicates that such interdependence is beneficial for both the library and faculty. The question that remains is how such relationships are established.

Universities in the US set the pace in the 1970s in creating posts in subject librarianship, a model subsequently adopted in other countries. In most cases, the activities of subject librarians were two-fold. They were to have a technical/bibliographic service function as well as public service function. As will be illustrated later, the automation of technical services diminished the technical services component of the subject librarian role and public and client services became the most significant component.

The role of subject librarians or subject specialist in the US was viewed primarily as that of collection development, liaison with a department or a faculty and related activities (Suresh, Ryans and Zhang, 1995). Lynch and Smith (2001) state that in the 1970s most libraries in the US operated a functionalist model. Emphasis was on technical services and collection development. They add that in the 1980s there was an increased number of subject specialist positions as libraries focused on service delivery (Lynch and Smith, 2001).

In the late 1990s China instituted a government programme to both reduce the number of institutions and to reform their administration and management. For university libraries the reform included the establishment of subject librarian posts on a contract rather then permanent basis (Ping and Zhang, 2001) with the aim of making them more accountable for delivery of service to clients and more responsive to their needs. The creation of subject librarians formed part of a strategy to streamline processes and reduce costs. In addition the restructuring process raised the qualifications of directors of university libraries. Directors of libraries had previously been employed from first-degree holders, however, in the new dispensation library directors are required to have advanced library degrees (Ping and Zhang, 2001). The duties of subject librarians were to serve as liaison to academic departments, provide library instruction and write instructional materials. The centrally directed nature of these changes is a contrast with the changes in other parts of the world, for example in the US where universities enjoy more autonomy and instituted their own programme for the creation of subject librarians. The common factor in each case is the need to make services more student-focused.

In Korea, Sejong University Library restructured its services from a functionalist to a subject division approach in 2000 (Shin and Kim, 2002). The restructuring aimed at improving quality of services. There was a move from placing learning resources according to forms to organising them according to subjects. There were three distinct collections, monographs, periodicals and reference collections. The reorganisation process created subject divisions in which subject librarians took responsibility for collection developments and client services in faculties. Their main task of the restructuring was to merge the three collections by subject. The reorganisation process also improved on communication channels reducing the hierarchical structure to a flatter structure that facilitated quick decision making. It was envisaged that a move to a subject approach would improve the quality of service.

In Nigeria, Port Harcourt University set up subject librarianship in the 1980s. The subject librarian was to provide service in two broad categories, collection development and service to faculty (Oliobi, 1994). The subject librarian serving an individual faculty had to have a first degree in the appropriate subject plus a postgraduate qualification. The rationale for this requirement was that with these qualifications, librarians would have in-depth knowledge of subjects taught in the faculties they served, and therefore would be effective in supporting them. A similar idea was implemented at the University of Botswana in the 1980s (Jenda, 1994). In Botswana the role of subject librarians was to perform tasks that included a combination of collection development and public services roles. In South Africa, University of Pretoria started subject reorganization in the 1980s (Gerryts, 1991).

Subject Librarianship emerged in Canada in the 1980s. In common with developments in the UK and Australia the role of the subject librarian has changed to include a substantial amount of teaching. (Julien and Leckie, 1997; Marfleet and Kelly, 1999; Bruce, 2001). However, the teaching contribution of subject librarians is not always recognised. In Canada, the teaching role of academic libraries is disguised, according to Julien and Leckie (1997). The content they teach is described in non-academic terms, often referred to as user education or bibliographic instruction. Kuhlthau (1994) coined terms to highlight the teaching role of librarians. Librarians giving extensive bibliographic instruction were called instructors while those who provided orientation were called lecturers. The advent of information literacy as a term for teaching retrieval and critical evaluation of information has gone some way to meeting the concerns with labelling and naming of the teaching process (Rowe, 1994).

Canadian subject librarians were contending with issues of status. Crowley (1997) recommends that the issue of status of librarians could be resolved by employment of subject specialist librarian with a higher degree in a subject. Such librarians could have peer relationships with faculty and be referred as 'Discipline Research Librarians'. Debate on the status of librarians included debate on whether librarians should teach. However, while the debate raged, librarians in Canada continued to teach.

Bernstein, (1997) argues that in Canadian universities, while the responsibility for user education lay with subject librarian, the co-ordination lay with reference librarians. Bernstein established that not all colleges and universities had adopted subject librarianship. Colleges in particular retained a functionalist approach. In such colleges, the reference librarians who gave bibliographic instruction were also responsible for publicising bibliographic instruction in the faculties. The study further showed that the extent of integration and collaboration of bibliographic instruction was largely dependent on the contacts reference librarians had with faculty.

Ducas and Michaud-Oystryk (2003) state that in Canada close faculty/library collaboration have positive impact on the student learning. Collaborative teaching and co-operation of faculty and libraries enhance student learning. The areas in which faculty and librarians collaborated were teaching/instruction, information services, research, and information technology and collection development.

Bernstein, (1997) further showed that changes in technology have influenced the content of bibliographic instruction sessions resulting in more instruction on how to use technology for information retrieval. This view is corroborated by Jenda (1994) and Ping and Zhang (2001) who both state that changes in technology have changed the role of the subject librarian significantly. The automation of routine work such as cataloguing, classification and purchasing has created a space for subject librarians to engage in the expanding task of training end users.

In Australia and in the UK the empowerment of the end user with computer skills before entry into university, enabling them to access online resources, has created a phenomenon commonly referred to as disintermediation (Biddiscombe, 2002). A growing concern is that disintermediation is rendering subject specialists 'dinosaurs'.

The end users are largely able to access online resources (Rodwell, 2001). While Dickinson (1979) had argued that in the later twentieth century and twenty first century there would be no role for the subject specialist, Rodwell (2001) argues that subject expertise is what librarians need in the disintermediated environment. Furthermore, it is emerging that not only is expertise required in the subject, but also breadth of knowledge and expertise on the dynamics of production, dissemination and storage of information in a subject.

In the UK in particular, prevalence of digital libraries and online resources demands that librarians need to become learning support personnel. The new role of librarians is to focus on user education that goes beyond information retrieval. Biddiscombe (2002) indicates that subject librarians need to be integrated in web-based teaching. They require good information technology skills to effectively utilise virtual learning environments (VLEs) such as Blackboard and Web CT.

Atton (1996) cautions though that the emphasis of the information retrieval training role of the librarian is at the expense of need to train users in critical thinking. Critical users of the library would be active contributors to knowledge not merely consumers. Goetsch (1995) contends that librarians are well positioned and trained to encourage critical thinking. The idea of encouraging critical thinking was a cornerstone of development of information literacy skills (ILS). The US (List, 1999) attempted to include it in the curriculum. This author's concern is that library schools may not be producing critical thinkers. Are the modern-day librarians significantly different in thinking from those of the turn of the twentieth century? How and where would librarians acquire critical thinking, which they would then teach clients?

It emerges in the literature that, while many countries in the world have adopted subject librarianship, the role and function of those librarians is dynamic. It has changed over years to focus on information retrieval skills training. In developed countries, developments in information technology (IT) have significantly altered the activities of librarians, requiring them to polish their IT skills and work in areas that are beyond information retrieval and traditional end user training. Many users entering universities already have sophisticated computer skills. Librarians therefore have to find new ways of serving their clients besides end user training. The challenge is to find those other ways of doing other business.

Creation of subject librarianship in Southern Africa

The University of Pretoria Library in South Africa marked its change in type of support with name change from Library Service in the late 1970s to Academic Information Service in the 1980s (Gerryts, 1991). The transition to an information service was achieved through four phases of development and a series of project plans. Subject Librarians were created as part of the change process, but before the end of the 1980s they had been transformed into Information Scientists. Gerryts (1991) argues that the transition of libraries had to be from collection-centred libraries to service-centred libraries.

At the University of Botswana, Jenda (1994) suggests that the information explosion, advances in computer and communication technology, proliferation and sophistication of user needs, and the need for improvement in efficiency and effectiveness of library service contributed toward the development of subject-centered librarianship. Subject-centred librarianship was adopted by the University of Botswana in 1981. In this arrangement subject librarians performed both technical and public services activities in faculties that they served. Each subject librarian supported a number of departments. Their role included collection development, information organization, user education, reference and faculty liaison in the departments for which they are responsible. In 1996, the University of Botswana introduced course-based Information Literacy Skills (ILS) (Mbambo and Rosselle, 1998). Subject librarians took responsibility for the teaching of information skills. While the initial ILS was course based, ILS has grown to become part of an independent compulsory credit course GEC (www.ub.bw/Library). In a major review of subject librarianship at the University of Botswana, subject librarians reaffirmed the value of subject librarianship to faculty and to delivery of services. More importantly they highlighted recommendations to improve their quality of services, faculty liaison, marketing, collection development and ILS. They also called for staff development programmes to enhance the quality of work of subject librarian.

Faculty support in Southern Africa: results of a survey

Background

The boundary and limitation of Southern Africa is defined by context. The Southern African Development Community (SADC) include Tanzania in their definition, as shown in Figure 12.1. The Library Association of East, Central and Southern African Countries (SCECSAL) includes Tanzania in East Africa. For the purposes of this study the countries of Southern Africa include Botswana, Lesotho, Namibia Swaziland, South Africa and Zimbabwe.

Except for Namibia, those countries share a common history. They are all former colonies of the UK. Namibia, on the other hand, had been a colony of Germany. South Africa, though, had been a colony of the Dutch and has some Dutch heritage. Most of the countries share a common history and a common official language, English. South Africa has 10 other official languages besides English. English is the commonest language of instruction in higher education in Southern Africa.

The countries studied have varied university entry levels. They all have seven years of primary education. However, years of secondary school education and entrance to university differ. In Botswana and Lesotho, entrance to university is after Ordinary Level. In South Africa, it is after an additional year to Matriculation. While in Zimbabwe it is a year beyond Matriculation, at Advanced level. Universities of Botswana and Lesotho offer four-year degrees. Most universities in Zimbabwe offer three-year degrees unless attachment to industry is a requirement, as happens

Figure 12. 1 Map of Southern Africa showing all Southern African Development Community Countries
Source: Southern African Research and Documentation Centre (SARDC).

with some practical programmes. South African universities largely offer three-year degrees with some exceptions.

University libraries in Southern Africa are well established. They have come together to form the Standing of Conference of University and National Librarians of Eastern, Central and Southern Africa (SCANUL/ECS) (www.scanul-ecs.org). They hold biannual conferences to deliberate on issues pertinent to their delivery of service. In the last few meetings they have been concerned with issues of information literacy, usage of statistics and setting up of standards.

Survey Results

The following section reports the results of a survey conducted in 2004, looking specifically at the types and forms of library support delivered to faculties in universities in Southern Africa. As was discussed earlier in this chapter, surveys of this type have been infrequent and so this research gives unique insight into Southern African university libraries at a time of change. Broadly it is an accurate picture; however, for various reasons no responses were received from university libraries in Namibia and Swaziland and a limited number of responses were received from university libraries in South Africa. At the time of writing, 2004, South African universities are engaged in a process to reduce the number of universities from 35 to 21 through a process of merger.

The survey reviewed a number of factors, the number of universities in each country, the age of the universities, the size of each faculty, the number of library posts and the type of support offered. Each factor was analysed to look at whether any individual factor was significant in influencing the choice of model in each country for either a subject-based structure or a functional-based structure.

The issue of the number of universities in each country raises interesting questions. South Africa has 35 universities, or 21 universities post-reorganisation, Zimbabwe 11 registered universities while Lesotho and Botswana have one university each. Broadly, while South African universities promote a subject-based model, in Zimbabwe there is a mix of practices. Botswana adopted a subject-based model in 1981 while Lesotho has a function-based model. The question not answered in the survey but perhaps an area for future research is whether having a choice of universities within one country encourages competition for students. One possible conclusion might be that a student-centred model, more attractive to potential students, would predominate where universities compete for students.

Higher education is well established in Southern Africa. The majority of South African universities and the national universities of Lesotho and Botswana were created over 25 years ago. In Zimbabwe, one university, the University of Zimbabwe, was chartered in 1955. The other eight universities in Zimbabwe have been created in the last 15 years.

Lesotho reported in the survey that it is in a period of transition moving away from a functionalist structure to more student/subject focused approach. In Zimbabwe there is a mix of functionalist and subject-based structures. The results of the survey indicate that older institutions prefer a subject-based model. In writing on this subject Jenda (1994), from the University of Botswana and Gerryts (1991), from the University of Pretoria give the reason for their transition from functional to subject-based models as the need to provide a student-centred service, lending support to the conclusion that established institutions naturally progress to student-centred modes of service delivery.

The size and number of faculties has no direct relationship to the size or type of support services. The majority of Southern African Universities have six to ten faculties. Newer universities in Zimbabwe are smaller with five or fewer faculties. The number of students generally does not exceed 15,000. The exceptions are the two open universities in South Africa, University of South Africa (UNISA) and Zimbabwe Open University (ZOU) that have in excess of 20,000 students each. UNISA adopts a subject-based approach, ZOU a functionalist approach. Looking across the region, the size of the university and the number of students does not appear to be significant in determining how the library is organised.

While there is no exact correlation between the number of professional Library posts and the number of students, most universities reported the number of professional library staff to range from 15–20. A notable exception to this are the two open universities – UNISA, which has a subject-based structure, has 83 professional library staff and ZOU, which has a functional-based structure, has 27. This lends support to Jenda's (1994) argument that subject librarianship is expensive in terms of human resources and can only be supported where sufficient human resources are available.

When reviewed in detail a number of models emerge. ZOU operates on a regional library model. Each of its regional centres is serviced by a single librarian. The National University of Lesotho is moving from a functionalist to a subject-based approach. The majority of universities in South Africa operate a subject-based model. Within this there are different practices. Botswana operates a subject teams approach with subject librarians working under the leadership of a Faculty Library Co-ordinator. The majority reported that where a subject based model was used, one subject/faculty librarian worked with each faculty.

The term used to refer to these librarians also varied from one institution to another. In Lesotho, when the transition is complete they will be called Subject Specialists. One institution in South Africa called them Information Librarians. In Zimbabwe they are referred to as Faculty Librarians. In Botswana they are referred to as Subject Librarians. In other institutions they are referred to as Subject Specialists.

Whatever term is used to describe them, the librarians who provide services to faculty perform a common range of activities including: book selection; information organization; library marketing; teaching ILS; collection development and reference; and faculty liaison. When asked how they rated their own services, respondents were positive. Lesotho, currently in the process of reorganising expressed concern at the level of service they provided to students. Areas that would underpin an improved service to students were an increase in staff numbers and better communication between staff. Asked how they perceived faculty could be served better, the demand for staff was again an issue. Other issues raised were a closer liaison with academics, strengthening partnership with faculty; recruiting personnel with ICT skills; and completion of the transformation of the university. Respondents also commented on other areas of concern in their relationship with faculties and academics:

- academic institutions must take faculty librarianship more seriously;
- role of faculty librarians still needs to be accepted by faculty;
- more co-operation with faculty will enhance support;
- more library staff would enhance the quality of service to faculty;
- faculty appreciate having a contact person in the library;
- faculty status would enhance librarianship;
- use of more user-friendly words is encouraged instead of words that refer to clients as 'Readers'.

Summary

Out of the results of the survey it seems that no single pattern of subject support is emerging. The concept of librarians dedicated to supporting faculty is widely accepted in universities in Southern Africa. However, the model of practice varies from institution to institution. Except for countries with single universities, there was no national 'model' of subject librarianship. Each institution within one country developed its own practice. What maybe helpful to the practice and implementation of subject librarianship in each of the countries in Southern Africa would be the establishment of a standard for best practice. Newer universities would then benchmark themselves against those practices.

Most institutions requested for more staff to improve the service but also to meet the demands of tasks that are performed across faculties.

The wide ranging call for closer partnership with faculty implies that faculty librarianship has not become institutionally recognised as a service. Furthermore, while the university structure may have a position for a librarian or assistant librarian, Faculty librarian or Subject Librarian is an arrangement internal to the library. This is so in Botswana and Zimbabwe for instance. Perhaps institutionalisation of the position of Faculty Librarian or Subject Librarian may provide recognition within the university structures.

Subject librarians in Southern Africa continue to perform end-user training tasks as well as some technical service tasks. The disintermediation phenomena are not prevalent as the majority of users are not sophisticated computer users. The role of subject librarians is largely to equip users with information retrieval skills. End users still need training in information retrieval. All institutions emphasise this as an important role for the subject librarian. In the light of developments in Australia and North America, and Western Europe, proactive librarians in Southern Africa need to begin to prepare for the eventuality of doing business differently. What will happen when users become sophisticated users?

Another issue that requires attention is that of critical thinking skills. Are current users being taught information retrieval skills or is critical thinking included? It is not enough to teach information retrieval skills: a good information literacy programme needs to include critical thinking skills; that is, it needs to equip students with skills that will enable them to critically evaluate the information that they retrieve.

Conclusion

This brief survey report indicates the adoption of subject librarianship is common among university libraries in China, Korea, Nigeria and Southern Africa. The literature review and the survey both confirm that the adoption and practice of subject librarianship is a preferred model. However, what remains varied are the models of the practice, and in some cases the title by which they are called. The survey of Southern African institutions however, proved beyond doubt that the practice of subject librarianship is widely accepted in institutions of higher learning in Southern Africa.

In the twenty-first century, librarianship in higher education institutions seems to be client focused. This is reflected in the trend towards the establishment of dedicated librarians to support specific faculties. Various names and titles are given to these library practitioners, but the common denominator is that they are dedicated to providing service to faculty. The varied labelling of these practitioners is indicative of a transition of the type of service model adopted by university libraries. University libraries themselves are in a state of transition with names ranging from Academic Information Services to University Library and various other titles in the middle. This transition is necessitated by the need to be responsive to faculty needs. The advent of information and communication technology has further compounded the transitionary nature of the practice and profession of librarianship. What remains constant is that librarians remain central to higher education in Southern Africa whatever name they are called.

References

Atton, C., 1996. Towards a critical practice for the academic library. *New Library World,* 97 (5), 4–11.

Bernstein, E., 1985. Library services at the Hugh Macmillan Medical Centre, *Bibliotheca Medica Canadiana*, 7 (3), 115–116.

Biddiscombe, R., 2002. Learning support professionals: the changing role of subject specialists in UK academic libraries. *Program,* 36 (4), 228–235.

Bruce. C., 2001. Faculty-librarian partnerships in Australian higher education: critical dimensions. *Reference Services Review,* 29 (2), 106–116.

Crowley, B., 1997. The dilemma of the librarians in Canadian higher education. *Canadian Journal of Information and Library Science*, 22 (1), 1–18.

Dickinson, D.W., 1979. Subject specialists in academic libraries: the once and future dinosaurs. *In* R.D. Stewart and R.D. Johnson, *New Horizons for Academic Libraries: Papers presented at the First National Conference of the Association of College and Research Libraries, Boston, Massachusetts*, 8–11 November 1978, Saur, New York, NY 438–444.

Ducas, A.M., and Michaud-Oystryk, N., 2003. Toward a new enterprise: capitalizing on the faculty/librarian partnership. *College and Research Libraries,* 64 (1), 55–74.

Gerryts, E.D. 1991. Managing organizational development in modern university library environment. *IATUL Quarterly,* 5 (3), 167-184.

Goetsch, L., 1995. Reference service is more a desk. *Journal of Academic Librarianship,* 21 (1), 15–16.

Jenda, C.A., 1994. Management of professional time and multiple responsibilities in a subject-centred academic library, *Library Administration and Management*, 8 (2), 97–108.

Julien, H., and Leckie, G.J. 1997. Bibliographic instruction trends in Canadian academic libraries. *The Canadian Journal of Information Science*, 22 (2), 1–15.

Kotter, W.R. 1999. Bridging the great divide: improving relations between librarians and classroom faculty. *Journal of Academic Librarianship*, 25 (4), 1–20.

Kuhlthau, C., 1994. Students and the information search process: Students and the Information Search Process: Zones of Intervention for Librarians. *In* Irene P. Godden (ed.), Advances *in Librarianship 18*, Toronto: Academic Press, 57–72.

List, C., 1998. *An introduction to library research*. New York: Prestige.

Lynch, B.P., and Smith, K.R., 2001. The changing nature of work in academic libraries. *College and Research Libraries*. 62 (5), 407–420.

Marfleet, J. and Kelly, C. 1999. Leading the field: the role of information professional in the next century. *The Electronic Library,* 17 (6), 359–364.

Mbambo, B., and Rosselle, A., 1999. Integrating information literacy skills instruction into the curriculum: a comparison of two approaches. *In* K.J. Anderson et al. (eds), *LOEX of the West: collaboration and instructional design in a virtual environment Stamford, Connecticut:* JAI Press.

Miller, L., 1977. Liaison work in academic libraries. *RQ*, 16 (3), 213–215.

Oliobi, M.I., 1994. Tapping the subject background of librarians: the University of Port Harcourt Library experience. *Library Review* 43 (3), 32–40.

Ping, K., and Zhang, S.L., 2001. Toward continual reform: Progress in academic libraries in China. *College and Research Libraries*, 63 (2), (5) 164–70.

Proceedings of a workshop on Subject Librarianship, 27–29 July 1999, Gaborone (Unpublished).

Rodwell, J., 2001. Dinosaur or dynamo? The future of the subject specialist reference librarian *New Library World,* 102 (1), 48–52.

Rowe, C., 1994. Modern library instruction: levels media trends and problems. *Research strategies*, 12 (1), 4–17.

Shin, E.-J. and Kim, Y- S., 2002. Restructuring library organizations for the twenty-first century: the future of user oriented services in Korean academic libraries. *Aslib Proceedings,* 54 (4), 260–66.

Suresh, R.S., Ryans, C.C. and Zhang, W., 1995. The library-faculty connection starting a liaison programme in an academic setting, *Library Review,* 44 (1), 7–13.

Townley, C.T., 2001. Knowledge management and academic libraries, *College and Research Libraries,* 62 (1) 44–55.

Vondracek, R., 2003. Going beyond selection. *Library Journal,* 128 (12), 20.

Walter, S., 2000. Engelond: a model for faculty librarian collaboration in the Information age. *Information Technology and Libraries,* 19 (1), 34–41.

PART IV
Conclusion

Chapter 13

Conclusion

Penny Dale, Matt Holland and Marian Matthews

'Help yourself,' said Harry. 'But in, you know, the Muggle
world, people just stay put in photos.'
'Do they? What, they don't move at all?' Ron sounded amazed. '*Weird*!'
(J. K. Rowling 1997) [Editors' note: Muggles are non-wizards]

Overview

In the introduction, we stated our aim of using the publication of this book to provide snapshots of subject librarianship; of the people involved in the wide ranging activities of the posts in their many and various incarnations and to reflect some of the postholders' hopes and, in some cases, fears for the future of the role. We were aware from the outset that, like Harry Potter's wizard photographs, the snapshots do not stand still. Librarianship as a profession moves constantly to respond to changing needs; government policy, institutional demands, quality assurance, supporting and contributing to research as well as working in partnership with academics and other support staff to enhance the learning experience for students. In this final chapter we will look at some of these drivers for change and the impacts, both positive and negative, that they have on subject librarians.

Change drivers

The future of the subject librarian in the increasingly *electronic environment* of the academic library has been referred to by several contributors to this book, and is the subject of wide debate within the profession. The process of disintermediation, direct end user access to resources, threatens the subject librarians' relationships with students and staff as well as providing opportunities for change. There is a move away from providing access to resources, although that remains important, to a less defined role of providing a supportive environment for teaching and learning. There are also exciting opportunities, for example the development of virtual learning environments, offering considerable scope to 'reinvent' the subject librarians' role in a new context. Several chapters in this book take up this theme, indicating areas where there are opportunities for personal and professional development.

Increased *subject specialisation* offers another possible route for the development of subject librarianship. The policies and initiatives of the Higher Education Funding

Council for England, such as the Quality Assurance Agency Subject Review and the Research Assessment Exercise, increasingly address higher education as a collection of subject groupings. So too does the subject network of the Higher Education Academy, as does JISC with resource enhancement activities, specifically in the Resource Discovery Network. In a climate of intense competition for student places encouraged by league tables, such collaborative activity can see almost contrary. However the possibilities of economies of scale that can be achieved by subject groupings of information professionals are recognised by the funding bodies and need to be embraced by library professionals. Subject-based communities of practice are already well established but there is still scope for development of new communities as some subject areas are not covered and others might need re-focussing to reflect changes in the curriculum.

Several chapters refer to the growing contribution of subject librarians to *learning and teaching*, working in partnership with academic and support staff to enable students to become motivated and independent learners. It is perhaps the right time to respond to Alan Bundy's challenge 'to be daring' and create opportunities to be more proactive in learning and teaching. This has implications for the training and continuing professional development of librarians. A number of contributors to this book have endorsed membership of the Higher Education Academy, referring to the credibility membership brings and also the usefulness of its services, notably the subject network. We recognise the progress that the Chartered Institute of Library and Information Professionals has made since inauguration, but we urge continued action to support the information literacy agenda. Our professional association must also monitor the provision of relevant professional training, and ensure that appropriate continuing professional development opportunities are available to enable subject librarians to respond to the changing environments in which they operate. Institutions also have responsibility for this, and we hope that the Framework for Professional Qualifications will enable individuals to decide how best to use the training that is available and to lobby for appropriate provision where gaps need to be filled.

As institutions from across the higher education sector focus on, and compete for, *research funding* and *knowledge transfer* opportunities, subject librarians need to be actively involved in the processes from the outset to ensure not only that resource funding is considered but also that security protocols are in place from the beginning. We are sure that colleagues across the profession will relate to the situation where 'access to all full text electronic resources' has been promised to a potential partner with no consideration of licensing restrictions. Working creatively and responsively at this level can be perhaps one of the most effective ways to positively address another concern raised by some authors in this book, that of *status* and *credibility* within academic institutions.

The electronic library

Whilst embracing change, subject librarians also need to be critical and ensure that new directions are informed by adequate reflection. For example, the transition to *electronic resources* without considerations of usage, dissemination and access can create confusion and hostility with end users. The skill of introducing and exploiting electronic resources can be overlooked in the rush to make services available or to save money (or more probably space). Communication with all of the stakeholders and reflective intermediation as and when necessary will not only ensure the provision of robust and value-for-money resources, but also the co-operation and buy-in of users. Paradoxically, to introduce and develop successful electronic resources, subject librarians need to be good verbal communicators and fully integrated with academic as well as library networks.

Networking

Subject librarians have proved the value of *partnership* working both within their own institutions and across regional and subject sectors. They are uniquely placed to develop the role of knowledge broker, working with students and academics, to consolidate and enhance their contributions to learning and teaching. The need to collaborate and find new ways of working with faculty and students is one of the themes of this book. This also means working across subjects to provide quality resources and also across traditional sectoral boundaries.

Socio-economic factors

Higher education in the UK is part of a society that endeavours to be *inclusive*, promoting equal access to education for all regardless of their background. To illustrate this, in 1962 only 6 per cent of under 21s went to University, When the DfES published *The future of higher education* in 2003, 43 per cent of those aged 18–30 went on to higher education and this figure is set to rise to 50 per cent by 2010. Numbers of students with *additional learning needs* continue to increase, as do numbers of *mature students* returning to study, or entering for the first time after, or in conjunction with, work or family commitments. A further dimension to this profile is added by rising numbers of *international students*, and also home students from increasingly varied *ethnic and cultural backgrounds*.

Government policy

In 2003, two Government White Papers *The future of higher education* and *Widening participation in higher education* stated Government objectives for the development of higher education in the UK. Some of the implications of these White Papers are discussed in this book; how librarians in academic libraries can best support increasing numbers of individuals with different life experiences and varying levels of education is a theme running through many of the chapters, as are the challenges of supporting the delivery of higher education in institutes of further education. Librarians have a proven record of responding to the challenges of widening participation, but there is no room for complacency as the expectations of students, their parents, and in many cases their employers, continue to rise. Partnerships not only with librarians in further education but also in public libraries are already providing opportunities for subject librarians.

As this book goes to print in 2005 the debate about charging for undergraduate tuition is largely over, at least in England and Wales, and students entering higher education from 2006 will have to pay fees of up to £3000 for their course. Just how much of an impact the introduction of fees will cause remains to be seen, but as academic libraries have been working with fee-paying users (such as postgraduate and international students) for many years, any ramifications for services may well be already covered by existing policies. The transition of short loan collections to electronic resource provides a good example of increasing access to books and journals without increasing staff and other costs. This does mean however that subject librarians need to ensure that their collection management skills cover electronic resources.

Quality assurance

Quality assurance offers exciting opportunities for subject librarians. Benchmarking in some shape or form is with us to stay. It has become embedded in institutional processes, informing academic development and business planning. The advantages and possibilities of active involvement are described in this book, but we would like to add our own endorsement. There is much discussion within librarianship about professional values and job satisfaction. Being part of the quality assurance process within an institution ensures that systems and resources are indeed fit for purpose. We may find the meetings too frequent and too long, wording for the self-evaluation documents too short and buy-in from some colleagues difficult to achieve. The result, however, justifies the effort if it leads to a service that is responsive to need, and is understood and supported by faculty and the institution.

It has been a stimulating experience to commission the chapters in this book, and to read them as they arrived on our PCs, each one reflecting a different aspect of subject librarianship. Sometimes the movement in the snapshots referred to at the start of this chapter was so rapid that we wondered if it was possible to complete the book in the way we had envisaged. Engagement with learning and teaching, changes to the quality assurance process, and the development of virtual learning environments are all challenges to the job that subject librarians do; they are also presenting us with unique opportunities.

References

Bundy, A., 2005. Changing and connecting the educational silos: the potential of the information literacy framework. *LILAC 2005.* 5 April 2005. *Imperial College.* London: LILAC.

Department for Education and Skills (DfES). 2003. *The future of Higher Education.*

London: HMSO.

Department for Education and Skills (DfES). 2003. *Widening participation in higher education*. London: HMSO.

Rowling, J.K. 1997. *Harry Potter and the philosopher's stone*. London: Bloomsbury.

Index